Anonymous

Antiqua Mater: A Study Of Christian Origins

Anonymous

Antiqua Mater: A Study Of Christian Origins

ISBN/EAN: 9783744652230

Printed in Europe, USA, Canada, Australia, Japan

Cover: Foto ©Lupo / pixelio.de

More available books at **www.hansebooks.com**

ANTIQUA MATER:

𝔄 Study of Christian Origins.

'He had an earnest intention of taking a review of the original principles of the primitive Church: believing that every true Christian had no better means to settle his spirit, than that which was proposed to Æneas and his followers to be the end of their wanderings, *Antiquam exquirite Matrem.*'
The Life of Mr. A. Cowley, by Dr. Sprat.

LONDON:
TRÜBNER & CO., LUDGATE HILL.
1887.
[*All rights reserved.*]

Ballantyne Press
BALLANTYNE, HANSON AND CO.
EDINBURGH AND LONDON

Dedication.

TO

W. R.

IN TOKEN OF LONG AND VALUED FRIENDSHIP.

CONTENTS.

PREFACE . . . ix.-xx

Part I.

THE EXTERNAL HISTORY.

CHAP.   PAGE

I. PAGAN SOURCES—THE REIGN OF TRAJAN — PLINY AND TACITUS ON THE CHRISTIANI AND CHRISTUS—SUETONIUS—THE 'AUTHOR OF THE CHRISTIAN NAME' . 1

II. REFERENCES TO THE JEWS IN THE ROMAN LITERATURE OF THE SECOND CENTURY 20

III. CHRISTIAN SOURCES—JUSTIN MARTYR . . . 32

IV. CHRISTIAN SOURCES—THE 'HÆRETICS' (OR SECTARIANS) DURING THE FIRST HALF OF THE SECOND CENTURY . 44

Part II.

THE INTERNAL HISTORY.

I. THE HAGIOI, APOSTLES AND PROPHETS—THE CHRISTIANOS AND THE CHRISTEMPOROS 52

II. THE ECCLESIA—'THE VINE' . . . 69

III. RITES OF THE HAGIOI 78

CONTENTS.

CHAP.		PAGE
IV.	THE NEW CREATION, THE NEW PEOPLE, AND THE NEW LAW	94
V.	THE SEAL OF THE NEW COMMUNITY	107
VI.	MORAL TEACHING AMONG THE HAGIOI—THE 'TWO WAYS'.	131
VII.	THE EVANGELION AND THE EVANGELISTS	151
VIII.	THE IDEAL AMONG JEWS AND GENTILES	189
IX.	THE GNOSTIC THEOLOGY	213
X.	THE CRITICS AND THE APOLOGETES OF CHRISTIANITY	243
XI.	CELSUS AND ORIGEN	272
	ADDENDA	303
	INDEX	305

PREFACE.

THE present tract has been written in answer to the following inquiry :—

'*What may we learn—apart from the books of the New Testament—from the old Christian and the Græco-Roman literature of the second century, in respect to the origin and the earliest development of Christianity?*'

It seemed to the writer convenient, and even necessary for the sake of clearness, to understand the question as referring to the origin and early history of the people called *Christiani*, and of their beliefs and practices. The term *Christianity* seems of too vague and vast an import to be fitted for introduction into a historical investigation of this kind; moreover, it is something of an anachronism to use so abstract a denomination in connection with the new-forming religious life of the second century.

Now, on examining the literary evidence of the first two centuries on this question, one searches first for certain historic *data* of time, place, and persons; and speedily discovers how few these data are, and how slight the information they can be said, in any sense, to yield on the subject of our inquiry. If one has approached the literature of the period with the assumption that something definite could be made out respecting the lives of Christ and the apostles independently of the New Testament, one assuredly has been brought, sooner or later, to the consciousness of a complete illusion. The pagan writers betray no knowledge of such particulars, nor can they be found in the writings of the so-called 'apostolic fathers.' What has long been admitted with reference to the so-called epistles of 'Barnabas' and 'Clement,' and the apocalypse of 'Hermas,' is that they are for us *anonymous* documents. What must further be admitted is, that they are absolutely *undated* documents, and that learned guesses at their dates are of no service, but the contrary, to scientific inquiry. As for the literature inscribed with the names of 'Ignatius' and 'Polycarp,' there seems little reason for dating it in the second century rather than the third or the fourth. These documents, moreover, are open to the suspicion of serious *interpolation* or *corruption*. Truth is still truth, though it be but negative in quality; and we venture a strong protest against the practice of using materials so uncertain, for the purpose of favouring any assumed historical result whatever. The case with Justin Martyr is somewhat different. The *Apology* in his name contains a date, on the ground of which his literary activity may be ascribed to about the middle of the second century (147-167). The result of our examination of the sources is this: that, apart from the New Testament, the historical origin of the new faith must be sought primarily in Justin Martyr's accepted works. We know no other dated Christian literature so early as those works, to which we invite our readers' careful attention. They are accessible in a tolerable translation to those who read only in English. Any person of ordinary clear-headedness has the materials of judgment before him; and if he takes the usual view of what Evidence is, and of what is *not* Evidence, he will, as we believe, come to the conclusion that Justin of Flavia Neapolis had no exact knowledge, whether of the 'Apostles' in general, or of him whom he calls the 'Apostle of God.' He had an Idea before his mind, but not actual Persons, of whose life and teaching any accurate particulars had been recorded.

If we extend the examination to Irenæus and Tertullian, we find that they were unable to supply the *lacunæ* in Justin's knowledge. The Twelve Apostles remain for them a legendary group, whose existence belongs to the shadows of the Old Testament, and has no basis in historic *data* of our era. And with regard to Paul, Tertullian is our witness that, apart from the New Testament books, nothing authentic was known about him. It is that Father himself who raises doubts about the 'Apostle of the Hæretics' which cannot easily be dispelled. The bare result of the whole examination is, that from some time unknown, the statement that Jesus Christ had been crucified under Pontius Pilate, was repeated as a formula in connection with the rites of Exorcism and Baptism, and that coæval with this belief, was that in His resurrection, ascension, and second coming. With whom did this tradition originate? While the old Catholic fathers figure to themselves Twelve Apostles, founders of true or apostolic churches, without being able to authenticate those Apostles, they unanimously refer the origin of the powerful Gnostic schools or churches which dissented from the 'great church,' to Simon of Samaria, called by them a Mage, and said to have flourished in honour at Rome in the reign of Claudius. We consider this to be the most distinct and most remarkable fact that can be elicited from the evidence before us. We see the figure of the Samaritan through a distorting medium of envy and fantastic exaggeration, and no defence of their Master by his numerous followers has come down to us. Yet, on the reluctant testimony of his passionate opponents, he stands forth as the truly original spirit of the first century, the great Impulsor of the religious movement from which Christendom arose. And the manner in which the commanding figure of the Paul of modern imagination, flits before us in the Clementine romance as a sort of *alter ego* of Simon, though the writer names him not, is a point that must arrest attention, until the historic truth beneath these representations shall at last be laid bare.

We hold that the Christian world has for ages been content for the most part, and is still content, to beg the question of the historical origins of Christianity, under the influence of the 'old Catholic fathers;' that is, under the influence of men who were ignorant of the history of the Ecclesia or Ecclesiæ, which they administered with so much skill; men who were content to fill the void in their knowledge with poetical fancies, and who probably encouraged the circulation of historical fictions, which tended to support their 'apostolical' pretensions with their flocks. Those to whom the great principles of Protestantism are dear, can no longer, when once their eyes are opened, consent to abet these delusions. The so-called Hæretics, that is, the Dissenters from the 'great church,' were in reality *before* the Catholics, both in point of time and of originality. It is in the Gnosis and among the Gnostics that we must seek above all for the distinctive notes of Christianity as a Religion distinct from Judaism and from the decaying forms of heathendom. And if this be so, then our ecclesiastical histories and our apologies—if, indeed, they be necessary—should be rewritten from this standpoint. And it will be a great gain if such a reconsideration of the subject shall lead to the disappearance of old hates and prejudices from the field of letters, and if those whose dearest memories are bound up with the Christian name shall be able gratefully to recognise their debt in just proportions alike to Jew, Greek, and Roman, for the rich experiences which they have contributed to the common religion of civilisation. Certain it seems, that the great complex we call 'Christianity' can be traced to no mere local origin, to no village idylls, but only to that great world of religious passion and imagination revealed to us in the study of the letters of the first two centuries of our era.

But the reader may ask, Of what value can deductions be, which *ex hypothesi* exclude the New Testament books as evidence? Though this question is not strictly our business, we cannot refrain from saying a word about it, because clearly our results are all but worthless, if it can be shown that the New Testament books are older sources than the rest of our early literature. But here again we have suffered ourselves to become the victims of age-long delusions. With patient toil, the author of 'Supernatural Religion' has examined and stated the evidence upon this subject. One may perhaps venture the criticism that he has rather overdone than underdone his work; for by massing so formidable an array of references to modern writers, he has perhaps excited a diffidence in the ordinary reader, who may suppose that he is not competent to judge of the merits of the question unless he has spent laborious years upon the 'critics.' This is not so. The question really lies within a narrow compass. The reader may practically confine himself to Justin of Neapolis as a dated witness from the middle of the second century. He knows no authoritative writings except the Old Testament; he had neither our 'Gospels' nor our Pauline writings; his imagination was a blank where our own is filled with vivid pictures of the activity of Jesus and of Paul.[1]

---

[1] The late Bruno Bauer, who has long been treated by the theological world as an outcast, but who has been recently vindicated in a most candid spirit by Professor A. D. Loman (*Theol. Tijdschr.*, 1882-3),

Professor Harnack of Marburg, in his lately published 'Handbook of the History of Dogmas' (1886), has with great candour sketched the true history of our New Testament literature, according to the scientific probabilities of the case; only, his admissions seem to require the rewriting of the earlier sections of his work. These writings were originally anonymous, the deposit of anonymous sayings; only gradually were authors found for them, whose names, when found, were wafted over the world by the breath of 'Tradition.' The Professor has dwelt upon the sudden appearance of the 'Canon' at the end of the second century, on the ignorance of any New Testament until after the middle of that century, and the want of a universal recognition of such a Testament even at the beginning of the third century.

The numerous biographies of Jesus and the 'Acts' of apostles must have been mainly composed during the age of the Antonines, and were doubtless called forth by a public need in the churches, analogous to that which has called forth a multitude of Lives of Christ during our own time. There was an intense craving, both in the interests of spiritual satisfaction and in that of controversy, to emerge out of the atmosphere of vague intuition and reminiscence into the daylight of historic portraiture. And, frankly, there is in the nature of things, little more reason for approaching these documents with an awe-struck respect, as for

dates the New Testament literature in the period 130-170. Cf. on his views the testimony of H. Schiller, *Gesch. d. Röm. Kaiserzeit*, 1883, p. 446. See also Graetz, *Gesch. d. Juden*, 2. Aufl., 3. 225.

something of Divine inspiration in a special sense, than for so approaching the 'Lives' which have proceeded from the pens of our modern evangelists and historians of the 'apostles.' What have the latter, especially Ernest Rénan, done for us? They have brought us nearer and yet nearer to two great Figures, Jesus and Paul. They have performed the same kind of service for early Christian traditions, that our immortal dramatist performed for the early traditions of our English kings. But for the most part this has been done at the expense of that strong supernatural element in which our New Testament literature is steeped. In spite of all the efforts of the Evangelists of the second century to humanise Christ, to bring Him into intimate relations with flesh and blood, the outline of the story remains ghostly, spiritual, supernatural in the proper sense—the story that could alone, as we hold, have stirred the pulse of mankind. Working our way back through the fascinations of Art to that prime basis of religion, Belief, from which all great art springs, we find that it was the Gnostics, from Simon to Marcion, who truly grasped the principle that the new Religion was the revelation of a Mystery, and referred to relations between Heaven and Earth and Hades, not to be detected by the eye and ear of sense—a spiritual revelation made to the spiritual part in man.

We have striven to write with coldness on a subject which demands coldness in the inquirer all the more, if there is no subject in which his interest is more deeply engaged. We promise ourselves correction and enlargement of our views from the judgment of others. But, whatever mistakes we may have, nay, must have fallen into, in matters of detail, there can, in our humble opinion, be no mistake so wholesale and so stupendous as that of seeking to extract an accurate history of their past from the Christian writers of the second century. The first thing to be ascertained in matters of evidence is the character of the witnesses; and witnesses more passionate and more fanciful, less informed, or less scrupulous as to matters of fact, can be hardly found. Those who beg a good character for their witnesses at the outset beg the whole question at issue; and unfortunately, this is the common proceeding of writers who do not enjoy or do not exercise the freedom of their thoughts in these matters.

Not but that we keenly sympathise with those who cannot willingly part with the illusions of ages. But to surrender illusions on any vital subject means a momentary pain exchanged for a permanent good. What is life but an 'education by illusion?' What is the pursuit of Truth but the pursuit of light, through all eclipses never quenched? *Veritas, laborans nimis sæpe, extinguitur nunquam.* When once the New Testament books shall be assigned the place in literature and in ecclesiastical history which belongs to them, their varied contents will assume a new significance, and receive a critical appreciation denied to them, so long as the artificial assumptions as to their date and character continue.

It seems hardly an honest question to ask whether

our religion can continue to hold its ground in the faith and affections of the people, if the negative truth concerning its early literary records be candidly avowed by Christian teachers. Probably, however, the question has vexed the mind of many of our eminent men of letters since the time of the poet Cowley. And certainly it is a question that must be faced sooner or later by serious men. Some interesting discussions on this point have been held of late years by some Dutch theologians, mainly in consequence of the publication of Professor A. D. Loman's researches on Pauline questions. For ourselves, if we ever felt in early years that there was something in the Christianity of the heart that defied alike assault and defence; if we have observed with others that our religion continues to survive the apologies offered for it, and to flourish upon free criticism of its documents and the institutions connected with it, we have been confirmed in such persuasions by the results of our present inquiry. Our interest is in spiritual and enduring realities rather than in names and labels; and a better confession than that of *Christianus sum* in Tertullian's sense is that of *Homo sum* in the sense of Seneca and the gentle emperor, Marcus Aurelius. Citizens of a greater empire than even the Roman, it is well if we can understand that the religion we have inherited from our forefathers, was not in its inception provincial, and should now be interpreted, according to its history and genius, as the humane and the universal faith.

Be this as it may, we share strongly the feelings of some Churchmen of our time,—that the habit of cultivating critical acumen to the highest degree, in reference to classical letters and history, in our schools and universities, and of blunting its edge when brought to bear on Christian letters and history, is the source of great moral evil in the educated world. Ecclesiastical institutions are on their trial in our time; and to us it seems that they cannot retain their hold on the conscience and affections of the people by the promotion of chastity, temperance, thrift, and every possible virtue—except candour and truthfulness in the treatment of the documents and history of the Christian religion.

The history of the Church and of its dogmas properly begins with the period of the Antonines, 138–180 A.D. Here we find ourselves still in the midst of a legendary atmosphere. The foundations of the 'Ecclesia,' in the new sense, are being laid upon the Rock-man, and the college of Hierosolymite apostles. The counter-legend of Paulus is being elaborated from opposite polemical standpoints. Amidst the haze stands out with clearness the historical figure of Marcion alone. The name of Irenæus is of significance only as the reputed author of a work against the Hæretics, which is a monument of their influence as the first Theologians of the Innovation. Clement of Alexandria already adopts the broad principles of the Gnosis.

The study of the Hæretics and of the sources of

their Doctrines leads to far-reaching perspectives, and brings to light the wide basis of ancient spiritual Belief on which the new Creed and Rites were built. In short, the Innovation resumed and purified the religious life of the great peoples of antiquity. Egyptians, Persians, the mixed populations of the Levant, the Greeks, and the Romans all contributed to it. Not without reason does the writer of the 'Acts of the Apostles' give so extensive a map of the area affected by this great revolution.

Its history, we repeat, is no provincial tale. There is a true sense, as Augustine remarked in his *Retractationes*, in which the Religion existed from the beginning. According to our modern way of speaking, it is the great expression of the ideal life in mankind, not to be confounded with particular and positive facts, but lending an undying charm to the poor and sorry chronicle of those facts.

'*La mère, c'est la Tradition même,*' said the brilliant author of *La Bible de l'Humanité*. And in the poetical sense it is true that the modern quest of the 'ancient Mother' means the renewed study, not so much of the antiquities of this or that people, as of the common heart of Humanity which throbs in all.

ANTIQUA MATER.

Part I.

THE EXTERNAL HISTORY.

CHAPTER I.

PAGAN SOURCES—THE REIGN OF TRAJAN—PLINY AND TACITUS ON THE CHRISTIANI AND CHRISTUS—SUETONIUS—THE 'AUTHOR OF THE CHRISTIAN NAME.'

DURING the reign of Trajan (98–117), Tacitus was writing his *Annals*, Suetonius was composing his *Memoirs of the Emperors*, Juvenal his *Satires*. Pliny the younger was 'legatus pro prætore' of the province of Pontus and Bithynia under the same emperor.

Plutarch (ob. c. 125), whose writings contain so rich a mine of moral and religious lore, flourished during this and the following reign.[1]

Pliny is supposed to have written his famous letter to Trajan in the autumn or winter of A.D. 112.[2] He was then proprætor of Pontus and Bithynia. In the

[1] Müller and Donaldson, *Hist. of Lit. of Ancient Greece*, 3. 179.
[2] Mommsen, *Hermes* iii. 53, for 1869. See Ep. 10, 28. Bruno Bauer, *Christus und die Cäsaren*, 2 aufl., 1879, p. 268 f.

year 93 or 94 he had been prætor at Rome, but never having been present at judicial inquiries concerning Christians, he says that he was ignorant of what was customary in respect to the trial or punishment of them.[1] He has great hesitation as to whether he should make some distinction in point of the age of the accused or not, whether those of tender and those of robust years should be placed on one footing. Ought the convicted to be pardoned on repentance? Or was no indulgence to be shown to those who had once been Christians, and then had desisted from their profession? Was he to punish the *mere name* of Christian, though dissociated from crime, or only the crimes that might be associated with the name?[2]

Pliny goes on to describe the procedure he had hitherto adopted towards those who were brought before him on this charge. Thrice he put the question to them, with threats of punishment: Were they Christians? If they persevered in the affirmative answer, he ordered them to be led away to execution. For he felt assured that, whatever the nature of their belief might be, 'their pertinacity, their inflexible obstinacy,' ought to be punished. Some of those senseless fools, he adds, were Roman citizens, and, on that ground, he marked them out to be sent to Rome.

But soon, as the governor found, accusations increased, and that in consequence of his own action in the matter. An anonymous *libel* was brought to his notice, containing the names of many persons. Different

---

[1] Cf. Plini et Trajani Epp. 10. 96, 97, ed. Keil, Lips. 1870.

[2] The resemblance of this argument (under the form of inquiry) to Justin Martyr, *Apol.* 1. 4, should be noticed. Cf. also Athenag, *Leg. pro Christ.*, 2; Tertull. *Apol.* 3; Lactant. 4. 7.

kinds and degrees of this widespread criminality were ascertained. Some denied that they were or had been Christians. In the presence of the governor[1] they called on the gods, made supplication to the image of the emperor, which had been placed for that purpose among the *simulacra* of the deities, with offerings of incense and wine. They invoked maledictions on Christus, such as no real Christians could be forced to utter. They were then dismissed. Others who had been named by an informer confessed they were Christians, but presently denied the same; they had been such, but several years ago, in one case so far back as twenty years, had abandoned their confession. All these were put to the same test before the image of the emperor and the *simulacra* of the gods.

So far then as this testimony goes, if it be genuine, we learn that the Christian name and confession had been known in Asia Minor about as early as the year 90. The genuineness is, however, mere matter of opinion. For the moment we will assume it. A few years later than Pliny's testimony comes that of his friend Tacitus, who is writing (c. 112–115) a narrative of the great fire at Rome, which occurred in the reign of Nero, when the annalist was about ten years of age. To divert from himself the suspicion of having caused the conflagration, Nero arraigned and cruelly punished 'those called by the common folk Christiani, hated because of their *flagitia*.'[2] Suetonius, a contemporary of Tacitus, writing perhaps some years later, simply tells us that the Christiani, a 'genus hominum superstitionis novæ ac maleficæ,' were severely punished in the reign of Nero.[3]

[1] He 'dictated the words' (prœeunte, cf. Ep. 10. 60).
[2] *Ann.* 15. 44.   [3] *Ner.* 16.

The important question here arises, What is the exact value of this testimony in reference to the rise of the generic name *Christiani?* It is certain only that Tacitus when he wrote knew the name, and attached to it the same odious and contemptible significance that was current among Romans of his class. He had been a Roman magistrate in Domitian's reign (81–96)[1] when *Jews* were persecuted, but not—so far as we can ascertain—Christians as a 'class of men' distinct to the Roman eye from Jews. Tacitus must have known of the condemnation of Flavius Clemens and Domitilla, the relatives of Domitian; and there is no proof that this pair were branded by the Romans with the name *Christiani*.[2] They were converts to Judaism, according to Dion Cassius, while Suetonius only characterises Clemens as a man of 'contemptible sloth.' The relatives of Domitian may, for aught we know to the contrary, have been, nay probably were, believers in the Messianic *parousia* and kingdom, and hence in part drew suspicion and accusation upon themselves.[3] The listlessness towards mundane business, said to be so disgraceful in Clemens, might well be, as with others, the effect of his enthusiasm. But he, with others, is not charged with *Christianity*, but with *atheotes*, and divagation to the customs of the *Jews*.[4] There is absolutely no evidence in the historians that during the fifteen years of Domitian's rule there was any animadversion against

---

[1] Teuffel, *Gesch. d. Röm. Lit.*, § 332 ff., ed. 3.

[2] Dion., 67. 14 ; cf. H. Schiller, *Gesch. d. Röm. Kaiserzeit*, 1883, pp. 537, 577.

[3] The real motive of the condemnation was doubtless political. On the turbulent Cynic mob orators of the time, and the atmosphere of conspiracy in which the Flavian emperors lived, Suet. *Vesp.* 13 ; Tacit. *Dial. de Orat.* 10 ; Suet. *Dom.* 10.

[4] Xiphilinus (Dion. *Cass.* 67. 14).

the *Nomen*, which to confess and persist in confessing, was an offence punishable with death in the eyes of Trajan and of Pliny.

Ignore for a moment the disputed places in Tacitus and Suetonius, it then becomes apparent from the concurrence of evidence in Pagan with Talmudic writers, that it was not till near the close of the first century that a schism among Jews of the Circumcision and new religionists, never thenceforth to be closed, began to be revealed. The weight of evidence is therefore overwhelming against the assumption that so early as the reign of Nero (54–68) the *nomen* and the stigma existed, the origin of which is one of the main points of our inquiry.

But is there any fair and reasonable explanation of what was in the minds of Tacitus and Suetonius when they imagined *Christiani* to have existed in Rome in Nero's reign? We believe there is. Tacitus was aware that the designative word was derived from the name *Christus*. To speak of Christians was to speak of the followers of the *Auctor Nominis ejus*, who suffered death under the procurator Pontius Pilate, in the reign of Tiberius. Tacitus says nothing of Jesus: Christ is the *proper name* with him of the Head of the Christians. In the *Histories* Tacitus had given a strangely fabulous and vague account of the early history of the Jews, taken probably from unfriendly Greeks of Alexandria. He could have known nothing of the distinction between believers in *a* Messiah, and believers in *the* Messiah, Jesus. In writing of the event of the year 70, he enables us to understand how the Messianic expectation shaped itself to the thought of a Roman. 'Many (at Jerusalem) were persuaded that in the ancient books of the priests it was contained, that the Orient should prevail at that time, and those who went from Judea.'[1] While the Jews interpreted the *ambages* in their own favour, the event showed that Vespasian and the Flavian house were intended.[2] So Romans reasoned, having no inkling of that great struggle for empire over the imagination of mankind, signified by the opposition of Christ and Antichrist, which was going on, in scenes remote from the battlefield and the popular tumult. But if at that epoch and long before there glowed in multitudes of Jewish breasts a proud and triumphant faith in the Anointed of the Lord, in the King seated on Zion's sacred hill, to whom the heathen had been decreed as His inheritance and the whole world for His possession, and who should dash His enemies to pieces as a potter's vessel, what wonder if such faith broke forth into irrepressible and exultant self-manifestation, when Rome was in flames, and the beginning of the end seemed to be near at hand? Now, in a single day, the superb queen of the Seven Hills had been smitten with death and mourning and hunger, and should be burned with fire according to the *fiat* of the mighty divine Judge. Such belief must necessarily appear to every loyal Roman to be the effects of an *exitiabilis superstitio*, and the feelings reflected therefrom must bear the colour of a 'hatred of the human race.'

Our explanation then of the passage in Tacitus is that the term *Christiani* had for him a value altogether different from that which it has long borne for us and for the history of the world since the great Messianic

---

[1] Hist. 5. 13.
[2] Cf. Suet. *Vesp.* 4; Joseph. *B. J.* 6. 5. 4. Dion. (Xiphilinus) 66. 4, 7, 8. [Holtzmann, *Judenth. u. Christenth.* 479.]

illusions faded away, toward the end of the second century. The sufferers under Nero were Messianists, 'Fifth Monarchy men,' it might almost be said, of whom a large number were probably proselytes to Judaism, and who were inflamed with those ardent and passionately confident hopes of the downfall of the Roman empire and of the establishment of the kingdom of the Hagioi and the Elect, which are reflected in the Book of Enoch and in the Apocalypse.

What the Neronian government struck at with a severity so appalling was a political creed and a political faction, to which modern Fenians, Anarchists, or Nihilists, furnish a certain analogy; only that an intense religious zeal supplied fuel to the Messianic politics in a manner or degree unparalleled in our times. That the *Christiani* who were first seized admitted their guilt,[1] that they informed against others, and that a vast multitude were convicted, not so much on the charge of incendiarism as of hatred of mankind, Tacitus further tells us. Nor is there anything incredible in this, when we compare the history of epidemics of enthusiasm. By no means easy of credence, on the other hand, is the part assigned to Nero in this horrible drama.[2] It is for us a sober inference that here as elsewhere the imagination of Tacitus, who was a great poet, but a timid man, has projected those horrible representations of a mad

[1] *Qui fatebantur* may of course be understood of their confession of *incendiarism*, or of being *Christiani*. We take the latter view, on the basis of the evidence as a whole. The word seems copied from Pliny's letter; and the obscure use of it is a strong ground of suspicion against the passage.

[2] Cf. the silence of Josephus, no friend of Nero, *Ant.* 20. 8. 2, 3. H. Schiller, *Nero*, 425, cf. his remarks on Tacitus, 16. Joel, *Blicke,* 2. 143, who cites Stahr in Westermann's *Monatshefte*, 1875, 583.

tyrant upon a canvas, on which he works with the peculiar zest of an historical artist.

We cannot presume positively to assert at this stage of the inquiry that Tacitus and Suetonius ante-dated the use of the name *Christiani* from the reign of Trajan into that of Nero,[1] but only that both at the later and earlier epoch the name was a vulgar designation of a faction on whose lips, whether they used Greek or Latin, the name *Christus* or *Chrestus* was frequently sounded, and who connected with that name a *superstitio* novel and of deadly tendency in relation to the order and stability of the empire.[2]

We pass upward from the reign of Nero to that of Claudius (41–54). Here a brief notice of Suetonius informs us that the Jews, incessantly rioting under the impulsion of *Chrestus* (if such be the true reading),[3] were expelled from Rome. But Josephus has no reference to this matter; and Dion says that the Jews were forbidden to meet together and practise their rites, but that they could not be expelled because of their great numbers. Under this conflict of testimony little stress can be laid upon the passage in Suetonius. It is not certain that he meant by the instigator of the riots the *auctor nominis Christiani*,[4] but if he did he must have imagined him as a Roman Jew, and all that can be safely inferred from his statement, if its historical character be not questioned, is that the Messianists and their preaching excited the jealousy of the Roman authorities, and called for the interference of the police. It is known that about this

---

[1] That is, from the mere language they employ.
[2] Cf. Renan, *L'Antichrist*, 160, for the obscurity of the evidence.
[3] Only one MS. has this form. Others, *Cherestus*, &c.
[4] The word *impulsor* implies continued action. H. Schiller, *Gesch. d. Rom. Kaiserzeit*, 1883, p. 447, note.

time the Clubs (*hetæriai, sodalitia, thiasoi, synods, klinai*) were suppressed both at Rome and at Alexandria.¹ And in that fact we may find a suggestive hint of the manner in which the order of the empire was being undermined by forces which worked all the more dangerously in repression and in secret.

To resume the results of our inquiry up to this point: our two leading witnesses, such as they are, Tacitus and Suetonius, carry back their reminiscences of the *Christiani* to no earlier date than about 64, on the occasion of the fire at Rome. Their sufferings, as a sound historic criticism of the passages in question shows, were the result, not of a religious persecution, but of a police prosecution. At the time of their writing our witnesses certainly knew that *Christiani* were in some sense distinct from *Judæi*; but it by no means follows that at Rome fifty years before, that distinction was recognised outside the circle of Orientals. Tacitus in advanced life was probably aware that the *superstitio* was of Judæan origin, and was also aware that the fire in the time of his boyhood began in the quarter of the Orientals at Rome.² It is therefore highly probable that he connected these two facts in his mind, and transferred the Christian appellation by an anachronism to the year 64. And this conclusion becomes almost a moral certainty when we examine our other witnesses from the reigns of Trajan and of Hadrian. Plutarch, who was learned in Greek and Roman religion, touches on Jewish abstinence in food, and on the 'mysteries of the Hebrews,'³ but is silent as to Christians.

---

[1] Tac. *A.* 14, 17; Dion C. 60. 8. On Judaism at Rome in general, cf. Baur, *Die Christl. Kirche*, 60; Hausrath, *Ntl. Ztgesch.* I. 84.

[2] H. Schiller, *Nero*, 435 ff.

[3] *Sympos.* 4. 4. 4; cf. 5. 1; 6. 12; Tacit. *H.* 5. 5, 23; Levit. 23. 40.

Pausanias has some vague knowledge of the Jews, but is silent as to Christians, whether at Corinth or elsewhere. Juvenal, amidst several striking pictures of Jewish life and manners at Rome,[1] would certainly have introduced the Christians if their beliefs had made any noise in his time, but he too is silent about them.[2] Epictetus has but a single contemptuous reference to the obstinacy of the 'Galilæans;' it is like an echo of Pliny's sentiment. Pliny himself is assumed, as we have seen, to have been in sore need of a precedent for dealing with the Christians; how could he have been ignorant of precedents,[3] had *cognitiones* concerning their religious opinions been held, when he was prætor, or before? And how can the silence of a man in high place like Seneca, Nero's minister, about Christians, be explained, if they had made any impression on the social and public life of Rome?

It is just conceivable that theirs was a secret existence, and that they were secretly leavening the mass of Jews amongst whom they were lost to the Roman eye. But we wait for clearer and more abundant dateable evidence from subterranean Rome than has yet been supplied to the historical student.[4] Nor until we have ascertained the phænomena of the daylight, as described by contemporary witnesses, should we amuse our fancy with speculations upon burial clubs (*collegia funeraticia*) and their supposed analogy to the first Christian communities.[5]

As the question at present stands, it cannot be too

---

[1] Satt. 1. 155; 3. 13; 6. 390, 542; 14. 97.
[2] Cf. Merivale, *Hist. of Romans*, 6. 277.
[3] Cf. his boasts of experience in Ep. 1. 20.
[4] The oldest Christian inscription is said to date from 71 A.D. De Rossi, *Inscr.*, 1 ff. This is doubtful.
[5] H. Schiller, *Gesch. d. Röm. Kaiserzeit*, 448.

firmly stated, that the Christians as a distinct *religious* community, Christianity as a *religion* distinct from Judaism and from Paganism, stand out to the gaze of the world for the first time in the second decade of the second century. And for this conclusion we have but two doubtful texts.

What was then known by Romans of the authorship of the Christian name? The answer runs in Tacitus' words: *Auctor nominis ejus Christus Tiberio imperitante per procuratorem Pontium Pilatum supplicio affectus erat.*[1]

The statement as to the 'authorship' is vague, because there is no other evidence to show that in the earliest time Christ gave this name to His followers, or that they adopted it for themselves.[2] Setting aside the New Testament, there is evidence that the earliest Catholic Christians loved to call themselves, even as the Hellenist Jews of Alexandria, by such names as *Hagioi* and *Eklektoi*, and *Brethren*; and where the name Christianos appears, it is in some connection which hints that the new people are accommodating themselves to it, as the characteristic name alone recognised of their profession in the Roman world. In the *Didaché* (*Doctrina Apostolorum*),[3] the name only once occurs, and then with a kind of slur, as if the reproach of inertness had fastened on the 'Christians' in the midst of a poor and hard-working community. This part of the tract, according to the average opinion of critics, belongs to the later half of the second century. Justin Martyr, writing during

---

[1] *Ann.* 15. 44.
[2] The name is probably of Roman origin, like *Herodianoi*, and was originally sounded Chréstiani, nay, was still so pronounced in Lactantius' time.
[3] 12. 4. προ νοήσατε, πῶς μὴ ἀργὸς μεθ' ὑμῶν ζήσεται χριστιανός.

the same period, plays upon the name, and endeavours to make some capital out of the resemblance in sound of χριστιανοί to χρηστιανοί.[1] Apparently he recognises no earlier name of the people whose cause he has undertaken to defend. He charges the Jews with having 'chosen out select men' (ἄνδρας ἐκλεκτούς) and having sent them forth from Jerusalem into the whole world to declare that a godless Hæresis (αἵρ· ἄθεον) of *Christians* had arisen; and that this was said by all who were not acquainted with the *Christians*.[2]

This statement is illustrated later by Tertullian[3] and by Eusebius.[4] The Apostles of the Sanhedrin, furnished with epistles or encyclic letters, went, it is said, everywhere through the world, denouncing the teaching of Christ as a new and godless heresy. 'Apostles,' in Jewish definition, were still, in Eusebius' time and later, those who were supplied with such encyclic letters from 'the Rulers.'

At what time were these Jewish missionaries sent forth by the Sanhedrin? Neither Justin Martyr nor Eusebius fix the date: the former says it was 'after the resurrection and ascension was known to the Jews;' the latter says merely that he had found the statement in the 'writings of the ancients,' but mentions no epoch.[5]

But here Jewish scholars, students of the Talmud,

---

[1] ὅσον γε ἐκ τοῦ κατηγορουμένου ἡμ. ὀνόματος, χρηστότατοι ὑπάρχομεν. *Apol.* i. 4.   [2] *Dial. c. Tryph.* 17; cf. 108, 117.
[3] *Ad Nation.* 1. 14; *Adv. Marc.* 3. 23; *Adv. Jud.* 13; *Apol.* 16.
[4] Euseb. *in Jes.* xviii. 1, p. 424; Epiph. *H.* 1. 2. 4; cf. Graetz, 4. 304, 476.
[5] It is not proved by Justin's statements, nor by those of later writers, that the Jewish heretics (Minim or Nazarenes) of 80–100 were the spiritual progenitors of the *Christiani*. The Gnostics, as we shall see later, were not only the great Anti-nomians, but the great Anti-nationalists from the beginning of Hadrian's reign.

come forward to assure us that no division respecting the Messianic question or the Law so irreconcilable as that above indicated, occurred in the Jewish camp; no fatal quarrel, no 'rent in the family table-cloth,' until the time of Trajan.[1] Here we have (according to Joel) a date sufficiently precise, the cessation of the feast-day called 'Jom Trajanus' by the Jews.[2] This evidence we are bound to respect and receive, until it be convincingly rebutted. And thus we are brought to the same historic result as before. The epoch at which the 'godless Heresy' of the Christians or their precursors is revealed to the view of the Jamnia Sanhedrin is a little earlier than the epoch at which the same movement presents itself as a novel, extravagant, and mischievous *superstitio* to the observation of Pliny, Tacitus, and Suetonius. The seed-bed of the new religion is to be found in the spiritual conditions of the world, especially in Syria and Asia Minor, at the close of the first and the beginning of the second century of our era.

But now it must follow that if the name of the new people was not an object of public knowledge until that epoch, neither could a historic founder have been the object of public knowledge before that epoch, who bore the proper name 'Christus.' For in Tacitus this is a proper name. He does not think of the Auctor as an ideal being, both human and divine, like an Asklépios, the auctor of the Asklepiads, or other

---

[1] Graetz, *Gesch. d. Juden*, 4. 104 ff. Joel, *Blicke*, 1. 14 ff., 2. 87 ff. Derenbourg, *Essai*, 408, 422.

[2] Against Joel's view that Christianity was at first a Jewish *national* movement, see Oort, *Theol. Tijdsch.*, 1883, p. 509. He admits, however, that the dissension between the orthodox Jews and the heretics who claimed freedom in the interpretation of the Law dates from Gamaliel II., 80–117. See *Addenda*, 1.

eponymous founders, but simply as a man who had suffered, through the agency of the Roman procurator, in Tiberius' reign. He ignores the name Jesus; and yet surely had any authentic records of Pilate's proceedings existed among the Roman archives, the Auctor would have been described as Jesus, who was called Christ or King of the Jews. The title would not have been given as the proper name. But there is no proof, as is well known, that any genuine 'Acts of Pilate' ever existed.[1] Whence then did Tacitus derive his information? Was he acquainted with Josephus personally or with his *Antiquities?* Either he had seen the passage in that work relating to the good man who had suffered under Pilate, or he had not. If he had seen it, he must have known that His name was Jesus, or must have rejected the passage as spurious. If he had not seen it, he must have informed himself from some other source, Jewish or Christian. An anti-Christian Jew would not have given him Christus as the proper name of the Auctor, for this was to ignore the titular use of the word. Tacitus' source then was probably Christian.[2] In any case, his omission of the name Jesus shows how distant and inaccurate was his view of the fact of the death of the Founder, as compared with the representations in our Gospels.

[1] Cf. on the *Gesta Pilati* or Gospel of Nicodemus, *Supernatural Relig.* (6th ed. 1875, 1. 325, 338).

[2] Since writing the above, and after much consideration and reconsideration, we are constrained to express a strong doubt as to the genuineness of the passages in Pliny and Tacitus. Whether derived from Christiani, or Christian interpolations, their value as evidence is much the same. Dr. A. Pierson, *Die Bergrede,* 87 ff., thinks these accounts interpolations. The student should consider above all whence and at what time the self-damning boast *Christianus sum!* is said to have arisen.

It is most disconcerting to our prepossessions when for the first time we realise that the all-stupendous Event of the Passion, on which Christendom has for so many ages fixed its devout gaze, has for its reality as distinct from its ideality no earlier literary evidence than the bald statement of one so little exact in his information as Tacitus. Had he read our Gospels, or even been acquainted with the conciliatory temper manifested in them towards the Romans, he could never have denounced the Christians in the terms he has used. Yet were those details of the Passion in the Gospel causing multitudes of hearts to vibrate all around him when he wrote, and he wholly ignorant of them? We cannot but remind ourselves in passing that the date of the New Testament books is the great question really *sub judice* in such inquiries.

Omitting those books, we inquire what particulars were known to the world concerning the life and death of the 'Auctor,' at the beginning of the second century? The loss of the books of Tacitus referring to the period after 29 is lamentable and irreparable, and excites suspicion no less than regret. However, there is no reason to suppose that they contained any ampler account of Christian origins than that which lies before us in his later page. Possibly, in those lost Annals he 'traced, in a few burning touches, the fierce unyielding character of that marvellous people to whom, as the surest of human depositaries, were committed the oracles of God;' and gave more particular details concerning 'the false and offensive statements regarding the origin of the intruders from Palestine, which circulated among their enemies, and which, as we discover from the allusion of Tacitus himself at a later period, were accepted by the Romans with the prone credulity of national exasperation.'[1] It is our Jewish brethren who must most keenly feel that literary and historical loss.[2]

But to return to the passage in the Annals (xv. 44). It is the part of the historical student to discover dates if possible, but not to invent them. After all the labours of chronologists, the year of the Passion remains unknown, and the date of the birth of Jesus.[3] The conjectural dates assigned to the Crucifixion vary, ranging from 27 to 33. The statement of Tacitus is no more than the statement of the 'Apostles' Creed,' concerning the Founder. 'He suffered under Pontius Pilate.' And this statement dates from nearly three human generations after the presumed event.

Jewish sources (we may hardly cite the questionable passage in Josephus as evidence) contain none of those events which are supposed during 30–70 to have agitated the Orient.[4] At the latter date, as we have seen, an expectation of something great from the Orient prevailed. From the year 80 only, as Talmudists assure us,[5] is there evidence of disputes in the interior of Judaism with the *Minim*[6] and Denunciants, as the heretics and apostates were called. At the end of another generation, in the reign of

[1] Merivale, *Hist. of the Romans*, 5. 414.

[2] Cf. Joel, *Blicke*, 2. 96.

[3] V. Clinton, *Fasti Ro.*, and the works of Sanclemente, Ideler, and A. W. Zumpt (1869); H. Schiller, *Gesch. d. Röm. Kaiserzeit*, 1883, p. 460; Merivale *Hist. of the Romans*, v. 351.

[4] Cf. Loman. *Theol. Tijdschr.*, 1882.

[5] Joel, *Blicke*, 1. 30; Graetz, *Gesch. d. Juden*, 4.

[6] Joel would explain this as = οἱ πιστοί, which is doubtful. Jerome identifies (*Ep. ad Aug.*) the Minæi with Nazaræi as Jewish heretics of the Eastern Synagogues of his time. The word Christian is anathematised as Nazarene. Ib. c. 5; v. 18. Toland, *Nazarenus*, c. viii.; Selden, *de Synedr.* 1. 8.

Trajan, these controversies reached their acme. The Sanhedrists forbade the instruction of the youth in Greek, and officially opposed the new translation of the Scriptures by Aquila to the Septuagint, which they considered to be a garbled version; and their Apostles went forth through the Diaspora upon their errand of warning and of repression. Thus again we return to the time when Tacitus was listening from his study window to the ominous sounds which were beginning to fill the air. A sect was being everywhere spoken against, was bringing bitter discord into the bosom of Jewish households, because of its attacks upon the Law and the Temple, was becoming the object of official prosecution at the hands of the Romans. The peculiar and essential dogmas of a sect are never sharply defined, until it is attacked and its existence threatened. In the case of the Jews and the Denunciants the strongest causes of antipathy between men and men were at work; for the fate of Judaism itself, its national customs with that simple and sublime Theology on which those customs were based, was at stake. The controversy was embittered by the fact that both parties appealed to the same sacred Scripture, and used the like weapons of controversial exegesis.[1] The Romans, on the other hand, faced the new Power with a weakened religious conscience; and perhaps dimly perceived in the spiritual Head of the Christians a rival to the emperor.

So far we have reached a negative result, but one of great importance. There is no reference in the literature of the first century to *Christiani* at all. And of the literature of the earlier years of the second century, the only historical or quasi-historical passage,

[1] Joel, *Blicke*, 2. 48 ff.; Oort, *u. s.*

that in Tacitus, yields no proof that the Christians existed as a religious sect distinct from the Jews, or had been exposed to religious persecution in the time of Nero, or at any time before the reign of Trajan. The so-called persecution under Nero was but a continuation of the measures taken against Orientals under Tiberius and Claudius.[1]

Nor have we a single notice of the Founder of the *Christiani*, or their supposed Founder, until the same epoch. His proper name was unknown to the Romans; and there is no dateable repetition of the statement by the Roman writer that he suffered under Pontius Pilate, until it is met with again in the writings of the Christian apologist, Justin Martyr, c. 147. But the Simonians, and other sects of Gnostic *Christiani*, were before Justin. If we can trust his statement (repeated by Irenæus) that their legendary head, Simon Magus of Gitton in Samaria, flourished in honour at Rome so early as the time of Claudius, then Gnostic mysteries, magic, and theosophy,—a system first developed in Samaria by teachers imbued with Alexandrian or Platonic wisdom, and which thence spread through Syria and Asia Minor to the shores of the Euxine,— was the real beginning of the Christian revolution. The Gnostics appear to have had from the first a tradition of a crucifixion of Jesus, though they denied that their *Christus*, a spiritual and impassible being, could be subject either to birth or death. This novel *cultus* was that which Pliny, Tacitus, and Suetonius correctly described, from a Roman standpoint, not as a *Mos*, but a *Superstitio*, the introduction of the worship of a new god.

And now we take the unusual course of turning

---

[1] Cf. Schiller, *Gesch. d. Rom. Kaiserzeit*, 449.

back upon ourselves and criticising our own arguments. The kindly reader will not accuse us of 'recklessness' in our treatment of the much-disputed passages in Pliny and Tacitus. We have endeavoured, on the assumption of their genuineness, to ascertain their purport; but must now remark that these texts cannot be made to yield anything certain or even probable, in point of historical information. And so far we will anticipate, and say, as the result of our whole inquiry, that the notion of a 'name' and the 'confession' apart from any other guilt as punishable by the Roman government, seems an absurdity on the face of it. Further, that the original names current with the Greek and Roman vulgar were *Chréstianoi, Chréstus,* connected with the use of the words τὸ χρηστόν, χρηστός, χρηστότης; and that the assumption of the form *Christianoi*, with the clumsy and self-betraying attempts to explain it as connected with the *unction* of Christians, or with the Jewish *Messiah,* were part of that great usurpation of Old Testament antiquity which began, on the part of the 'great church,' in the latter half of the second century.[1]

---

[1] The embarrassed attempts of the Fathers to explain the name Chrestiani, or Christiani, are remarkable. Cf. Jerome on χρηστότης in Gal. v. 22. 'Those who have believed on Christ are χρηστοί.' The question arises whether *Chrestos*, as name of the Auctor, the 'Good' or 'Blessed One' (like Μακάριος), was not earlier than Christos,—an epithet of the 'good God' believed by the Gnostics.—Chrestos: a Religious Epithet. By J. B. Mitchell, M.D., 1880.

CHAPTER II.

REFERENCES TO THE JEWS IN THE ROMAN LITERATURE OF THE SECOND CENTURY.

BUT now, that we may have a distincter view of the limits of Roman knowledge of the sources of our religion at the era beginning with Trajan, let us cast a rapid glance at those pictures of Jewish life in Rome which we find in the *Satires* of Juvenal, and elsewhere.

From 63 B.C., when Judæa was subdued by Pompey, and many Jews were carried to Rome as slaves, we may date a quiet but considerable influence exerted by them in the affairs of the city.[1] Their numbers, their concord amongst themselves, and their influence in public meetings, are dwelt upon by Cicero in his oration for Flaccus, delivered in B.C. 59.[2] On the other hand there must have been counter influences at work upon them in their exile from Jerusalem, which tended to relax the strictness of their religious practice and of their principles.[3] After 35 B.C., when Sosius had taken

---

[1] From this period dates the Messianic *Psalter of Solomon.* Edersheim, *Life of Jesus,* 1. 31. 1. 74; *Christos Kyrios,* Ps. 17. 36. Cf. Lament. Jer. 4. 20, LXX.

[2] Cf. Tacit. *Ann.* 2. 85; Philo. *Leg. ad Cai.*, 2. 568. On the *Pons Judæorum,* Graetz, 3. 142, ed. 2, cites Basnage, *Hist. des Juifs.* 4. 1047; Frankel, *Monatschr.*, Jahrg. 3. 437.

[3] *Vide* the tractat. Pesachim, 53a, 66a, 70b., cited by Graetz, *u. s.*

Jerusalem, the number of Jews in Rome must have increased. In the quarter called the Vicus Tuscus we find them settled in the time of Horace; and in the engaging companionship of the poet and his friend, the man of letters, Aristius Fuscus, we may gaze upon a Sabbath scene similar, perhaps, to that which presents itself in the Ghetto at the present day.[1] Horace terms the holiday the 'thirtieth Sabbath,' thus evincing but a confused acquaintance with Jewish customs. Yet it is remarkable that he should, even in jest, represent his friend as 'one of many' who had scruples about offending the *curti Judæi* by disregard of the sacred day. In another satire he alludes to their cogent zeal in controversy; they prevailed by turbulence and numbers;[2] and in another he has a sketch of a superstitious mother who vows that her sick boy, if he recovers, shall on the fast-day (probably the Monday or Thursday fast of the Pharisees) stand naked in the Tiber. In another place he alludes to the superstitious credulity of the Jew Apella, probably a freedman. Horace himself is not impressed by respect for the people;[3] yet we may well suppose that there were many, even among educated Romans, who were struck by their disdainful attitude toward the pagan deities, and by their unbending character amidst the spiritual decrepitude which prevailed.[4]

A letter of Augustus (in Suetonius) makes a confused allusion to a *sabbatis jejunium* of the Jews;[5] and

---

[1] *Sat.* I. 9. 70; cf. Dernburg, *Die Institutionem des Gaius*, 1869, p. 18.
[2] *Sat.* I. 4. 142; cf. Friedländer, *Darstell.* iii. 509.
[3] B. Bauer, however, somewhat fancifully finds his *conversion* in *Car.* I. 34.
[4] Gens contumelia numinum insignis.—Plin. *N. H.* 13. 4 (9), 46.
[5] Octav. 76; cf. 93, and Justin, 36. 2. The Day of Atonement is perhaps meant, Levit. 16. 31; Joel, *Blicke*, 2. 133.

it seems questionable whether either Suetonius or Tacitus or Seneca drew always clear distinctions between Egyptian rites of Isis and those of the Jews: the phrase 'that superstition' covers them both. They were in common suppressed by a *senatus consultum* in the reign of Tiberius, and the sacred utensils and vessels were burned. Jewish freedmen to the number of 4000 were enlisted in the army and transported to Sardinia and other unhealthy regions; while those who continued their 'profane rites' were threatened with expulsion from Italy by a fixed date (A.D. 19).[1]

In the East, although Syria and Judæa were wearied with their burdens, and had prayed for the remission of the tribute (A.D. 17),[2] there was, says Tacitus, 'rest under Tiberius;'[3] and he makes no allusion in this his earlier historical work to Christ or His followers, about whom Philo is also silent. Josephus has the suspect passage.[4]

The accession of Gaius (Caligula), and the attempt to set up his effigy in the temple, provoked the people to arms; the commotion ceased with the emperor's death. And one cannot but demand, if the sect supposed to have lived in amity with the Romans during the previous reign were increasing in Judæa in the time of Gaius, what part did they take in this commotion, and where is the record of it? The testimony of Tacitus has been destroyed, and the resentment of the Hagioi against the worship of the emperor has

---

[1] Tacit. *Ann.* 2. 85; Suet. *Tib.* 36. Cf. Senec. *Ep.* 108; Philo, *Leg. ad Cai.* 24; Joseph. *Ant.* 18. 3. 5.
[2] Tacit. *Ann.* 2. 42.   [3] *Hist.* 5. 9.
[4] *Ant.* 18. 3. 3. For the discussion of it recently, cf. G. Volkmar, *Jesus Nazarenus*, 1882; J. H. Scholten, *Theol. Tijdschr.*, 1882; B. Bauer, *Christus*, 8.

possibly found expression in the undated 'Wisdom of Solomon,' as well as in Josephus and Philo.

When the broken narrative of Tacitus is resumed in Claudius' reign, there comes before us the figure of Antonius Felix (*A.* 12. 54), whom he had painted in the *Histories* in strong contrasted colours as a man who wielded the power of a monarch in the spirit of a slave, a man cruel and vicious to the last degree. He must have tyrannised in Judæa for many years; but Tacitus is silent as to any religious disputes which might have come before him, while he notices the guerilla warfare which went on between the Galilæans under Ventidius Cumanus, and the Samaritans under Felix, and the intervention of Quadratus, governor of Syria (A.D. 52). He knows of no stream of *Christiani*, nor any apostle of their creed passing Romewards.[1]

To revert to Rome. Already we have seen that the Jewish riots at Rome a year or two before (c. 48) cannot, by any fair interpretation, be understood to have had reference to Christians. Much more probably distress or outrage was the cause, or most probably a too great confidence in their numbers, and a desire to quell those hopes of sovereignty over Jerusalem and the East, which dazzled the upper classes, and were encouraged by mercenary astrologers.

But as to the distress and poverty of the Jews at this period, the picture in Persius, drawn from the life, stands before us *en evidence*,—the picture of 'Herod's Day.'[2]

In the reign of Nero, the city, according to Tacitus,

---

[1] Cf. Joseph. *Ant.* 20. 6 ff. He names Simon a Mage in the reign of Claudius, but makes him a Cypriote Jew, 20. 7. 2. Cf. the Cypriote Mage, 'a Jew,' in Acts 13. 6 ff. The encounter seems a reflection of that in chap. 8. (the two Simons).

[2] Sat. 5. 180. Cf. Sen. *Ep.* 95; Juvenal 3. 14, 6. 542.

had become a sink of atrocity and shame. And who that recalls the splendid commonplace (*Homo sum*, &c.) with which the world has been thrilled from the Roman stage; who that feels the real no less than the nominal nexus of 'humanity' with the Latin tongue and institutions, but must sympathise with the generous dismay of enlightened Romans if they discovered after the fire that the city harboured vast numbers who hated Rome's noblest ideal? But how could such a phænomenon have escaped the notice of Juvenal and of Seneca? How is it that no particulars are given of the forms which this misanthropy assumed? If there is no 'substantial evidence' that Tacitus was here guilty of an anachronism, there is 'substantial evidence' that he had a very lax conception of the duties of a historian,[1] and no substantial evidence that a notice is correct and unconfused, which stands out isolated amidst the silence of his predecessors and contemporaries.

Here the notices in Juvenal, who also wrote during Trajan's reign, may be introduced.[2] He refers to the punishment of the *Tunica molesta* in connection with attacks on Tigellinus, which was also the punishment of incendiaries; so do Martial and Seneca;[3] but there is not a word in either to connect this punishment with the *Christiani*.

Then we have the picture in Juvenal of the settlement of Jews—

"Quorum cophinus fœnumque supellex,"

in the grove Egeria, close to the Porta Capena, during the reign of Domitian. To this reign also belongs the

---

[1] See Nipperdey's Introduction to the *Annals*.
[2] 1. 155, 8. 235.   [3] *Ep.* 14; *De Ira*, 3. 3.

notice in Suetonius[1] of the severity with which the Poll-tax was levied upon the Jews through the empire, and of the outrages to which they were thereby subjected. Nor do our accounts of this period from writers of the third and fourth century establish that the Christians were distinguished from Jews in the persecution of the latter. It is idle, when we are asking for evidence on certain questions of fact, and when we have ascertained that the evidence is small in amount and dubious or negative in effect, to insist that this or that may have been known or may have occurred. For the Flavian period our pagan sources are silent as to Christians, and our late Christian witness, Eusebius, is a man who contradicts himself and cannot be trusted.[2] Writing in the reign of Constantine, he was naturally eager to claim for the new religion the gentle world-wearied spirits of Domitian's time as confessors and martyrs. They had much in common with the pure and peaceable spirit that we love to associate with Christianity, but to call them Christiani is an assumption and an anachronism. Once more the course of our inquiry has brought us back to the reign of Trajan and to the standpoint of Juvenal. He, with Tacitus, had a distinct knowledge of some of the external peculiarities of the Jews. He alludes to Oriental kings observing the Sabbath feast, with bare feet; to the begging Jew at Rome who interprets the laws of Jerusalem and the will of highest heaven; to Jews who sell for a trifle whatever dreams you will; to those who adore naught but the clouds and the spirit of the sky, and who think that swine's flesh is

---

[1] *Dom.* 12.
[2] On the Flavian period and the influence of refined Judaism at Rome in conjunction with ascetic Stoicism, see B. Bauer, *Christus in die Casaren*, 240 ff.

of the same value with human flesh. He alludes to circumcision, to the contempt of the Roman laws, to the reverence for the Law handed down in a mysterious volume by Moses, which they have by heart. He says that they will not show the way except to a fellow-worshipper, and that they lead the circumcised alone to the fountain sought; where, says a scholiast, they are baptized.

Tacitus,[1] after a legendary account of supposed Jewish migrations, tells us that Moses instituted new rites, contrary to those of other mortals. 'With them all things that with us are sacred are profane; allowed among them those which with us are polluted.' He adds fables about the worship of the ass, and the cause of their abstinence from the swine and other matters on which we need not dwell. Amongst various calumnies he bears witness to their 'persistent good faith, and their ready compassion amongst one another;' to all others they cherish the hatred of enemies. It will be noticed how closely this corresponds to the account of the *Christiani* in the *Annals*. Tacitus goes on to speak of the lustfulness of the Jews, so that though they abstain from intercourse with stranger women, *inter se nihil inlicitum;* of their separateness from others, of the institution of circumcision, the object of which is to distinguish them from others, and which is adopted by those who pass over to their Mos (*transgressi in morem corum*), of the first principles in the instructions of these proselytes. To contemn the gods, to lay aside patriotism, to hold parents, children, brothers cheap. They aim at the increase of their numbers. To slay a kinsman is forbidden; and the souls of those who perish in battle or by the exe-

---

[1] *Hist.* 5. 1 ff.

cutioner are believed to be eternal. Hence their love of offspring and their contempt of death. They are distinct with the Egyptians in their disposal of the dead, practising burial rather than cremation; they have the like belief concerning the infernal powers. As to the celestial powers, while the Egyptians worship animals and effigies formed by art, the Jews believe with the mind alone, and own one Divine Power;[1] think them profane who fashion after the likeness of human beings and with perishable material, images of the gods; that supreme and eternal spirit, they say, can neither be imitated, nor be subject to destruction. Therefore they set up no *simulacra* in their cities, much less their temples. Not to kings do they render this flattery, nor this honour to Cæsars. Some, continues the historian, have thought, because their priests sung to the flute and the drums and crowned themselves with ivy, and because a golden vine was found in the temple, that they worshipped Father Liber, the subjugator of the Orient.[2] But the institutes are widely different. Liber appointed festive and joyous rites; but the *Mos* of the Jews is absurd and sordid.

Here Tacitus seems at his best, enjoying that peculiar power of characteristic remark in which he excels far more than in the accurate narration of distant facts. In his time Jewish writings were widely diffused; and it is probable enough that he had read the protest against the idolatry of the Gentiles in the Wisdom of Solomon.[3] The calumnies which he repeated were,

---

[1] "Mente sola unumque numen intelligunt."

[2] See this view in Plutarch, *Symp.* 6, referring as it seems to the use of wine at the Feast of Tabernacles.

[3] Chaps. 13. 14.

on the other hand, doubtless derived from Greeks of the type of Lysimachos and Apion. Still, it is observable, he expresses only distaste for the "Custom" of the Jews; he does not brand their belief as a deadly *superstitio*. Nor does he make the slightest allusion to the Messianic hope. Incidentally he notes the fact that the Jews made proselytes; and on other grounds it may be believed that they were numerous, in the lower if not in the higher ranks of society.

And now once more we return to the famous passage in the *Annals*, which came late from the pen of Tacitus. Only by repeated glances at the horizon of this writer and his contemporaries, only by noticing the light and shade, the eminences and the hollows of the scenery, so to speak, can we be fitted to give the correct importance to his testimony concerning the *Christiani* and *Christus*. We hold that he could have meant no more than that a new class of men, Messianists, followers of Messiah, whom he believed to be an individual, were then, in Trajan's time, about 116,[1] making themselves felt in the empire; that the vulgar scoff-name *Christiani* then current, marked them off from the *Judæi;* and that Tacitus transferred the name, on the ground of an identical hatred to mankind, to the reign of Nero, and to the Messianist zealots who took part in the burning of Rome. The whole review tends to warn us against the illusion and fallacy of giving precise meanings upon terms vaguely used by our witnesses. The name Christianus of itself conveyed nothing which an orthodox Jew might

---

[1] Cf. B. Bauer, *Christus, &c.*, 153. The criticisms of Gibbon, Merivale, Schiller, Keim, &c., all show how impossible it is to find *history* in the passage.

not accept, until it came to connote beliefs incompatible with reverence for the Law and the Temple and with strict monotheism. And since it is the object of our inquiry to trace the early history of beliefs which inspired and consoled, in other words, to obtain if possible a real definition of the contents of a creed and life vaguely labelled by Romans *Christian*, it is well to revert to the other and earlier names by which the new people were recognised among one another, before the breach with Judaism was observed.

We have disposed of the solitary passage in Greek and Roman writers of the second century which seems to favour the assumption that Christians as distinct from Jews were known and marked before the reign of Trajan. For the letters of Pliny and Trajan, externally unattested, unquoted by Justin Martyr (a silence that tells most gravely against them),[1] awaken, on internal grounds, doubts too serious and too numerous in the historical student to be repressed. It is needless to press the point, because when it is once realised how wanting in the external notes of genuineness those documents are, the hand of an apologist becomes at once apparent, skilfully contriving to represent the Christians in the most amiable light to the Roman governor, the governor and the emperor in the most amiable light to the Christians.[2] This is a 'subjective' reason for refusing to accept the letters as evidence upon a point of chronology; for it is a controversy which must turn upon subjective grounds

---

[1] As to Tertullian, *Apol.* c. 2, it cannot be said that he "attests" these letters, as Bishop Lightfoot, *Apost. Fathers*, 2. 1. 55, says. On the contrary, he speaks of Pliny as having degraded some of the Christians,—which is not in the letter.

[2] Analogously, Tertullian, *Apol.* 21, makes Pilate a Christian 'in his very conscience.'

only. The simple truth is, that the MS. is non-extant, and that the letters were first published in France at the beginning of the sixteenth century.[1] Under those conditions Tertullian must be regarded as the first witness, not to *the* letters before us, but to the fact of *a* letter relating Pliny's dealings with the Christians;[2] and in this witness there is little or no more value than in that of Justin Martyr to non-extant 'Acts of Pilate,' the existence of which Tertullian also assumes. Writers who are so delighted with the verisimilitude of the letters in question that they require no further proof of their genuineness, certainly exhibit a charming *naïveté;* but they appear to forget that fictitious art is very poor unless it can give life-likeness to its creations; and that a romancer of even moderate genius was quite capable of framing a *pastiche* of the kind from the slight data of a correspondence believed to have taken place between Pliny and Trajan, and which may actually have taken place in respect to *Christiani*. As the matter stands, the burden of proof rests upon those who maintain, not upon those who doubt, the authenticity of the letters in question, as they now stand.

The general silence of the classical writers is infinitely more significant than the ambiguous voices from which we have in vain sought to wring a certain meaning. And if at this point we glance forward,

---

[1] Bishop Lightfoot, *Apost. Fathers*, 2. 1. 54 (1885), after asserting that forgery is here 'inconceivable,' says in the next sentence that it is 'extremely improbable,' a curious anti-climax. If the reader has a clear notion of what evidence is, the matter may be safely left to his judgment. Cf., however, in addition to Aubé, *Hist. des Persecutions*, 215 ff. (1875); Havet, *Le Christianisme*, 4. 425 (1884), whose critique seems to us to be that of mere common sense; B. Bauer, *Christus*, 268.

[2] Cf. *Apol.* 5. The expression about Christ as 'God,' also savours of Tertullian, *Apol.* c. 21.

from Tacitus to Lucian, over an interval of half a century, the slight reference of the latter to the 'poor wretches' in Syria and Asia, the victims of impostors who trade on their illusions, who still believe in the impaled one of Palestine, is one of the most valuable indirect criticisms upon any accounts we have from before this time.[1]

[1] We have allowed what we have written on the passage in the *Annals* of Tacitus to stand. But the evidence against its genuineness seems overwhelming. 1. Clement of Alexandria has not the passage among his collections from pagan writers. 2. Nor has Tertullian, who cites with an instructive comment the passage from the *Histories*, and who roundly calls Tacitus a prating liar, *Apolog.* 16. 3. Sulpicius Severus, *Hist. Sacr.* 2. 29 (c. 422, A.D.)—*nomen et omen!*—has a description of the tortures of the Christians almost word for word identical with that in Tacitus. This was probably the source of the interpolation. 4. Eusebius has not the passage in his miscellaneous collection of 'evidences.' 5. Our knowledge of the MS. depends on Joh. de Spire, 1468, who dates that which he published at Venice from the eighth century only.

The manner also in which the reference to the *Christiani* and their tortures under Nero is inserted amidst irrelevant matter in Suetonius, *Nero*, c. 16, betrays interpolation. Cf. c. 12, as evidence against the charge of wanton cruelty on the part of the emperor.

CHAPTER III.

CHRISTIAN SOURCES—JUSTIN MARTYR.

JUSTIN is our earliest known or *onomast* witness from among those who had accepted the designation *Christiani*.[1] His first *Apology* probably dates from about the year 147, or some thirty years after the much discussed passage of Tacitus. What the latter did not know with respect to the *nomen*, we must look to find supplied in Justin; for we know of no other dated document of the second century in which the name occurs.[2]

What has Justin to say of the rise of the Name? He says that Christiani are so named from their 'Teacher who is the Son of the Father of all and Lord God, and His Apostle, Jesus Christ.'[3]

Omitting the theological statement, we here learn for the first time that the Teacher of the Christians was Jesus, surnamed Christ, designated also Apostle of God.

What did Justin know of the life of Jesus? We omit for the present the theological and supernatural statements. He says that Joseph, the betrothed of

---

[1] Cf. *Supernat. Relig.*, vol. I.
[2] Bishop Lightfoot has begged a date for the Ignatian epistles (cf. Harnack, *Expositor*, 1886) where the name occurs; as also *Christianismos*.
[3] *Apol.* I. 12.

Mary, who was known by him to be pregnant by another, set out, at the time of the first census in Judæa under Cyrénius, from Nazareth where he lived, to Bethlehem, because he was of the tribe of Judah by blood, and this tribe dwelt in the country of Bethlehem. In an incoherent sentence Justin proceeds: 'The child was born in Bethlehem, and since Joseph had no place in the village to lodge in, he took up his quarters in a cave close to the village, and when they were there, Mary brought forth the Christ and placed Him in a manger, where He was found by the mages coming from Arabia.'[1] The time of the birth was '150 years before' that of Justin in writing the first Apology.[2] As the Apology is not dated, so neither is the birth of Jesus.

Further, Justin says that Jesus was hid from other men until He came to manhood; He was then believed to be a carpenter and the son of a carpenter, Joseph. In fact, He made ploughs and yokes. He was baptized, and His baptism was attended by prodigies, which need not here be related; because such witness is of no more historical value than that of Livy to prodigies which occurred at about an equal distance of time from his own during the second Punic war.

Christ had a brief and concise mode of teaching: He was not a sophist,[3]—as, it may be added, the author of the *Apologia*, whether consciously or unconsciously, was.

As we have seen, Justin agrees with Tacitus in asserting that the Author of Christianity was put to death under Pontius Pilate; but we are ignorant of

---

[1] *Dial. c. Tryph.* c. 78. Cf. *Apol.* 1. 34.   [2] *Apol.* 1. 46.
[3] Lucian, in the *Philopseudes* 16, refers to the Syrian *sophist* from Palestine who exorcised dæmons.

any genuine document from which the information could have been derived. After all discussion, the bare fact that Tacitus' work contains this statement, unconfirmed by his predecessors or contemporaries, about eighty years after the time of Pilate, is all that remains. And since Tacitus knows no proper name of the Founder, we must take his statement, iterated by Justin, to prove no more than the existence of an idea or opinion in the mind of Tacitus that the Founder had so suffered under Pilate. And in the absence of further historical evidence, we must already come to the probable conclusion that the belief of the Christians in the middle of the second century rested upon a foundation purely Ideal. This is no hasty and rash conclusion; though it is one which constrains every thoughtful mind to a long pause of silence and of reflection.

There is no need for us to tread over again ground so thickly marked and perhaps obscured by the footprints of modern scholars. There is good reason why we should abstain from overloading our pages with references to their writings, and so lend any further countenance to the notion that no man is competent to form a judgment on these questions until he shall have perused a whole library of learned letters. The data are few; the scope of the investigation is within the range of every clear-thinking person.

Justin cites certain 'Memorabilia of the Apostles.' The Memorabilia do not coincide on their contents as a whole with any work that has come down to us; nor are 'the Apostles' identifiable with any known historical persons.[1] As we have seen, the term Apostle (שלוח) is of Jewish origin;[2] and the

---

[1] *Supernat. Religion*, I.

[2] In Greek *Silas*, which becomes a proper name in the *logos* of the 'Acts of the Apostles.'

Memorabilia are generally moral sayings, the like of which, as may be gathered from other sources, constituted the doctrinal stock, in great part, of the wandering teachers of the *Diaspora*.

Neither in these Memorabilia, nor elsewhere in Justin, is any historical statement of the origin of Christianity to be found. For the five generations which lie between him and the supposed date of Jesus' birth—so far from their being any unbroken chain of testimony to that or any event of Jesus' life —Justin, through all his laboured *Apologia* and his *Dialogue*, has no individual nameable witness for the historical reality of his assertions at all. His silence about Paul,[1] when he had every reason to cite him in his anti-Judaistic reasonings, is a silence that speaks—a void that no iteration of unattested statements, no nebulous declamation, can ever fill. Justin is one of those men who, incapable of sound dialectic, imagines that others must be blind to the truth if they do not start with the same ideal premises with himself; and who is the very type of that kind of reasoner who would persuade himself and others by mere incessant repetition of the same thing, over and over again. His method can only be convincing to those who have been convinced beforehand. All this is instructive, because it brings to light the process by which the popular mind has, since Justin's time, been brought into that fixed attitude of awful reverence toward the Ideals of Christendom, which is commonly, but erroneously, confused with Belief in the 'facts of the Gospel.' The Ideals commend themselves as

[1] We can neither admit guesses as to the reason of his silence, nor correspondences with 'Pauline' passages as evidence of anything, so long as it remains unproved that the Pauline epistles are exceptions from the pseudepigraphic character of second century literature.

sublime and beautiful to common intuitions and feelings, and therefore as 'true,' in the sense in which dreams are true, while they last. Here the tacit assumption creeps in that what is thus ideally 'true' must have been historically 'real'—an amiable assumption often, but which the slightest attention to common experiences suffices to dispel. The ideal truth of painting or of poem teaches us nothing of itself as to the reality of the persons, acts, and sufferings that may be there painted or described. All that the noblest work of art can accomplish is to set before us the likeness of life, in general forms of intuition and modes of feeling—that life being either natural and open to common perception, or supernatural, and revealed only to the intuition of poetic phantasy. We may admire and love the representation, but cannot be said to 'believe' it, without a confusing abuse of words. If we say, without evidence, that we believe the representation to be that of historic fact, we simply mean that we prefer an easy acquiescence to a troublesome dispute.

Justin accepted tales afloat in his time concerning Jesus on no evidence

'Worthy to warrant the large word—Belief.'[1]

Still less can we.

What deprives Justin of all credit as a historian of Christian origins, apart from his ignorance of sources, is the habit he has of inventing facts to correspond with poetic ideals. This is the reverse of the scientific process, which seeks to ascertain the origin of poetic ideals in the pathos with which human nature invests the common facts of life and spiritual experience.

[1] Robert Browning, *Ferishtah's Fancies*, p. 18. The whole parable is full of point.

Justin assumes the Hebrew prophetic Scriptures to be axiomatic—above all demonstration; an assumption which ignores the plastic quality of poetry, and the fluid nature of poetic thought. Such material admits still less than wax or clay of precise definition; it may be shaped into any form, at the pleasure of the exegete, as the famous allegorising fancies of Philo had shown. The nobler prophetic oracles of Israel contain adumbrations of a Coming One, undefined as to the epoch, and the place (unless with one exception) of his origin. Justin, assuming the authority of these oracles, assumes further that they must have been fulfilled in a precise manner, and further, that they must have been fulfilled about a century and a half before his time. A prophet makes distinguished mention of Bethlehem in this relation; therefore the Christ Jesus must have been born in Bethlehem. And because in a passage of the same prophet, mistranslated by the Greeks, 'He shall dwell in a lofty cave of a strong rock,' and misunderstood by Justin of the Messiah, a reference was supposed to a cave,—Jesus must have been born in a cave. This story, which doubtless flattered Justin, owing to its resemblance to stories of the births of Mithras or of Greek gods and heroes, by which he is so much influenced, is repeated by subsequent writers.[1] It is found in two *evangelia*, 'apocryphal' so called.[2] The difference, however, between 'apocryphal' and 'canonical' is to the critical student merely ecclesiastical, as the ecclesiastical distinction itself is founded on interested considerations. We are

[1] *Apol.* I. 34; *Tryph.* 70. 78; Origen *c. Cels.* i. 51; Micah 5. 2; Isa. 33. 13 ff.
[2] *Protev. Jac.* 18; *Ev. Infant. Arab.* 2. 3; *Hist. Jos.* 7; *De Nativ. Mar.* 14; Origen *c. Cels.* I. 51, Jerome to Sabinian.

entitled to assume that the idea of the cave birthplace was the current idea in Justin's time, and that the omission of it belongs to a later epoch.[1]

Because Justin found in a Psalm the description, 'They opened their mouth against me as a raging lion,' he thinks that this must have been 'Herod, King of the Jews,' successor of that Herod who destroyed the babes born near Bethlehem 'about that time;' or else—the devil. (Justin is ignorant of the distinctive name Antipas.) Similarly, the massacre of the babes is made to tally with an oracle in Jeremiah[2] about Ramah, connected in a fanciful manner with one in Isaiah about Damascus and Samaria.[3]

The prophet speaks of his mystic child named 'Speed-spoil-Hasten-booty.' 'Before he shall have knowledge to cry, My father and my mother, the riches of Damascus and the spoil of Samaria shall be carried away before the king of Assyria.' Justin finds this fulfilled in the coming of the 'Magi from Arabia' at the birth of 'our Christ.' The king of Assyria stands for Herod, on the ground of his wickedness. Samaria means the sinful power; Damascus the seat of the wicked dæmon who was to be overcome by Christ as soon as he was born,—it was formerly in Arabia, though now in Syrophœnicia. The Magi themselves are the spoils signified. They showed by coming to Christ that they had revolted from the dominion of the evil one in Damascus. Tertullian, with amusing wit, makes use of the passage in a similar way against Marcion.[4]

Without commenting on the remarkable feat of

---

[1] Cf. *Supernat. Relig.* I. 312.   [2] Jer. 31. 15.
[3] Isa. 8. 4; *Tryph.* 78, 103.   [4] 3. 13, cf. *adv. Jud.* 6.

exegesis, we may remark, especially as Justin so frequently thrusts Greek parallels before us, that the idea of the dispossession of the evil power from his old seat by the new-born god, strongly resembles that of Apollo dispossessing the Pythian fiend from the Manteion at Delphi. The 'Magi from Arabia' have a close relation to the origin of the new religion; and Samaria and Syrophœnicia were among its earliest seats, as we believe subsequent inquiry will make probable.

Who does not applaud the retort of the indignant Trypho, 'The words of God are holy, but your interpretations are artificial, or rather blasphemous.'[1] At times, indeed, one is tempted to suppose that in putting forth such nugatory stuff, Justin was indulging in elaborate irony against the sophistical interpretation of Scripture, of which Philo is the great master. Certain it is, that Trypho appears throughout in a more respectable light than his opponent. It is needless to make an inventory of the passages in which Justin begs or borrows his assertions of fact from the imagery of the prophets. If his writings are not an elaborate piece of satire, then they are an elaborate piece of sophistry.

Trypho says such interpretations are artful and blasphemous. It seems still impossible to determine whether the hallucinations Justin seeks to propagate are shared by himself or not; for we know too little of the author to form a correct impression of his character.[2] He seems, however, to stand alone among Christians of that early time in the exercise of this

[1] *Tryph.* 79.
[2] It is difficult to believe in the sincerity of Tertullian, a man of really vigorous understanding. We cannot shake off strong suspicions as to the genuineness of the 'Justin' we have before us.

peculiar craft, in which he has never, we believe, been excelled.

Perhaps a moment's attention will not be wasted on his account of the death of Jesus, since this is the solitary fact of which Tacitus was, or appears to have been, cognisant. Justin speaks of Pilate as *Epitropos* in Judæa in the times of Tiberius Cæsar.[1] This is the *proper* Greek term for *procurator*. The first and third of our gospels employ the term *Hégemon* for Pilate's title, which is also given to Felix and to Festus. *Epitropos* is never used for a procurator in the New Testament. Plainly, therefore, Justin is not following our New Testament, but ordinary Greek usage, in respect of the term.[2] An incidental point, yet worth attention; because it is strange that, if there had been a common tradition from the first of an event under the rule of the procurator, there should not have been agreement as to the proper Greek rendering of his title.

A more important point is that Justin first tells us that the punishment suffered by Jesus was *crucifixion*. Here, again, a mere statement, unsupported by antecedent or contemporary writers, can have little value, coming from such an one as Justin. It was easy to *infer* that the punishment was by crucifixion; especially since the memory of the siege of Jerusalem by Titus —seventy years before, when numbers of Jews were scourged, tormented, and crucified amidst the jests of the Roman soldiers—had left its awful impressions behind.[3] But what reason is there to suppose that a deed so public, so wantonly cruel, disgraced the reign

---

[1] *Apol.* I. 13, cf. 61 ; *Tryph.* 30.

[2] Josephus also terms Pilate 'Hegemon of Judæa.' *Antt.* 18 3. 1, if the reading is not suspect. [3] Joseph. *B. J.* 5. 11. 1.

of Tiberius, when there was quiet in Judæa, according to the express testimony of Tacitus?

Here again a long pause of reflection is demanded. If it was true that Pilate caused the *Auctor nominis* to be cruelly put to death, there must have been a cause for his action. Knowing what we do of Roman administration in the provinces at that time, we cannot believe that the hatred of a party in the Sanhedrin, or of a mob in the city, could have constrained the most wicked Roman governor to torture to death, without consulting the emperor, a Jewish teacher, who was no enemy of the imperial power. Moreover, Jewish records supply no evidence of such a hatred towards sectarians at that time. Suppose for a moment that Tiberius or Pilate saw in the Auctor an enemy of the imperial power, whose influence was to be dreaded, is it the least credible that his execution should have left no trace in the public records, from which Tacitus might have drawn a fuller account,—no mention in that interesting narrative which Philo has given of his visit to Gaius, a few short years later (40)[1] —no mention in the life of Josephus, nor among the calumnies of Apion, and but a single tame notice, all questionable, in the *Antiquities*, instead of a volume?

And here we may point out the fact that Lucian, whose 'Peregrinos' dates from about the same time as the Dialogue of Justin (c. 160), alludes to the Object of the Christians' worship as 'the man who was *impaled* in Palestine;' a discrepancy which hints the vagueness of the notions which prevailed at that late date respecting the mode of the death of the Auctor.[2]

---

[1] The genuineness of this piece is not universally received.

[2] τ. ἄνθρωπον τὸν ἐν τῇ Παλαιστίνῃ 'ανασκολοπισθέντα, c. 11. τὸν δὴ ἀνεσκολοπισμένον ἐκεῖνον σοφιστήν, c. 13.

In brief, it must appear to the simple historical student, as distinguished from the professional apologist, that the cruel death of 'the faithful witness,' the arch-martyr of early Christian intuition, belongs, like the death of Stephen, of Ignatius, of Justin himself,— to the category of the ideal, rather than to the common objective real. It was an age which, as is abundantly proved from its literary monuments, habitually construed the past from the passionate ideals of the present. Knowing what we do of that century, and its modes of imagination and customs of literary fiction, the assumption of the critic must be that the persons and the events of which the writers of that century said to themselves—

"'Twas a hundred years since,'

are poetic, until they are proved substantially real. And the proof of substantial reality fails, when, instead of an imposing mass of contemporary testimony, we are confronted by a great void, and a scarce broken silence.

Justin is no historian at all. The broken narrative he actually tells is unvouched for in its details by preceding or contemporary writers. It is enveloped in a confusing haze of the writer's own fancies and reasonings, and attestation is sought for it in quotation from 'the Sibyll' or in analogies from heathen poets, which only betray the absence of matter-of-fact knowledge.[1]

We pass from this part of the subject with the remark, that Justin Martyr, in his effort to explain and defend Christianity in the presence of the Jew and the Greek, only succeeds in awakening irrepressible

---

[1] *Apol.* I. 20.

doubts as to the very existence of any individual Founder at all. The real founders, it may be inferred, were certain roving teachers called 'Apostles,' reminiscences of whose instructions had been preserved in certain note-books accessible to Justin.[1] These he treats as of no divine authority. The Jewish prophetic Scriptures furnish the actual materials out of which he constructs the poem of the incarnation.

Already then we are in a position to affirm, that the origin of the Christian symbol, and its explanatory tradition, was not in verifiable Fact, but in Cravings, Imaginations, and Aspirations of the soul. The nature of these it must now be our business to endeavour to trace out. It is in the history of these alone that we recover from our disenchantment and discouragement, and that the real grandeur of the subject is disclosed.

[1] The distinction of an apostolic and a post-apostolic age therefore falls away. There is no age which is not 'post-apostolic.' Let the reader carefully consider our other earliest witnesses to 'apostolic' tradition, before a 'Canon' was talked of: Irenæus 1. 8. 1, 2. 30. 9, 3. 9. 1, 17. 4. Tert. *præscr.* 6, &c. Clem. *A. Strom.* 1. 1, 9, 7. 16; *Pæd.* 3. 12. Cf. Euseb. 6. 12. If these 'witnesses' be closely scrutinised, there will appear little reason for admitting the existence of a *Canon* in the modern sense before the fourth century. The recent *Introductions* of Haltzmann (1885) and of Weiss (1886) build upon the old illusions; less so, Harnack, *Dogm. Gesch.* 1886.

CHAPTER IV.

CHRISTIAN SOURCES—THE 'HÆRETICS' (OR SECTARIANS) [1] DURING THE FIRST HALF OF THE SECOND CENTURY.

THE hæretics were, historically speaking, the predecessors of the Catholics, in spite of the assertions of Tertullian to the contrary. His 'churches of apostolic census,' like the apostles themselves, are unknown.

The writings of Justin Martyr cover the period from c. 147 to c. 167.

Casting now a glance backward through the haze of his reminiscences, we now ask, Who preceded him as teachers? What names did they bear? What was their doctrine? Who were the spiritual genitors of the *Christiani?* Our inquiry here concerns the reign of Hadrian (117-138), and Justin's *Apologia* (147) reflects a certain amount of light upon that time.

Justin says that 'after the ascension of Christ into heaven,' the dæmons put forward certain men to declare that they were gods; and that these men were not only not persecuted by the Romans, but were thought worthy by them of honours. One of these was Simon the Samaritan, who in the time of Claudius Cæsar wrought magic miracles by means of the art of dæmons operating in him, and this 'in your royal

---

[1] *Haeresiotes,* Justin calls them, *Tryph.* 80.

city of Rome.' He was thought to be a god by the Romans, and honoured as such among them with a statue, which was erected on the Tiber between two bridges, and inscribed with the Roman inscription *Simoni deo sancto*.[1]

It is almost needless to point out that *Semones* was the general Sabine name of tutelar genii or lares;[2] and that the temple of Semo Sanctus or Sancus stood on the Quirinal at Rome, founded (according to Dionysius) in 466 B.C.[3] There could be no more absurd anachronism than that by which Justin confounds an archæologic fact of Roman religion with a reminiscence of a Samaritan 'a hundred years since;' no greater paralogism than that which confounds a supposed human person with a spirit, such as a Semo, Lar, or Genius was. Mistakes as gross are constantly committed by mystical mythologists in our day; but we do not reckon men of that class as good witnesses to matters of fact.

Almost all the Samaritans, continues Justin, and some of other nations, confess that *Simo sanctus* is a god, and worship him. One Helena, who followed him 'about that time,' and who had formerly been a common prostitute, is said by them to be his 'first notion' or conception.[4] It does not concern us to unravel the perplexities of these fancies, which were rife enough during our period: witness the 'Proteus' of Lucian and his *Pseudomantis*, and above all the Apollonius of Philostratus. There was an immense craving for *sôteria*,[5] for assured weal of body and soul; and mages,

---

[1] *Apol.* i. 26. [2] Cf. *Dius* in Dius Fidius; Preller, *Röm. Myth.* 79.
[3] Ovid. *Fast.* 6. 213, with notes in Merkel, Peter, or Paley's edition.
[4] ἔννοια πρώτη: a personification in the Gnostic system, confounded with an actual person. See the jest against the stoic *Pronoia* as an old woman, Cic. *N. D.*
[5] *Heilssucht* and *Heilsmanie*, Lippert terms it.

thaumaturges, *manteis* and *pseudo-manteis*, like the Alexandros and the Peregrinos denounced by Lucian, swarmed in the world, practising on the wretched credulity of the ignorant. These men were regarded, like modern spiritualists, as semi-divine, and at a little distance of time were confounded with the divine.[1] All that results from the allusion of Justin is, that he was aware of some heathen cult or cults widely diffused, the origin of which in his own land he knew, but which he felt to be powerfully antagonistic to the dogmas he was defending. Menander, another Samaritan, and a disciple of Simon, who was also under dæmonic inspiration, deceived many at Antioch by magic art. He even persuaded his followers that they would never die;[2] and there are still, says Justin, some of this confession, disciples of his, at the present day. Marcion of Pontus is still alive, and teaches his disciples to own some other god greater than the Demiurge. Marcion 'among every race of men has succeeded, by the assistance of dæmons, in causing many to break out into blasphemies, and to deny God the Creator of all, and to profess that *another greater god* has wrought greater things.'[3]

The statement now follows, that all who take their rise from these teachers are called *Christiani*, just as the various schools of philosophers bear the common name of philosophy. Whether these Christian sects are guilty of the dark charges of Thyestean banquets

---

[1] Lucian says the Christiani regarded Peregrinos 'as a god,' also as their lawgiver and *prostates*. *Peregr.* c. 11.

[2] 'The wretches (the Christiani) have persuaded themselves they shall be immortal and live for ever.' Ibid.; cf. *Hist. Jos.* 26.

[3] Lucian says that the 'great one who was impaled in Palestine' was still honoured because he brought *this new religion* or cultus (τελετή) into existence, c. 11.

and Oidipodean incest or no, Justin cannot say; but this he knows, that they are not harassed nor put to death by the Romans on account of their opinions.

Later, Justin repeats himself in reference to Simon and Alexander, the Samaritans. They still hold many deluded by their magical works of power,—a delusion which in the case of the 'sacred Senate' and the Roman people had gone so far, that they set up a statue to Simon, as aforesaid.[1] Justin hopes that the holy Senate and the Roman people will learn their error, and cast the statue down! '*Num furis, Justine, an prudens ludis nos, obscura canendo?*' An uneasy suspicion will steal upon the mind, as if we were being made the victims of an elaborate jest.

Still, setting aside this nonsense about Simon Magus, we must remember that Justin at all events knows of a contemporary sect of Simonians and another of Marcionites, both of them bearing the common name of *Christiani*. From Irenæus the list of these 'Gnostic' sectarians is considerably increased. We hear of Nicolaitans, disciples of Cerinthus, of Saturninus, of Cerdo, of Carpocrates, Basilides, Valentinus, of Ophites, Perates, and others. Alexandria, Antioch, Rome, were the centres of their activity, and their period is the reign of Hadrian and onwards. But the legendary Archimage, Simon of Samaria, is the spiritual father of them all.

Let us once more return to our old standpoint, the commencement of the reign of Hadrian. There is now revealed to our view a swarm of teachers bearing that common name with the Roman vulgar,

[1] *Apol.* 1. 56.

passing from city to city on the errand of novel doctrinal disseminations. These men were proud of the Greek *gnosis*, contemptuous of the Jews, of their Scriptures and of their Theology, and of their very God, the Demiurge, and eagerly bent on securing the spiritual empire for Hellenism. Or, to shun abstractions, this was the national struggle of Greeks with Jews in the heart of civilisation, and under a people whose laws afforded them a common protection. The notes of the Gnostic in general are antinomistic feeling and anti-Judaistic Theology. The attack upon the conception of the Demiurge, or Creator, in other words, the God of the Old Testament, could be regarded as nothing less than extremest blasphemy by strict adherents to the Law. And equally opposed to the pure monotheism of the typical Ebionites were the new Christologies of Gnostic speculation.[1]

We find ourselves, then, in the midst of a time when the common name of Christiani covered antagonisms the most violent, differences of feeling and of dogma the most irreconcileable. The synagogue was at war with the ecclesia; Ebionites and apostles of the Sanhedrin, Jewish hagioi, prophets and teachers were ranked against Hellenic or Hellenist sophists of the type of Justin of Neapolis and his Gnostic opponents. Under such conditions the more scholastic Gnostics, with a poetical system that had relish only for a limited class of educated men, had little chance of wide or enduring popularity.

We must now follow the clue of internal evidence. We must seek for traces of that purer Judaism or Ebionitism which preceded Catholic Christianity, and which may be detected by the resemblance of its spirit and forms to the later prophetic and moral literature of the Jews; and negatively, by the absence of Hellenic Christology and other Hellenic modes of intuition of the Divine. We must then trace, as far as the too scanty evidence permits, the process by which the material of tradition assumed the intelligible forms of popular Greek and Roman thought.

We have avoided so far knowingly taking a single step into the region of mere inference and conjecture. We have confined ourselves to named and dated witnesses. The course of our investigation has brought us back, again and again, to the standpoint of Tacitus, c. 116. The brief account he gives of the death of the Auctor some eighty years before, we must conclude to have been derived indirectly from the Christiani themselves. But it is historically without certification; nor does the belief ascribed to Marcion (c. 138) respecting the '15th year of Tiberius,'[1] nor that of Justin (c. 147), no more than that in the anonymous and undated pseudo-Clementine 'Recognitions,' furnish any additional evidence in the historical sense.[2] At present, it must be maintained that at the beginning of the second century, while the title 'Christ' was known in the like general sense that the titles Cæsar, Arsaces, Pharaoh were known, Jesus was not existent for History.[3] Not a single witness was then in old age forthcoming to declare, 'I was present at the Crucifixion' nor 'I knew one who was present at the Crucifixion.'

In the time of Vespasian there was a rumour con-

---

[1] Iren. I. 27. 2, 3. 12; Tert. *Adv. M.* I. 19.
[2] I. 6. The passage describes the vague and ever-swelling rumour in the Orient which took its rise in Tiberius's reign.
[3] Clem. *Recog.* I. 45.

cerning the future rise of an Oriental king, fulfilled only in the Flavian house itself. Forty-five years later rumour is busy again, in a darker time, with a good message derived from a more ancient time concerning the kingdom of God, yet to be realised. Wherever hope and ambition live in oppressed hearts, the inarticulate music from the distance will be heard; and it will gradually resolve itself into articulate words, and corresponding images of grandeur will be begotten in the general mind. For

> 'Rumour is a pipe
> Blown by surmises, jealousies, conjectures;
> And of so easy and so plain a step,
> That the blunt monster with uncounted heads,
> The still discordant wavering multitude
> Can play upon it.'[1].

Not until late in the second century is a light cast back by Irenæus and his disciple Hippolytus upon the mist in which Christiani are enveloped, by their informations concerning 'the Gnostics' from Cerinthus (c. 115) and those who followed him. From these sources we learn that a mighty effort at spiritual innovation had been going on in Asia Minor, in Antioch, in Samaria, in Rome and Alexandria. The Gnostics had proclaimed a new religion, a new rite, a new God, at war with the Creator and God of the Old Testament, a Gospel of liberation from the present world and its 'beggarly elements,' a doctrine of 'knowledge, faith, and immortality,' a sublimated creed, in which the fleshly actuality and suffering of Jesus was disdainfully denied. The ideal figure of Simon Magus doubtless represents the 'glorification of Christianity' in the Gnostic preaching. And the conclusion is probable that in the Gnostic movement we see the real beginning of the conquests of the Christiani, in other words, the victory of Hellenic religion and speculation over the narrower and less flexible spirit of Judaism.[1]

[1] See Hilgenfeld, *Ketzergesch.*, and R. A. Lipsius, *Die Apokr. Apostel Gesch.*, 1883.

Part II.

THE INTERNAL HISTORY—EVIDENCE OF THE OLD CHRISTIAN LITERATURE.

CHAPTER I.

THE HAGIOI, APOSTLES AND PROPHETS—THE CHRISTIANOS AND THE CHRISTEMPOROS.

WE have here before us a number of documents which remain, after all the study lavished upon them by modern scholars, only the more distinctly undated, anonymous or pseudonymous. Our study of them must therefore be directed to the *characters* they exhibit, that is, in respect of names, notions, practices, sentiments, and dogmata. One negative character at once arrests attention in connection with our preceding study of the *Christiani*, and that is the absence (with slight exceptions) of this designation of the new religionists. And we have therefore to ask, By what names were they known before the Roman term became current at the beginning of Hadrian's reign?

THE HAGIOI, THE APOSTLES AND PROPHETS.

The *Hagioi, Sancti*, Saints: this is perhaps the most distinctive, the most honourable and endeared name of the Jewish ancestry of the *Christiani*. Excluding the rich evidence of the New Testament books on this matter, we may point to the Book of Enoch, the date of which is unknown, but which probably falls within our era: a book imbued with Jewish enthusiasm, and strongly coloured with Jewish imagery. Here the Hagioi and the Elect are profusely mentioned, and in a way which shows how profoundly these names suggested the most exalted status in the Messianic kingdom believed to be approaching. The book is of great importance as shedding a powerful light on the inner history of Judaism of the time. If these ideas had long been fermenting in the Jewish breast, we need no longer wonder at the allusions to the Orient in the Roman historian.

Again in the Wisdom of Solomon, a book of another cast, lit up with an expression of sober wisdom and of refined piety, referred, as we have seen, by Jewish critics, to the reign of Gaius (Caligula), the designation *Hagioi* frequently occurs. It is found also in the Book of Siracides (Ecclesiasticus), and in the Book of Tobit, which has been referred to the reign of Hadrian. The writers of these so-called Apocrypha stand on the border-line between orthodox Judaism and Hellenism, and were, though greedily perused because of their glorification of Judaism, still 'doubtful reading for Jews' because of their broader tendency.[1]

The Hellenist name *Hagioi* represents the Hebrew חדשים, a designation especially given to the sacred ministers under the Law, in particular the Levites. It appears everywhere to connote that sacerdotal char-

[1] Edersheim, *Life of Jesus*, 1. 33.

acter which was stamped on the elect nation as a whole.[1]

Now in the *Didaché* (*Doctrina Apostolorum*) and in the 'Epistle of Barnabas,' through which a common vein of exhortation runs, we read, 'Thou shalt seek out day by day the face of the Hagioi (that thou mayest rest upon their words).'[2] The context in both cases bespeaks reverence for 'him that speaks to thee the *logos* of God (or of the Lord).' It may be inferred that the Hagioi were themselves teachers; in fact, every member of the communities whose life is here unveiled, was doubtless in some sort a teacher. The name *Hagioi*, however, is the most general characteristic appellation that we can discover in these early tracts, always with a significance of dignity. *Christianos*, as has been already said, once occurs in the *Didaché*, as it seems, with no such significance, but rather the contrary. In Barnabas it does not occur. From familiar names, such as 'sons' and 'daughters,'[3] or 'brethren,' we can glean little or nothing of historical worth. It may excite reflection that in 'Barnabas' and some other documents, there seems in general to be a designed abstinence from any distinctive name: the personal pronoun 'we' is indefinitely used, and there is no insistence upon the privileges of a new people, such as we find so marked in Justin. However, it may be said that where the Hagioi are, apostles, prophets, teachers are not far off; and to these names we may turn for further elucidations.

'Apostles,' as we have seen, is a term of Jewish

---

[1] See the exhaustive discussion in Count Baudissin's *Studien*. 2.
[2] *Did*. 4. 2; *Barn*. 19. 10; Const. *App*. 7. 9. 12; *Jud. Pctr*. 99. 16. 18.
[3] *Barn*. c. 1; Apostol. Church Order: salutation.

origin;[1] and it has historical value as designating the emissaries of the Jewish Sanhedrin, who were commissioned to regulate the feasts of the calendar and to transact other religious business throughout the Diaspora. But we cannot certainly date the *Christian* use of the term till the time of Justin. Who, then, were these teachers that to the Christian public of 150 appeared to have been the founders of their doctrine and way of life, and of whom the Head was the 'Apostle of God,' Jesus Christ Himself? Unless Justin can inform us, it is to be feared that no definite knowledge on this subject can be gathered from any other source. Justin, however, indulges in the usual phantasies on the subject of 'the apostles,' who, he says, were symbolised by the twelve bells (!) on the high priest's robe, and in whose person as it were speaking to Christ, Isaiah said, 'Lord, who hath believed our report?' &c.[2] But Justin could tell no more than he knew of the life and work of 'the apostles,' which was that men, in number twelve, set out from Jerusalem into the world at some undated epoch, men unskilled, with no faculty of speech, but who through the power of God declared to every race of men that they had been sent by Christ to teach all 'the logos of God.' This was in fulfilment of the prophecy in Isa. 2. 3.[3] In another passage he says that the prophets who are being sent forth ($\dot{a}\pi o\sigma\tau\epsilon\lambda$-$\lambda\dot{o}\mu\epsilon\nu o\iota$) to announce ($\dot{a}\gamma\gamma\dot{\epsilon}\lambda\lambda\epsilon\iota\nu$) the commands of God, are called *angels* and *apostles*. This is seen in Isaiah, for he says, *Send me* ($\dot{a}\pi\dot{o}\sigma\tau\epsilon\iota\lambda\dot{o}\nu$ $\mu\epsilon$)![4]

Here it will be seen that those who teach the logos

---

[1] שְׁלוּחִים, Mischna Sanh. 11. 4; Wuensche, *Neue Beiträge* 1878, p. 129; Graetz, *Gesch d. Juden*, 4. n. 21.
[2] *Tryph.* 1. 42; cf. *Proter. Jac.* 8.
[3] *Apol.* 1. 39.
[4] *Tryph.* 75.

of God are practically synonymous with the prophets, angels, or messengers, and apostles of Justin's retrospect.

In another place, the apostles of Christ are called 'His brethren.'[1] The name of one of them was changed to Peter; of two others, Zebedee's sons, to Boanerges, and that for a theological purpose, according to Justin,—that Christ might be identified with Him who called Jacob Israel and Oshea Jesus (or Joshua)![2]

The 'Memorabilia' of the apostles, as should be now well recognised, do not coincide with any 'Evangelia' which have come down to us. The latter term is not used for the literary sources by Justin.[3]

All that we can gather from him is that he had a shadowy notion flitting before his mind of twelve apostles, unlearned men, who had gone forth from the sacred city on a teaching errand. Of the epoch of this mission he could only say to himself ''Twas a hundred years agone,' and the names of these twelve he cannot supply. This is not history, but historicising mythology. The world swarmed before his time with a body of men, the first 'Propaganda,' then known as saints and apostles, or holy apostles. Historical reasoning, taking its start from current ideals of fancy, at length arrives at the conception of twelve original apostles, said to be correspondent to the Twelve Bells of the high priest. The next step was to fit these twelve with names. As Justin is not in full

---

[1] *Tryph.* 106.

[2] But this awkward digression is plainly an interpolation. Nowhere else does Justin name Peter or other apostles.

[3] *Apol.* 1. 66 clearly has been interpolated.

possession of them, we can only infer that they had not been found up to his time.[1]

But as to the actual missionaries of Justin's time we have an interesting glimpse of their mode of life and activity in the recently published book, the *Didaché* or 'Teaching of the Apostles.' Though we must refuse to beg a date for any portion of this Tractate, few will dispute that the life of communities of the second century is here in part reflected.

'Now concerning the Apostles and Prophets, according to the decree of the Evangelion, so do ye. Let every apostle that comes to you be received as the Lord (Kyrios). He shall remain but one day, but if there be need, another day. If he remain for three days, he is a false prophet. And when the apostle goes out, let him take nothing except a loaf, until he comes to his night-quarters. But if he ask for money, he is a false prophet.'[2]

Here the apostle is apparently all but synonymous with the prophet, and both with those 'that speak the logos of God' and 'the Hagioi.'[3] The 'decree of the Evangelion,' as the Evangelion itself, is unknown as a term to Justin Martyr. Had there been extant at the time of the writer any authoritative decree of an Auctor concerning the treatment of the wandering 'Apostles,' he would hardly have spoken of the 'dogma of the Evangelion.' It must be further remarked, that there seems no reason for assuming the word *Kyrios* to refer to any other than God, in the

[1] The play of the Talmud on the five names of Jesus' disciples which it gives (Sanh. 43a) shows how readily invention might set to work here. Edersheim, *Life of Jesus*, I. 154; Wuensche, *Neue Beiträge* 128.

[2] Cap. 11. 3 ff. Cf. on similar sentiments of the Jewish teachers, Aboth. I. 13, 2. 2, and further, Wuensche, p. 130.

[3] 4. 1 ff.

Old Testament sense.[1] The honourable reception claimed for these itinerants, as for the teachers in general, is based upon an almost supernatural view of their office.[2] But here, as elsewhere, we know nothing of historical individuals, but only of a class of men so spiritually exalted in their own esteem and that of their fellows, that if no authentic history of their origin were forthcoming one must necessarily be invented.

In a similar shadowy and unhistorical manner to that of Justin speaks the writer of the romance called the 'Pastor of Hermas,'—another undated, unplaced, and anonymous work. He alludes to 'The forty apostles and teachers of the preaching of the Son of God.'[3] If any proof were needed that we are here in the world of the ideal, the author will supply it. The number forty is fixed upon because there are forty stones in the building of his Tower; which is typical of the Church. 'The apostles and bishops and teachers and deacons are stones.'

With these passages may be connected that in Eusebius respecting the 'Evangelists.' This so-called historian looks back to the period of which *he* must say to himself, ''Twas two hundred years ago and more,' with the like wavering and wandering glance that we have noticed in his predecessor, Justin. After talking of 'Ignatius,'[4] who remains *nomen et umbra* merely for the modern student, a being imagined to have lived in the reign of Trajan, he goes on to talk

---

[1] The commentators on 4. 1, who explain ἡ κυριότης of a *Christology*, grasp at the air.

[2] 'Cleave to the wise and their disciples and I will regard it as if thou hadst fetched the Law from heaven.' Sifri on Deut. 11. 22; Wuensche, 130.

[3] *Sim.* 9. 15, 16. Cf. 9. 25. *Vis.* 3. 5.   [4] *H. E.* 3. 36.

of 'the Evangelists who were still then flourishing.' These too are described as missionaries to foreign parts. The Holy Spirit wrought wonders by them, and multitudes embraced the true faith with their whole minds. Eusebius continues: 'As it is impossible for us to give the numbers of the persons that became Pastors or Evangelists during the first immediate succession from the apostles in the churches throughout the world, we have only recorded those by name in our history, of whom we have received the traditional acount as it is delivered in the various comments on the apostolic doctrine still extant.'

This description has been called 'the best commentary on the "Apostles" in the *Didaché.*'[1] It only shows, however, that Eusebius thought of the missionaries of the beginning of the second century as 'Evangelists,' and that they present themselves to his imagination in the like nebulous indistinct plurality that the 'Apostles' had presented themselves to that of Justin more than a century before. In Eusebius, in fact, we see the process by which to the straining gaze of the eager spectator the mists of 'Tradition' begin to 'dispart, disperse,' and forms begin to reveal themselves and take on themselves name and local habitation. As for Ignatius and his martyrdom, we must agree with the candour of Harnack, that such a thing is in itself a mere possibility.[2] When compared with other products of martyrological fancy, the event has that merest possibility which any creation of sentimental imagination possesses. A multitude of impressive lives furnish the material for a few impressive ideals. And this is all that can be gathered from the

---

[1] The Oldest Church Manual, P. Schaff, 1885, p. 69.
[2] *Ignatius*, p. 71.

accounts before us of the 'apostles' or 'evangelists' of Trajan's and Hadrian's reign. And when, it may be asked in passing, did the term *evangelistes*, unknown to Justin, take the place of *angel*, which is, as we have seen, in him synonymous with *apostle?* Does not Eusebius, according to the trick of the time, antedate his *evangelists* into the reign of Trajan?

But to return to our 'Apostles.' The term denotes a special class of *Jewish* officials, and appears to have been so used by the Jews down to the sixth century.[1]

The question therefore arises, How were the 'Apostles' on whose Memorabilia Justin falls back, and to whose teaching the distinctively *Christian* religion owed its origin, marked off from the 'Apostles of the Sanhedrin' already noticed? If, as there is every reason to suppose, an antagonism sprang up between these two classes in the reign of Hadrian, what traces has it left behind? An antagonism to false apostles, prophets, and teachers is abundantly revealed in the *hagiographic* literature of our era. For to avoid confusion, we must not speak of *Christian* literature where that name is yet unowned and unhonoured. The *Didaché* says nothing of apostles of Christ; 'Hermas' speaks of 'prophets of God,' and of 'apostles and teachers of the Son of God.' And the true teacher is known by his morals. There are also denunciations of 'Hypocrites.' But the real grounds of antagonism are only obliquely disclosed in a manner to which we will refer hereafter.

[1] Mommsen, C. I. L. 9. 648 (Berol.), 1883, *Cod. Theodos.* lib. xvi. tit. viii., lex. 14 (of Jewish *presbyters* and those whom themselves call *apostles*).

The Prophets.

We have already seen that the term 'prophets' goes constantly in the society of 'apostles' and 'teachers' in our early documents. In what sense is 'prophet' a distinctive appellation in the second century? To revert to Justin. He makes it abundantly clear in his earlier *Apologia*, that in his opinion the Old Testament prophets are the true *magistri* to whose *verba* he is *addictus jurare;* that they are the true teachers of the Christian religion, certified by the fulfilment of their predictions. Here he is addressing the Gentile world.

In the later *Trypho*, where he addresses Jews, who own the ancient prophets like himself, but who reject *in toto* his exegesis of them, he is constrained to make dogmatism do duty instead of argument in support of that exegesis, and overwhelms his opponent with scriptural abuse because the latter cannot admit the soundness of it. The judgment of God upon the unbelieving Jews is still suspended, he says, because He knows that 'still daily there are some who are being discipled into the name of His Christ and who are quitting the Way of Error, and who receive gifts each one, according as they are worthy, being illuminated through the name of this Christ. For one receives a spirit of understanding, another of counsel, another of might, another of healing, another of foreknowledge, another of teaching, another of the fear of God.'[1]

This is a suggestive passage, helpful towards the comprehension of what was going on still in the

---

[1] *Tryph.* 39.

Diaspora about the year 160. Men of Jewish birth were being discipled into a new name, were renouncing one 'way' for another, were being illuminated, *i.e.*, baptized, and after their illumination were regarded as the recipients of gifts or 'spirits.' It is impossible not to admire the *naïveté* of this artificial distribution of 'spirits,' and the natural manner in which by laying hold on the strong (or the weak) points of each individual, it continued to realise the ideal of an inspired community,—'all the Lord's people prophets.' If a disciple has no more than simple common sense, or simple piety without common sense, he is still a dignitary among a child-like people. The analogy to the manner in which Methodist or Salvationist sects propagate themselves under our eyes to-day will not escape the observer of human social instinct.

'Amongst us,' says Justin in another place, 'even to the present time, prophetic *charisms* exist. And hence you yourselves should understand that those which in ancient times were in your race, have been transferred to us.'[1]

But there are shadows in this picture which Justin does not attempt to conceal. Even as among the Jews in the olden time there were not only 'holy prophets' but also *pseudo-prophets*, 'even so among us there are now many false teachers whom our Lord foretold that we should be on our guard against,' &c. False prophets filled with a lying and impure spirit, neither wrought nor do work the miracles like those of the ancient prophets; they do however 'dare to work certain miracles for the amazement of men, and they celebrate ($\delta o \xi o \lambda o \gamma o \tilde{u} \sigma \iota \nu$) the spirits of error and dæmons.'[2]

[1] *Tryph.* 82.   [2] Ib. c. 7.

Here then are strong traces of strife of the most embittered kind in the communities of the second century. It is noteworthy that Justin admits the reality of miracles by false prophets, ascribing them to the agency of evil dæmons. He also testifies to the existence of 'pseudo-Christs' as well as pseudo-prophets, in his time.

These representations of the prophets of the second century may be made clearer from references in undated and anonymous documents. In the *Didaché* we find the remarkable prohibition: 'No prophet that speaks in spirit shall ye try or prove; for every sin shall be forgiven, but this sin shall not be forgiven.'[1] It is a grave mistake to confound 'speaking in spirit,' *i.e.*, in an inspired or ecstatic state, with the idea of a personal Spirit and his dictation. It cannot be shown that the conception of 'the spirit,' 'the prophetic spirit' (frequent in Justin), is any other than that of a *numen* or influence. But to continue, 'Not every one who speaks in spirit is a prophet, but only if he have the manners of the Lord. From their manners then the pseudo-prophet and the prophet shall be known.' There follow some obscure allusions to practices of the Prophets,—'ordering a Table in spirit' and 'making assemblies for a cosmic mystery,' from which it may be inferred that in a time so strangely affected by cravings for the mystic and the symbolic, dubious, and perhaps half-pagan dramatic rites were occasionally introduced. Clearly also there were abuses of the prophetic ecstasy for interested purposes. 'Whosoever says *in spirit:* Give me money

---

[1] 11. 7. In the Mischna Sanh. 10. 1, those who deny the revelation of the Law through the Holy Spirit have no part in the *olam haba* or world to come. Wuensche, p. 156.

or any other things, ye shall not listen to him; but if he bid you give for others that lack, let no one judge him.' Here then we have a glimpse of those selfish and mercenary spirits who made gain of godliness, such as those branded by Lucian in his satirical 'Peregrinus.'

Some of these prophets appear like the apostles to have been itinerant; others were settled in particular places. And what particularly arrests attention in the case of these latter, is the sacerdotal status and privileges claimed on their behalf. 'All the firstfruits of the produce of winepress and threshing-floor, of oxen and sheep, thou shalt take and give to the prophets; for they are your arch-priests.'[1] Now the arch-priests (οἱ ἀρχιερεῖς) designated the Sanhedrin or the heads of the twenty-four courses of priests. 'The high-priests, the prophet and the Sanhedrin,' constituted the supreme judicial court at Jerusalem.[2] These 'prophets' then must ultimately derive from the same historical source as the 'apostles,' namely, the Sanhedrin in Jerusalem; and when we connect with this the term *Hagioi*, of associations so strongly Levitical, as we have already seen, the inference is forced upon us, that in the communities where the *Didaché* was received as authoritative, the Judaistic Hagiocracy prevailed.[3] We can find in Justin no passage which countenances the theory of a special sacerdotal order among *Christiani*, nor in any document which can be confidently referred to the time before him. In one point comparison is invited in this relation, between

---

[1] 13. 3 ff. Cf. *Berachoth*, fol. 10 b, where similar offerings to the learned are said to be equivalent to the daily sacrifice.

[2] Joseph. *Antt.* 4. 8. 14.

[3] Probably all that is meant by the allusion to 'high-priests' is the great dignity and worth of the inspired teachers. Cf. *Sanh.* 58 b.

the *Didaché* and Justin. The former, at the end of the Eucharistic prayers, adds the direction, 'Permit the prophets to give thanks as much as they wish.'[1] Justin, on the other hand, says that at the end of the congregational prayers, the *president* (ὁ προεστώς) offers prayers and thanksgivings according to his ability.[2] Where these sacerdotal prophets stand forth on an eminence so marked in the *Didaché*, there is a blank and a silence in Justin. We may leave these phænomena to bear their own witness. Amidst statements so frequent of the existence of true and false teachers, it seems impossible to find a sure criterion whether of doctrine or of manners to enable us to distinguish between the two classes. However, there are other denominational phrases from which some further hints may be collected.

Those that 'come in the name of the Lord.' The *Christianos* and the *Christemporos*.

The *Didaché* reveals to us, in chap. xii., the life of a poor and hard-working community.[3] It directs: 'Every one that comes in the name of the Lord let him be received; then ye shall prove, and know him, for ye shall have understanding right and left.' By 'coming in the name of the Lord' we understand coming in the name of Jehovah, that is, by divine authority and sanction; and it seems a gratuitous assumption of the commentators when they explain the phrase as referring to 'the profession of Christ.' Evidently all that is meant is one who comes to a community in the well-known character of true

---

[1] They, says Harnack, are 'die Virtuosen des Gebets.'
[2] *Apol.* 1. 67.
[3] On the great emphasis laid by the Talmud on the duty of hospitality to the teachers of the law, see Wuensche, 140.

'apostle,' 'prophet,' or 'teacher.' And the like direction follows as before: 'If the comer is an itinerant, help him as far as ye can, but he shall not remain with you but for two or three days, unless there be necessity. If he wishes to settle among you, being a craftsman, let him work and eat. But if he has not a handicraft, provide according to your understanding that not idly among you he shall live a *Christianos*. If he will not act thus, he is a *Christemporos*. Beware of such.'

The only place where the name *Christianos* in this book appears, uses it in a sense of reproach, as tantamount to the description of a contemptible idler, and sponger upon the charity of poor people. And to this is added the stigmatic name of 'Christmonger,' which is to be found also in so-called epistles of 'Ignatius.'[1] But this latter word belongs to the Fathers of the *fourth* century, and is probably an interpolation in this place of the *Didaché*.

Although we do not find elsewhere in early Christian tracts this stigma affixed to the name *Christianos*, we do find pointed references to a class of men who infested the communities, who are compared to birds of prey, who know not how to procure food for themselves by toil and sweat, but seize on that of others in their iniquity, and though wearing an appearance of simplicity, are on the watch to plunder others;[2] of men whose practice it is to carry about 'The Name'[3] in wicked guile, who must be shunned as wild beasts; of those who bear 'the name of the Lord' in hypocrisy.[4]

The picture in 'Hermas'[5] answers, trait for trait,

---

[1] *Ad Trall.* 6; *Ad Magn.* 6.   [2] *Ep. Barnab.* 10.
[3] Ign. *ad Ephes.* 7.   [4] Polycp. *ad Phil.* 6.   [5] *Mand.* 11.

to that in Lucian's 'Peregrinus' of the charlatan who lives in luxury upon the hard earnings of the people, who refuses to prophesy except for gain, and who may readily be distinguished from the true and lowly teacher, who lives in hard frugality, by the empty loquacity of his discourse, and the pretentious swagger of his bearing. Too closely, according to our observation, does the 'cap fit' Justin himself, who for the first time boastfully adopts the name *Christianos*, and frivolously makes capital out of his wretched puns upon it. His manners can be relished by no person of modesty or good taste. And it is impossible to attend to the internal evidence of our early 'apostolic' or epistolic writings (it seems a gross anachronism to term them *Christian*) without perceiving that the strictures of Celsus were, from his point of view, amply justified. During the whole of the second century there must have been a large class of contemptible impostors abroad who made a traffic and a commerce of piety, who traded upon the itchings after the supernatural of the mass, and who were odious alike to cultivated men among the Greeks and Romans, and to the godly and moral artisans of the Jewish *Diaspora*. Had the world heard no more of the *Christiani* after Justin, the name would have come down to us as the brand of a historical shame. Even if we cleanse away the dark stains which were flung upon the *nomen* as calumnies, there remains no association with it of modesty, simplicity of life, of clearness or force of intellect to win upon our regard. It was a name under which men often drove a miry business, and the conceit of Justin on 'the excellent people' is frowned down by the recollection of the *Christemporoi*, or Christ traffickers. To note these things can be no pleasing task to any who have been wont to associate the Christian name with the holiest and sweetest ideals of life. But our object is to guard against a confusing anachronism in the history of names and ideas, and to show that the pure godliness and the chaste manners of the time were connected with other names, and propagated by teachers of another stamp than that of Justin.

CHAPTER II.

THE ECCLESIA—'THE VINE.'

GLADLY we turn from the bombast of Justin to the pithy and pregnant teaching of the *Didaché*. The earlier six chapters may be regarded (with Bryennios) as a distinct document, and the most valuable part, intrinsically, of the book. Its stress lies upon 'the Way,' *i.e.*, the true life of piety and morality. In closing its directions on the 'Way of Life,' the book says: 'In ecclesia thou shalt confess thy transgressions, and thou shalt not come to thy *proseuché* in an evil conscience.'

An *ecclesia* represents a *q'hilah*, a congregation, and it is distinguished in the times under study from a *synagogue* in that the latter generally denotes a Jewish meeting, the former simply a meeting of a city or a community. And it is important to note that we have before us a Hellenistic *ecclesiastical* as discriminate from a *synogogal* literature and life. There is a history behind these words which we need not now explore. Internal evidence shows that at the earliest epoch during our era we can touch, there was a schism between the orthodox synagogue and the *ecclesiæ* which became the seed-bed of the new movement. The Jewish *proseucha* was an oratory or place of prayer, a substitute for the synagogue, generally 'at the seaside.'[1] Whether in the above passage 'prayer' or 'place of prayer' is meant, hardly signifies for our present inquiry. It is sufficient to note that the study of Christian origins teaches us from the first to hold aloof from the synagogues which were under strict subjection to the Sanhedrin or the *proseuchæ* indistinguishable from them, to those 'meetings' which in all probability were at first held in private houses, and shunned observation. The history of our English Dissenters, their illicit and persecuted meetings in the open air, their plain and barn-like buildings set up in courts and alleys, when the time of toleration set in, supplies an interesting analogy. But during the second century a distinctively and confessedly *Christian* place of meeting open to public observation cannot be well thought of. Under the shelter and name of Judaism, as a *religio licita*, the new movements must have gone on.

But passing from the use of *ecclesia* to denote a local 'congregation' to that wider and loftier sense in which it stands now for a pre-existent celestial being or for a spiritual community of the Elect, scattered abroad through the lands, but destined to be gathered together; this ennoblement of the Idea may be traced to the heterodox Jewish communities of the Diaspora.[2] In the Eucharistia they prayed, 'As this Broken Bread was scattered abroad upon the mountains and gathered together became one, so let Thy Ecclesia be gathered together from the ends of the

---

[1] Jos. *Ant.* 14. 10. 23.
[2] See Hermas, *Vis.* 1. 3. 4, 2. 4. 1. She, the Ecclesia, was the elder creation; the world was framed for her sake. For this Dream-life of Jewish phantasy, cf. Harnack, *Hdb. d. Dogmgesch.*, 1886, p. 67, 104. Analogously Ecclesia was an 'Aeon' with some of the Gnostics.

earth into Thy kingdom.'[1] And again, 'Remember, O Lord, Thy Ecclesia, to deliver her from all evil and to perfect her in Thy love and gather her together from the four winds, the sanctified, into Thy kingdom which Thou didst prepare for her.' 'Let grace come, and let this world pass away.'

The origin of the conception of the kingdom is traced especially to the *Malkhut Schamajim* (or *Elohim*) of the Jews, especially the Essenes, whose whole life aimed at its realisation, and the bringing in of 'the world to come,' the golden age, the *Olam-La-Ba*.[2] On this hope, the congregation of the Dispersed, as these Eucharistic prayers reveal, were fixing their waiting eyes. And in the Klasma or Broken Bread they see an eschatological allegory, apparently nowhere else found.[3] These prayers conclude, 'Hosanna to the Son (or God) of David. If any one is holy, let him come, if any one is not, let him repent, Maranatha. Amen!' The same strong impression of Jewish Messianism (whether it be specifically termed Ebionitism or Essenism) is on these words. We can hardly doubt that the original ascription was to the Son of David, *Ben David*, the one name which united the hope of all the Messianist sects, as identical with the Messiah. 'The Messianic fulfilment, it was universally believed (at the beginning of our era), must be secured through the return home of the tribes of Israel scattered to all ends of the earth, richly laden with presents by the peoples, in compensation for the long suffering laid upon them.'[4]

---

[1] *Didaché* 9. 4. Cf. 'una per omnem orbem terræ ecclesia diffusa,' *Fragm.-Murat.* v. 55 ff; Iren. I. 10. 1, 3. 12. 7; Tert. *Apol.* 37; adv. *Marc.* 3. 10; adv. *Jud.* 7.
[2] Graetz, *Gesch. d. Juden*, 4. 219, ed. 2.
[3] Harnack, *ad l.*   [4] Graetz, 4. 218.

The substitution of the phrase 'God of David' jars with the context. On the opposition of these names turned a bitter controversy, where the rift between this refined Judaism of the Diaspora and pronounced Hellenism is disclosed. This Son of David, or Messiah, was, it may be inferred from Philo, conceived by many as a supernatural and an angelic being, a vision for the eyes of the saints alone, by which they were to be drawn home from barbarian lands—a 'docetic' notion.[1]

But the 'Epistle of Barnabas' protests, 'Jesus was manifested both typically and in the flesh; He is not the "Son of man," but the "Son of God."' And the 110th psalm warned against 'the error of the sinners' who would affirm that Christ was the 'Son of David.' The reference to Ebionite or kindred opinions is unmistakable. Confusion must result if we apply the common label 'Christian' to documents so diverse in their tendency as this portion of the *Didaché* and the 'Epistle of Barnabas.'

The summons to those who bear the honoured name *holy* (*hagios*) to join the waiting community, and to others to repent, is not to be confounded with a summons to the sacred meal or supper.[2] The ejaculatory password, *Maranatha*, 'the Lord cometh,' announces the glorious return upon the clouds of heaven.[3] As we have already seen, 'the Prophets,' chief priests and teachers among the Hagioi, are permitted full liberty of extemporaneous thanksgiving in this place. It is not a community of 'Christians' in the sense of Justin, nor of those vaguely designated 'this people' in Barnabas, whose beliefs are here

---

[1] *De Execratt.* M. 2. 435.   [2] Cf. Harnack, *ad l.*
[3] Cf. Sabatier, Bisping, Harnack, *ad l.*

disclosed, but a purer and simpler community of Messianist Hagioi, whose traits may be in great part supplied from the description of Philo.[1] They are living in patriarchal simplicity and sanctity, in an elevation of spirit that admits not of backsliding into the old ways of error and sin. They partake of the divine grace, awaiting its more abundant and near outpouring, at the coming of the Lord. Here was the foundation laid of the Universal or Catholic Church, built on the 'apostles and prophets' of which Irenæus and the old Catholics speak, and of which a representative was later to be found in Peter.

THE HOLY VINE OF DAVID ($\dot{\eta}$ ἅγια ἄμπελος Λαβίδ).

To return to the Eucharistia in the *Didaché*. 'First for the cup: we give Thee thanks, our Father, on behalf of the Holy Vine of David, Thy Child (or servant), which Thou didst make known to us through Jesus Thy Child (or servant). To Thee the glory for ever.' This carries us back to the 'Song to the well-beloved,' the saints and favourites of Jehovah, in the Prophet Isaiah, concerning the Vineyard, and to the similar psalm which describes the Vine brought out of Egypt and planted among the heathen.[2] The Vine is the chosen people: a simile vigorous and beautiful, full of charm to the Judæan imagination. We are reminded at once of the Golden Vine figured above the doors of Herod's temple; of the similar work of art the 'thing of delight,' presented by Aristobulus to Pompey and deposited in the temple of Jupiter Capitolinus in

---

[1] Important in this connection is the 'holy and divine Ecclesia' of Jehovah in Philo 1. 536 M. Cf. 1. 289 M., and its spiritual identity with the Stoical Communion, 'the city of Zeus.' Havet, *Le Christianisme*, 3. 449.   [2] Ps. 80.

Rome; and of the vine-leaf or the bunch of grapes figured on the reverse of coins which bore on their obverse the legend, 'For the freedom of Jerusalem.' These are probably the true elucidations of the Vine symbol; luckless obscurations seem the attempts of commentators to explain it from the mystical allegories of the fourth Gospel or of Clement of Alexandria. When it is said that the Vine was 'a favourite symbol of Christ with the early Christians, and is often found in the pictures of the Catacombs,' we must demand who these 'early Christians' were, and what ground there is for thus mixing up fact and inference in a single statement.[1]

Jewish phantasy, religiously circumscribed in its activity and confined to the objects of the world of God, clung to the noble trees of the land, the cedar, the cypress, and the palm, to the fragrant flowering shrubs, and to the kindly plant that yielded the wine that maketh glad the heart of man. It was symbolic of a nation's lifeblood, of secular prosperity, and of spiritual good.[2] Thanks, then, for the holy Vine of David must substantially be thanks for a common sacred life, or a holy common weal. How this is 'made known' through the child or servant Jesus is not self-intelligible; nor has any satisfactory explanation of the text yet been offered. It is quite conceivable that it has been interpolated by an Ebionite 'Christian' in the distinctive sense. Justin, referring to the tortures to which 'they who have believed on Jesus' have been subjected through all the world, defies their adversaries to terrify them or reduce them to slavery. They are like the Vine which has been pruned and which puts forth more vigorous

---

[1] Schaff, note *ad l.*   [2] Cf. Ecclesiasticus, c. 27.

branches. 'For the Vine planted by God [and the Saviour Christ] is His people.'[1] The words we have bracketed are seen both by their position and their sense to be an innovation on the old imagery, which is thus despoiled of its simple force, that does not depend on theological details. So Horace in his Ode 'to the City of Rome,' employs the same analogy in substance:

> 'Duris ut ilex tonsa bipennibus
> Nigræ feraci frondis in Algido,
> Per damna, per cædes ab ipso
> Ducit opes animumque ferro.'[2]

We might dwell upon the like purport of the simile of the terebinth tree or of the shaken olive-tree in the Prophets, or the Talmud: but it is needless. All that we have to point out is the historical anachronism and the glaring fault in taste involved in the audacious polemic which adapts and accommodates the beautiful symbolism of the Vine to new names and associations. We must infer as probable that the hand of an adapter has made itself felt in the inconsequential reference to the Vine of David 'made known by Jesus.'

The internal evidence of the *Didaché* so far hints the existence of communities of *Hagioi*, as distinct from *Christianoi*. The analogy of Hagioi to Hosioi (probably another name of the enigmatic Essenes or Essæoi or Chasidim) should be remarked. The Essenes disappear as a sect after the year 70. But sentiments and ideas outline the dissolution of the sects inspired by them. And the probability is, that what was vigorous in the spirit of Essæism (and it may be added of Pharisaism) continued to work in the communities of the Hagioi. In the *Didaché*, the *Ecclesia*

[1] *Tryph.* 110.   [2] Carm. 4. 4. 57.

is the congregation of the dispersed, who are to be gathered into the kingdom; and there is no clear reference to any Christ who has appeared, and belief on whom is the condition of membership in the ecclesia. On the other hand, turning to Justin, we find the statement that those who believe on Christ are 'one soul, one synagogue, one church.' The logos of God addresses this ecclesia as a daughter; she has sprung from and partakes of Christ's name. 'For *Christianoi* we are all called.' And by the words of Ps. 45. 10–12, they are manifestly taught to forget the ancient institutes of the fathers: 'Listen, daughter, and incline thine ear and forget thy people and the house of thy father.'[1]

The reply put into the mouth of Trypho is instructive: 'Suppose the lord of you Gentiles to be ascertained a Christ and a God, as the Scriptures signify,—from whom you have acquired your name Christianoi: it does not follow that We, who are worshippers ($\lambda \alpha \tau \rho \epsilon \upsilon \tau \alpha i$) of the God ($\tau o \hat{\upsilon}\ \Theta \epsilon o \hat{\upsilon}$) who made Him also, should need to confess or adore Him.'

Let us revert for a moment to the Eucharistia of the *Didaché*. Thanks are addressed to the 'Holy Father' and to the 'Lord Almighty,'[2] because of His holy name, which He caused to tabernacle in the hearts of the worshippers, and who made all things for His name's sake. Here the resemblance in phraseology and thought to the Jewish paschal *Eulogiœ* is clear enough.

And we must leave to the judgment of our readers whether the blessings ascribed to the mediation of the 'child or servant Jesus,'—the *zoé* and *gnôsis*, or the

---

[1] *Tryph.* 63. Cf. 135, 138.
[2] 10. 2, 3.

gnosis and *pistis* and *athanasia*,[1] 'made known' (like the Vine) by Him, point to either Jewish or Christian sources, in the sense in which those terms are commonly understood. Whether these references be grafted on the original prayers or not, they at least prove that no such Christology as that of Justin was here dreamed of.

We are here on the traces of a class of Sectarians or Hæretics equally to be distinguished from the orthodox Jews, as from the orthodox Christians represented by Justin. Whether they were Ebionites or Gnostics is a question of secondary importance compared with the question of the attitude in which they stood towards the ancestral traditions of the Fathers, Circumcision, the Sabbath, the fast-days, the Temple and the sacrificial rites. These they have renounced; and they dream of an universal Jewish Church, into which the strangers shall have been gathered, as the new branch is grafted into the noble stock of the ancient Vine. Philo may well be called the first Father of such a Church.[2]

---

[1] These seem Gnostic thoughts.
[2] See 2. 433 M. on Deut. 28. 43.

CHAPTER III.

RITES OF THE HAGIOI.

WE may use the name Hagioi provisionally, as designating at all events a large class of Jews, whose views are reflected in apocalyptic literature like the Book of Enoch, and who must be kept distinct in thought from the Christiani of Justin, and from the stricter adherents of the Temple and the Law. In many respects they appear analogous to the Essenes or Hosioi, according to the recent investigation of Lucius.[1]

The first *nota* of this class of Jews of the Diaspora is the negative, but significant one, the silence with respect to Circumcision, or the reduction of it to a spiritual symbol. How great the temptation was towards the end of the first century to renounce or to disguise this badge of membership in the national covenant, may be inferred from the details of the exaction of the Jewish *fiscus*.[2] But this was an apostasy in the eyes of the teachers of the Law; a Palestinian authority, Eleazar of Modin, declared that he who was guilty of *epiplasmos* forfeited his blessedness or his part in the 'world to come,' even though he were

---

[1] *Der Essenismus*, 1881.
[2] The *improfessi*, Sueton. Dom. 12. See Graetz, *Gesch.* 4. 79; B. Bauer, *Christus, &c.*, 240.

instructed in the Law, and was of pious conversation.[1] Those who concealed, or who disavowed this national covenantal note, incurred excommunication from the ancient congregation of Israel, and must have found it impossible long to maintain a distinctive and superior position in face of uncircumcised Gentiles, who boldly announced that circumcision was no longer a sacrament, but was to be understood in an allegorical sense, of the interior disposition of the man. The stern denunciations of their strict compatriots and the taunts of Greeks like Justin must have tended to drive a multitude of waverers in one direction, on a path from which there was no return. Justin tells the Jews they must receive the truth from him, an uncircumcised man. The circumcision of the flesh was given for a distinctive sign, to mark out the Jews for suffering. It was not necessary, otherwise Adam and Abel, and Enoch, and Noah, and Melchizedek would have had it. Abraham was blessed in uncircumcision, because of faith. Women cannot receive the rite, which again proves that it is but a 'sign,' not a 'work of righteousness.' Justin cries out, as usual mistaking clamour for argument, 'the blood of that circumcision is obsolete!' He admits that Christ was circumcised, but not that He might be justified, but that He might perfect the divine economy.[2] It does not occur to Justin to explain *how* fleshly circumcision, which he argues against from the Prophet Jeremiah, was nevertheless a part of the divine economy at the time of Christ's birth. Christians, he says, have received the 'second

---

[1] On the other hand, see the neglect of Circumcision by the Jew Ananias in his teaching of King Izates, Joseph. *Ant.* 20. 2. 4. Cf. Strabo, p. 760; *Verisimilia*, by A. Pierson and S. A. Naber, Amstelod., 1886, p. 11.   [2] *Tryph.* 19. 23, 24. 67.

circumcision,' by means of the 'sharp stones' of the discourses of the Apostles on the sharp-cornered stone! And so their hearts have been circumcised from all wickedness.[1]

The writer of the 'Epistle of Barnabas' reasons in a similar way, adding some foolish conceits of his own.

Experience teaches that the soundest reasoning on any religious or political subject falls ineffective when the public mind is preoccupied with passions and interests adverse to the truth; and, on the other hand, that the feeblest sophisms are acceptable whenever they fall in with prevailing passions and interests. The confident assertion that the circumcision was abolished must have been good news to multitudes of Jews of the period, could they believe it to be true. Some passages of the Old Testament gave a colour to the assertion. Moreover, the teaching of facts lent its powerful aid towards this revolution in thought. Educated Jews, brought into converse with many races, had to explain to themselves the fact that the sacramental sign was not peculiar to them, but was shared by Egyptians, Edomites, Syrians. If circumcision was the seal of the covenant between Jehovah and the people of His possession, how came it that heathen bore the same? If the thing signified was different in the two cases, then the thoughtful mind must be the more forced back upon the inner significance, to grasp it as the core of genuine religion. At the present day, when our knowledge of the world has so vastly opened out, and every well-informed Christian is aware that not only is circumcision practised far and wide among the native peoples of the great continents and the islands, but that ideas which he was

[1] *Tryph.* 114.

taught to consider the exclusive property of his faith, are shared by barbarians as native religious traditions, he is forced from the ground of old apologetic to seek some broader basis for his faith. And so, we apprehend, it is probable that when our era opened, there were multitudes of Jews in the Diaspora whose interest in maintaining the circumcision of the flesh had long been from various causes weakened, and who were ready to be drawn into the current of that revolution which we almost see in course of accomplishment in perusing the exultant pages of Justin Martyr. We simply note, however, the attack made upon the validity of the rite by him and by the author of the 'Epistle of Barnabas,' and the general silence elsewhere observed on the subject.[1]

THE SABBATH.

When we recall the manner in which the observance of the Sabbath is treated in some passages of the later Old Testament prophets[2] as the very summary of true piety, and the manner in which the Romans of our time still saw in that observance one of the chief *notæ* of the Judæi, we are prepared to estimate the spiritual revolution implied in the abandonment of that observance and the substitution for it of that of the 'Eighth Day.'

The first dated reference to this change we find in the *Apology* of Justin: 'On the day of the Sun so called, there is a gathering together of all who abide

---

[1] The fierce struggle on this question revealed in the Epistle to the Galatians probably refers to the middle of the second century. There is no external evidence of the earlier existence of that epistle. Cf. Loman in *Theol. Tijdschr.*, 1882, 1883.

[2] Jer. 17. 19 ff ; Ezek. 20. 12 ff.

F

in the cities or fields into the same place.' The description of the service follows. And then, 'During the day of the Sun in common we all make the *syneleusis* (or meeting), because it is the first day on which God turned the darkness and the matter, and made the world, and Jesus Christ our Saviour on the same day rose from the dead. For on the day before the Kronic day they crucified Him, and on the day after the Kronic day, that is the day of Hélios, He appeared to His apostles and disciples, and taught those things which we have delivered for consideration unto you also.' This is the earliest known statement of the observance of Sunday among the *Christianoi* and the reason of it, dating from about a hundred years after the event said to be commemorated.[1]

Justin taunts the Jews with the observance of the Sabbath in the same spirit in which he speaks of Circumcision. The Sabbath was enjoined by God upon them as a sign, because of their iniquities and those of their fathers.[2] But Justin in vain seeks to evade the direct force of the prophetic words which set the observance forth as a prime article of piety, by pointing out exceptions to the rule.[3] He explains away the Sabbath, even as Circumcision, by spiritualising it. 'The New Law would have you keep perpetual Sabbath, and you, because you are idle for one day, fancy you are pious, not understanding why it was enjoined on you. And if you eat unleavened

---

[1] *Apol.* i. 67. The Day of the Sun appears to point to the cult of Mithras (cf. Orelli, *Inscr.* 911). The admissions of Tertullian, *Apol.* 16, are here important: the turning to the east in prayer, the observance of the Sunday, and the recognition of the Persian origin of these customs. Havet, 3. 327 ff. On the sacramental significance of the New Sun or Fire in old religions, Lippert, *Die Religg.* and *Christenthum* 4 is especially lucid.

[2] *Tryph.* 21. [3] Isa. 58. 13 ff; *Tryph.* 27.

bread, you say that you have fulfilled the will of God. Not in these things is the Lord our God well pleased. If there is among you a perjurer or a thief, let him cease; if an adulterer, let him repent, and he has kept the sweet and true Sabbaths of God; if a man has not pure hands, let him wash, and he is pure.'[1] The writer of the 'Epistle of Barnabas' seems to outdo Justin in audacity. He argues that the Sabbath cannot be observed, according to the Law, except with pure hearts: this observance then is still for a future and renovate time. And of the oracle in Isa. I. 13, 'Your new moons and your Sabbaths I cannot endure,' the following highly imaginative exegesis is given: 'You perceive how He speaks: Your present Sabbaths are not acceptable to Me; but that is, which I have made, when giving rest to all things I shall make a beginning of the Eighth Day, that is a beginning of another world. Wherefore also we keep the eighth day with joyfulness, the day also on which Jesus rose again from the dead.'

It is impossible not to wonder at the effrontery of innovators who thus seized upon the Old Testament Scriptures, appropriated them, and perverted their plainest sense in favour of their own dogmatic assumptions and the substruction of Christian story. That the observance of the day called in the planetary series Sun Day, or, according to Jewish reckoning, the Eighth Day, was a fact about the middle of the second century, is clear; also that it commemorated a revolution, 'the beginning of another world.' But the observance is no more proof of a historic fact of resurrection than the later feasts of the Annunciation or of the Nativity are proofs of historic facts. There is no chain of

[1] *Tryph.* 12.

evidence to link the day observed in Justin's time with the ghostly event conceived to have occurred a hundred years before. These things again invite silence and reflection. The answer to the injuries and sophistries of Justin is that unbroken respect for the Sabbath which has continued during all these centuries among the dispersed of Israel.

But there is undoubtedly another aspect of this subject. The literary history of our religion in early times, unpleasing as it is to the lover of historic truth and fairness of argument, reveals below the surface the bounding pulse of a new life and a new hope. The 'Eighth Day' owed its sacredness to the recollection of the rite of circumcision, which, abandoned in the fleshly sense, must none the less be made to yield up its spiritual content for the satisfaction of faith. It was a type of the circumcision of the heart from error and wickedness; therefore the 'eighth' day or first of the week is symbolic of the regenerate life. That life must have an Auctor and a beginning; therefore the Lord must have risen from the dead on that day.[1] This is really the implicit reasoning of Justin; and similar is that of the epistle to the Magnesians which passes under the name of 'Ignatius.' Those who were conversant with the ancient Scriptures or were brought up in the ancient order of things have come into a new hope. They can therefore no longer observe the Sabbath. They must observe a new day, the *Kyriac* day, in commemoration of the renascence of their life. This was the day that Abraham prophetically rejoiced to see. Let then the Sabbath be kept, but no longer in the Jewish manner. And after the Sabbath, let the *Kyriac* (Lord's) Day be kept as a

[1] *Tryph.* c. 9.

festival, the resurrection day, the queen and chief of all the days.

So eager is the writer to snatch at any shred of verbal argument from the Old Testament, he finds in the inscriptions of two psalms 'to the end of the eighth day,' a prophetic reference to the day on which our life both sprang up again, and the victory over death was obtained in Christ, whom the children of perdition, the enemies of the Saviour, deny.[1]

But information showing that the observance of the day was deduced from an event, not *vice versâ*, we have none. In the face of this silence, in presence of the overwhelming evidence of the manner in which the traditional narrative of the Birth, Death, and Resurrection was constructed from data of the Old Testament, mystically interpreted, the modern critic has no alternative but to conclude that here aspiration and phantasy begot or adopted the Idea, and clothed it with the form of fact.[2]

This supersession of the Sabbath by the eighth, or first, or Sun, or Kyriac day is a strong nota of the religious innovators. It was to proclaim, 'Where there is Christianity, there cannot be Judaism.'[3] The silence of the *Didaché* and other documents on this matter seems significant of a transition.

THE FAST DAYS.

We have seen how strongly marked to the eye of the Romans were the fasting observances as a note of

---

[1] Pss. 6. 12.
[2] On this distinctly *creative* activity in literature which only ceased with the fixing of the Canon, see Overbeck, *Ueb. die Anfänge der patrist. Literatur* in *Histor. Zeitschr.*, N. F. xii. 307 ff; Harnack, *Hdb.* 98.
[3] *Ad Magnes.* 10.

the Jews. The regular fast-days of orthodox Judaism were the Monday and the Thursday.[1] To remove these weekly fasts to the Wednesday and the Friday was doubtless a hæretical proceeding and implied an irreconcilable breach with the Sanhedrin. The bitter allusion to 'the Hypocrites,' by whom we can only understand those orthodox Jews of whom the Pharisees were the most numerous representatives, as well as the most strict, points in the same direction. 'As for your fasts let them not be with the Hypocrites; for they fast on the second of the Sabbath and the fifth; but ye shall fast during the fourth and the *parasceué*' (Wednesday and Friday).[2]

But this passage seems referable to a late date. Neither in Justin nor in the anonymous literature do we find any allusion to the bi-weekly fast. Rather the rite itself of fasting is evaporated, like Circumcision and the Sabbath, into a figure of abstinence from sin. Here the great Unknown Prophet, who may, for aught we know, have flourished at a time very near to our era, and may have imbibed that purer piety which we have long been accustomed to term evangelical, from a common fountain with multitudes of his compatriots, —furnished the great *locus classicus* on the true fasting alike to Justin and to 'Barnabas.'[3] It is indeed one of those passages of universal and undying import which speak to every conscience, reminding men that religious observances which are not besouled by love to humanity, as well as by the fear of God, must degenerate into a farcical play-acting; and that the noblest ideal of worship is the life-imitation of a

---

[1] *Mischna Taanith*, 2. 9 : for division of opinion among the Pharisees on the merit of fasting, *Taanith*, 11a; Wuensche, 476.

[2] *Didaché*, 8. 1.   [3] Isa. 58; see *Tryph.* 15, 40; *Barn.* 3.

beneficent and compassionate God. And similarly in the 'Shepherd of Hermas,' the Shepherd tells the writer, whom he finds holding a *station*, or stated fast on the mountain, that in this way he will do nothing for righteousness. 'Commit no wickedness in thy life, and serve the Lord in a pure heart. Keep His commandments, walking in His precepts, and let no wicked desire arise in thy heart. Trust in God. And if thou doest these things and fearest Him and abstainest from every wicked thing, thou shalt live to God. And if thou doest these things thou shalt perform a great fast and acceptable to God.'[1]

If we recall not only the passage in deutero-Isaiah but other oracles and psalms in which the like antiritualism is taught, we shall be reminded that the antagonism to Hypocrites and the hypocritical representation of piety arose within the bosom of Judaism itself. And the stigma which in this respect attaches to the memory of the Pharisees as a class, probably enough originated with Pharisaic teachers of the type of the great Hillel. In this doctrine of the spiritual as opposed to the external fasting, we are touching upon something which is common to enlightened Jews, Christians and Stoics, as we may see in the writings of Seneca, of Persius, and of Juvenal. The *Christiani* made way in the world, not by a sound exegesis of Scripture, nor by the substitution of a new ritual for the old, but by appropriating a fund of deep moral intuitions which were widely diffused in a time too often superficially described as one of utter viciousness and corruption.

We may notice in passing how 'Barnabas' cites, under the name of 'the prophet,' some obscure

[1] *Sim.* 5. 1.

rabbinical tradition concerning a fast with the offering of two goats, one as a burnt-offering, the other as a curse-offering. The latter is shown to be a 'type of Jesus.' These curiosities are adopted by Justin and afterwards by Tertullian.[1] And the phænomenon is one of a mass of evidences how vague to the mind of such men were the notions of 'prophetic scriptures;' and how, instead of offering historic facts concerning 'Jesus,' they grasped at any material which might seem to add confirmation to the idea of a suffering victim, whose death had put an end to the old economy. Similar remarks apply to the 'red heifer' of the next chapter,—another type of Jesus.

THE TEMPLE.

Perhaps the boldest of all the attacks upon the ancient institutions of Israel is that which makes the Temple itself its object, and those to whom it was endeared as the House of God. Writing from his anonymous obscurity, avoiding any name which might discover of what nationality or sect he was, the forger of 'Barnabas' declares that 'the wretched men' who wandered in error trusted not in God Himself, but in the Temple as the House of God; and that their worship was little better than Ethnic worship. Among his citations in proof that the Temple is doomed is one from the Book of Enoch, mentioned as 'Scripture.' He makes allusion, as we cannot doubt, to the intention of Hadrian to rebuild the temple; after the ruinous war with Barcochebas.[2] 'Through their going to

---

[1] *Tryph.* 40; *Adv. Jud.* 14; *Adv. Marc.* 3. 7.
[2] See the Proleg. and note *ad l.* in Harnack and Gebhardt's edition.

war, it was destroyed by their enemies, and now they, as the servants of their enemies, shall rebuild it.'

But is there still a temple of God? There is: it exists in the Heart of Man. Sublime sentiment! Would that it had come from the lips of an open and avowed confessor, and not from those, as we fear, of a stealthy and injurious renegade. Why, the reader cannot but ask, does he not tell us who the new people are, to whom so high a doctrine has been committed? But let us quote his words. 'I find then that there is a Temple. How it shall be built in the name of the Lord, learn. Before we believed in God the habitation of our heart was corrupt and weak, as a real temple built by hand. For it was full of idolatry and was a house of dæmons through the doing of all that was contrary to God. But it shall be built on the name of the Lord. Give heed that the Temple of the Lord may be gloriously built. How? Learn. When we received the remission of sins and hoped on the Name of the Lord, we became new men (καινοί), being created again from the beginning, wherefore in our dwelling truly God dwells in us. How? His logos of faith, His calling of the promise, the wisdom of the decrees, the commands of the teaching (*didaché*); Himself in us prophesying, Himself in us dwelling, to us enslaved to death opening the door of the temple, which is a mouth, repentance offering to us, He leads into the incorrupt Temple.

'For he who desires to be saved looks not unto man, but unto Him dwelling and speaking in him, at Him amazed, that he has never heard him declare such words from his mouth, nor himself has ever desired to hear them. This is a pneumatic Temple, being built to the Lord.'

The figure of the temple of the heart is not strictly kept up. But apart from that, the passage seems of great importance for the understanding of the great religious innovation of the second century. Here we have the unofficial manifesto of an unnamed community, which we shall not greatly err in designating a community of Hagioi, whether at Rome or Alexandria none can pretend to say.

1. The visible temple has been dishonoured and abolished.

2. A Pneumatic or Spiritual Temple is being built 'on the Name of the Lord' [that is God].

Observe that there is no reference here to 'Jesus,' named in the Epistle elsewhere.

3. It begins with the New Creation, that is, with those who received the remission of sins, and hoped on the Name of the Lord.

4. The Indwelling of God in the hearts of the community is the essential principle of this new faith.

5. The result of this Indwelling is prophetic gifts and activity.

6. More definitely: the mode of this Indwelling is explained, not by visions of Divine things, but by audition of Divine verities:

    i. The Logos of Faith.
    ii. The Calling of the Promise.
    iii. The Wisdom of the Decrees.
    iiii. The Mandates of the Teaching.

No one who studies the Greek vocabulary and phraseology here presented will fail to see that we are here neither on Pharisaic nor on Christian ground. The author is bitterly contemptuous towards the adherents of the letter of the Law, and the restorers of the Temple. On the other hand he ignores the name *Chris-*

tianos entirely. Nor does the name 'Jesus Christ' occur except in one passage which, considering that 'Jesus' alone is named some twelve times in the Epistle, is hardly free from suspicion.

In these principles of 'Barnabas' we find laid bare the 'foundation of the apostles and prophets' on which the *ecclesia* was to be built. The writer himself, under the pseudonym, assumes the part of apostle and prophet, though the conception of the *ecclesia* is but faintly marked under the allegory of the 'wool among the thorns.'

Most important in the enumeration of the principles of the new edification seems to be the 'word of faith.' It has been argued by some scholars that had the author or the readers been Jews, he would hardly have written 'before we believed in God.' Had he been a *Christian*, he would hardly have thus dated an epoch of conversion. The truth is that *Pistis*, Faith as a new principle in religion, opposed to works of the Law, is of Jewish and præ-Christian conception.[1] With regard to the rest of the terminology, the study of the expressions 'righteousness,' 'hope,' 'love,' 'promise,' 'wisdom,' 'decrees,' 'dogmata,' 'mandates,' 'doctrine,' 'gnosis,' lead to something inapprehensible in any distinct way by the modern reader,[2] who finds that he has to do with an allusive religious dialect, the value of which depends upon the association with which it is connected in the minds of those whose ear has been trained to it. In this respect it may be compared with some of the Puritan literature of the seventeenth

[1] Cf. Sirac. 2. 8, 13; 40. 12; 45. 4; 49. 10; Wisd. 16. 26; Faith and Hope in Philo, 2. 415 M, 435, 574 M. Cf. R. Akiba and his doctrine of Faith.

[2] Cf. the similar vague expressions, ἡ παράδοσις, ἡ δοθεῖσα πίστις, τὸ κήρυγμα, &c., in *Patr. Opp.*, ed. Gebh. and Harn., p. 133.

century. And just as we know that a turbid and unintelligible theology was held by men of the seventeenth century of the greatest force of character, so may it be well inferred that the rambling reasoning of the literature of the second century nevertheless proceeded from communities filled with men of passionate self-belief, and of energy and power of persuasion which such self-belief ever inspires.

The solitary and independent thinker is apt to assume that faith is for the mass what it is for him—namely, a state of mind produced by experience and by evidence; and that he who pretends to a high spiritual status and prospects on grounds that cannot be explained to another, must be a fanatic or an impostor. Yet this is too severe a way of judging human nature. So intense is the yearning for security and confidence in the souls of the many, so primary a necessity does it seem to them, that they are ready to grasp at any word of authority or any rite by which it is positively said to be assured to them. Or, in the most impassioned minds, the feelings themselves carry with them their own authority. We '*know* that we have passed from death to life because we love the brethren.' And similarly the implicit logic of these revolters from the Law, and all the *corpus sine pectore* of the traditions of the elders, was: 'A new life and a new law is an absolute necessity; the old has become intolerable. We find in the prophetic writings the promise of a new covenant, of laws to be written on the hearts and minds of the people. Such promises are consonant with our own present consciousness of the stirring of new life within us. We are then the new people; let the old pass away.' But there is absolute silence as to any

Founder, Father, Teacher, Apostle, or Prophet of a hundred years ago who had first sounded this note of revolution and of reformation; absolute silence as to one who had on the contrary declared that He came not to destroy but to fulfil, and that not one jot nor one tittle of the Law should pass away till all were fulfilled. The author of 'Barnabas' rests upon an ideal victim—Jesus; Jesus the Master he ignores.[1]

A pause of reflection is again demanded.

[1] If these passages are part of the original text, which is doubtful.

CHAPTER IV.

THE NEW CREATION, THE NEW PEOPLE, AND THE NEW LAW.

THE thought of the New People, the true human creation prophesied at the foundation of the world—'let us make man after our image,' and fulfilled by the suffering of the 'Lord of the World' in the flesh, is emphatic in 'Barnabas.'[1] They are 'renewed in the remission of sins,' they are 'another type,' a second plastic formation in the last days. So too when the rabbinical author cited, as 'the prophet' says: 'Let all the priests alone eat the inwards (of the goat) unwashed with vinegar,' the reason is, that to the Lord, who is to offer His flesh for the sins of *His new people*, gall is to be given with vinegar to drink; 'Eat ye alone, while the people fast and mourn in sackcloth and ashes.'

To believe, to receive the seal, to be *renewed* in spirit, is the sequence of thought in 'Hermas.'[2]

There is no explicit reference to baptism here. But in Justin's explanation to the heathen the reference is explicit to the manner in which Christians 'dedicate themselves to God, *made new* through Christ.' There is persuasion of the truth of the teaching, the

[1] 5. 7; 6. 12. [2] *Sim.* 8. 6.

promise to live in accordance with it: there is fasting and prayer for the pardon of former sins. Then they are led to the water and are born again, making the bath in the name of the Father of all, and Lord God, and of our Saviour Jesus Christ, and of a Holy Spirit.[1] He cites as a saying of Christ, 'Unless ye be born again ye shall not enter the kingdom of heaven,' neither using the words of the fourth Gospel nor alluding to Nicodemus.

However, our point was here simply to call attention to the boldness with which this mystical conception of a new birth is announced in 'Barnabas' and supported by perverted ingenuity from the account of the Creation in Genesis. As for Justin, he finds his support for the regenerating Laver in the first chapter of Isaiah, adding, 'We have learned the *logos* with reference to this matter from the apostles.' What history in any precise sense can be extracted from writers who answer one's inquiries as to the origin of a new Faith, or an all-significant Practice by allusions to legends of missionaries, unnamed, unknown? Turning back to 'Barnabas,' we find that the apostles chosen out by the Lord to preach His Gospel were superlative sinners, that He might show He came not to call just men, but sinners.[2] Again inaccurately citing a rabbinical tradition (Mishna, Para. 3. 1–11) he says that at the offering of the Heifer the 'boys who sprinkled' signified 'those who preached the Gospel to you of the remission of sins and the sanctity of the heart; to whom He gave the authority of the Gospel, being Twelve for a testimony of the Tribes (for twelve are the tribes of Israel), that they might

[1] *Apol.* 1. 61.
[2] 5. 9. We infer that he did *not* use the Synoptic Gospels here.

proclaim it.' As we have already seen, Justin adds the notice that they set out from Jerusalem. Neither writer knows their names or their dates. We must conclude that the noble conception of a New Life and a New People, born from the spiritual travail of a revolutionary time, was nourished by a fantastic and mystical exegesis of Scripture, including the Mishna, and was fixed as the inner meaning of the baptism of proselytes to the teaching and legends of the Hagioi or kindred sects.

What is Life without Liberty? A fleeting flower without lustre or perfume, as one of our poets has sung. It was the passionate yearning for spiritual liberty which gave rise to the conception of the New Law. So again did aspiration clothe itself in the form of fact, and the Ideal of desire was converted into the real for belief. Once more the inexhaustible oracle of the first chapter of Isaiah was drawn upon. Sacrifices, feasts of the new moon, sabbaths, all were done away,

'*That the New Law of our Lord Jesus Christ, being without the yoke of necessity, might not have the man-made offering.*'[1]

We dwell only upon the substance of the thought, believing the passage, from its phraseology, to be open to suspicion of interpolation where it stands. Tertullian is full of this New Law.

In "Hermas" the mode of conception is different, but the substance of the meaning is the same. The suggestive imagery of the tree is introduced. A large willow is seen overshadowing plains and mountains, and under its shade were assembled all those who were 'called by the Name of the Lord.' Its branches are pruned by a glorious angel and distributed among

[1] *Barn.* 2. 6.

the peoples; yet it still continues sound. It signifies the Law of God given to the whole world; and this Law is the Son of God proclaimed to the ends of the earth. And the people under its shadow are they who have heard the proclamation and have believed upon Him.[1]

Or again, 'A Vineyard has been planted by God, that is to say: He created the People, and gave them to His Son. The Son appointed His angels over them to keep them. And He Himself purged away the sins of the people, and showed them the paths of life by giving them the Law which He received from His Father.'[2]

Although the commentators speak of 'Jesus' or 'Christ' in discussing these passages, it should be strictly noted that 'Hermas' ignores these names and speaks only of 'the Son of God,' who is apparently in his thought a glorious Angel of God. This is not what we commonly understand by 'Christianity.' Nor is the preaching of the Son of God conceived as a Gospel, but as a Law.

The expression the 'paths of life,' like the 'Way of Life,' as we shall presently see, is a biblical and Jewish apocalyptic and didactic expression, carrying with it a strong ethical import.

The Universal Proclamation.

The idea of an universal Preaching or Publication of this New Law runs through our 'apostolic and prophetic' documents. In Arcadia the Pastor sees twelve mountains of diverse forms, rising out of a plain: these are the Twelve Tribes which inhabit the whole world. The Son of God was preached to them

---

[1] *Sim.* 8. 1-3. Cf. Gebhardt and Harnack, *ad l.*   [2] Ib. 5. 6.

by the Apostles. And even as the stones from these mountains, when placed in the building of the vision, became of one colour, so all the nations that dwell under heaven were called by hearing and believing upon the name of [the Son of] God. They received the Seal, they had one understanding and one mind. Their faith became one and their love one. A beautiful and catholic vision.[1] But to attempt to find historic forms for these apostles of the Twelve Tribes in the Diaspora, or to identify the 'Son of God' with a known human teacher, is as vain as to define the wraith-like shapes of clouds on Arcadian mountain-tops. We must again guard against the assumption that the author has either *Judæi* or *Christiani* in any ordinary external sense in view. He writes as a Hagios and a Klētos; and his conception is that of an Ecclesia of the Sealed from among the scattered tribes, —in short, of the true or spiritual Israel.

Again, in pursuance of the allegory, those who believed from the eighth mountain were 'apostles and teachers who preached to the whole world.' Other mountains are allegorical of various centres of false and hypocritical, self-seeking, and wicked teachers, distinguished, as usual, by subjective *criteria*. But where are the particulars of this magnificent universal mission, the names of the missionaries, the sphere of their operations, and the contents of their message ? The historical student can but conclude that here the prophetic tense of the past is to be understood of the present or of the future. Those passionate dreams of the unity of the ecclesia amidst all diversity of tongues and manners which hovered before the imagination of the Judaism of the spirit and its proselytes from the

[1] *Herm. Sim.* 9-17.

shores of Pontus and the plains of Libya and Mesopotamia to the imperial city, was felt in this new time to be in course of realisation. And there should be no difficulty in understanding how this splendid dream of the proclamation of a new law to every nation under heaven should gradually, from mere intentness of gazing, resolve itself into the shape of a phantom history. Perhaps it may be said that this poetical composition, judged by ordinary rules of literary criticism, may never have been intended to convey other than poetic images of what might be.

But hardly the same can be admitted of the statements of Justin. Addressing historical persons, the Emperor Antoninus Pius and the Senate and Roman people, he says that his clients are those who are unjustly hated and harassed, 'of every race of men.'[1] And 'out of all human races there are those who are expecting Him that was crucified in Judæa, after whom the land of the Jews was straightway taken in war and handed over to you.'[2] But we find, as usual, that Justin's *datum* is a verse of the Old Testament. When the Psalm says, 'Their sound is gone out into the whole earth,'[3] this proves that men 'out of every race' were to believe in Christ.[4] By what argument, he asks, could we have been led to believe in a crucified man, that He is first-born to the unbegotten God, and that He will hold judgment on the whole human race, unless—before He was made man and came—we find announcements made concerning Him, and see them fulfilled: the desolation of the land of the Jews, and those out of every nation of men who have been persuaded through the *Didaché* from his apostles, and have rejected the old customs in which they erroneously

[1] *Apol.* I. 1, 25.   [2] Ib. 32.   [3] Ps. 19, 2, 5.   [4] *Apol.* 1. 40.

lived, looking at us, and knowing that greater in number and truer are the Christians from the Gentiles than from the Jews and Samaritans?[1] The oracle (Isa. 54. 1) runs, that the barren and deserted woman shall have more sons than the wedded wife.

When the wicked dæmons knew that Christ was being believed on and expected 'in every race,' they put forward Simon and Menander of Samaria to deceive the multitude with magic miracles.[2]

In the *Dialogue* Justin often iterates the like statements to the Jews. And here the question may be raised, Do the assertions of a New and Universal Law promulgated by the Son of God that we find in 'Hermas' mean substantially the same thing with the assertions of the universality of the 'Christian religion' in Justin? If they do, why does the phraseology and the notional stock of the two writers so differ? If they do not, what was the origin of these universalist conceptions? The literature reveals incessant schism and strife of the most embittered kind, side by side with bold pretensions to catholic unity, now on the part of the 'holy and elect' of the Dispersed, now on the part of the *Christiani*. *Prima facie*, it looks as if intense mutual jealousy between rivals for the possession of the Beautiful Bride could alone explain these phænomena. For the story of the passion for the Ideal is analogous to the story of the passion for Woman. The great abstractions of philosophy and of piety and of patriotism assume to the grammarian the feminine gender, and become all but beloved persons to the glowing fancy of the impassioned heart. And for the sake of her they call Ecclesia men have hated and fought with one another, as for her not less beauteous

---

[1] *Apol.* I. 53.   [2] Ib. 56.

sister, Theologia, as if they could not endure that her praises should be sung by another tongue than their own. But to return.

'Into all the earth' there went out from Jerusalem elect men (Eusebius calls them apostles) to denounce the godless Hæresis of the *Christiani*.[1] This was a hundred years before Justin; and he says that the same calumnies are being repeated by ignorant men still. The latter statement can only be accepted, that is, for the time immediately preceding Justin. It is confirmed by the counter-attacks of the Talmud on the 'Denunciants' and the Minim. These mutual denunciations went on in the Jewish Diaspora. But Justin has a theory of a *Christian* Diaspora. 'After Christ was crucified, the disciples who were with Him were scattered abroad until He rose from the dead, and persuaded them that it had been so prophesied concerning Him that He should suffer. And thus persuaded, they went out into all the world and taught those things.'[2] And so *Christiani* 'hold their persuasion from "the prophets" and others seen to be pious men throughout the world.' The modern reader may wax indignant at the repetition of these empty phrases; yet when it is considered that the doctrine they were used to recommend had so much that was salutary and necessary to the souls of men, we need not doubt that acceptance of the latter carried with it unquestioning respect for the former. So it has ever been and will be with the multitude. Yet however credulous they may be in reference to the history of their adopted religion, they will not accept statements about the contemporary world which are in defiance of known facts. One does not understand how Justin

[1] *Tryph.* 17. [2] *Ib.* 53.

could have ventured to maintain the existence of 'the faith of the Christ' among all nations at his time, and the expectation of His coming again, had not the fact that Jews were everywhere, and everywhere spoke of Messiah been well known.[1] That conversion from 'vain idols and dæmons' was going on everywhere may well be believed; but by whose instrumentality?[2] We do not forget the later boast of Tertullian as to the numbers of the Christians; but must correct his declamation from the still later and soberer Origen. In truth these vainglorious *Christiani* appropriated to themselves the credit of a great spiritual movement among the nations, the origin of which would have been more modestly and more reverently traced to a Holy Spirit alone. But the most important passage in the *Dialogue* has yet to be cited. The *Christiani*, says Justin, offer the sacrifices handed down by Jesus the Christ, that is, at the Eucharistia of the bread and the cup,—in every place of the earth. God beforehand witnesses that they are well-pleasing to Him. Those offered by the Jews and their priests He refuses, in the words of the prophet.[3] 'You,' he continues, 'hitherto in your love of contention, say that the sacrifices in Jerusalem at the time the Israelites so called dwelt there, are not received by God, but that the prayers of those from that race that were then in the Diaspora were acceptable to Him, and that He called their prayers sacrifices.'

Here then we have evidence indirectly of the Jews themselves that there was a radical theological difference between those who upheld the ancient Law and the institutes of the Temple and their brethren of the

[1] *Tryph.* 52. [2] Ib. 91.
[3] Mal. I. 10–12.

Diaspora. The latter were equally aloof from the *Christiani* in Justin's sense.

'That prayers and sacrifices offered by worthy men, are alone perfect sacrifices and well-pleasing to God, I also admit. Christians also have learned to offer these alone,—even at the memorial of their food, both dry and liquid, in which remembrance is made of the sufferings suffered for their sakes by the Son of God. His name the high-priests and teachers have caused to be profaned through the whole earth, &c.'[1] 'You are deceived by yourselves and by your teachers, in interpreting the logos (in Malachi) of those of your race who are in the Diaspora, as if it said that their prayers and sacrifices were pure and well-pleasing in every place. Acknowledge that you lie and endeavour wholly to deceive yourselves; first because not even now from the rising of the sun to the setting is your race diffused, but the nations, among whom none of your race has hitherto dwelt.'

Contrast with this the statement put by Josephus into the mouth of King Agrippa about one hundred years before. Addressing the Jews of Jerusalem, he says, 'There is no people upon the habitable earth which have not some portions of you among them, whom your enemies will slay in case you go to war.'[2]

Finally, Justin proceeds to the circumstantial vaunt, 'There is absolutely not one race of men, whether barbarians or Hellenes, or whatever name they are called by—people who live in waggons, or "houseless ones," or shepherd-dwellers in tents, among whom through the name of the crucified Jesus prayers and eucharistiæ to the Father and Maker of all are not offered. Knowing that at that time when the prophet

[1] *Tryph.* 117.; Semisch, 2. 452.   [2] *B. J.* 2. 16. 4.

Malachias spoke this, your Dispersion in all the earth, where ye now are, had not taken place, as is shown from the Scriptures.'

Certainly we hardly need the commentator's warning not to take these big statements of Justin, or those of Irenæus, Tertullian, and Lactantius 'too bluntly' (*nimis præfracte*), especially as Origen flatly contradicts them.[1] Such recklessness forfeits all claim not to credence merely, but to respect. That men 'out of every race' have suffered and do suffer for the name of Jesus all things that they may not deny Him, is a statement that could only be made and only received by those who had no proper sense of the value of language.[2] The statement in the pseudo-Justin's epistle to Diognetus, that 'Christians are scattered through all the cities of the world,' has no historical sense for us, inasmuch as we know not whether this epistle was written in the second, the fourth, or the fifteenth century.

To conclude on this part of the subject. To claim an ideal universality for the New Law of the Son of God, as 'Hermas' does, is a very different thing from the assertion of the universal diffusion of the Christians through the world in Justin. This he could not have known to be a fact. He probably seeks to imitate or to outvie Jewish boasts which may be found in Josephus already a hundred years before. Josephus says that the earliest Greek philosophers followed Moses in their doctrines; and that the mass of mankind have long been inclined to follow the religious observances of the Jews. There is no city of the Greeks, nor of the barbarians, nor any nation whatever, whither the custom of the Sabbath has not

---

[1] *In Matth. tract.* 28. [2] *Tryph.* 121 ; cf. 131.

come, and by which the Jewish fasts and abstinences from food are not observed. They also imitate their mutual concord. 'Our Law has no bait of pleasure to allure men to it, but prevails by its own face. As God Himself pervades all the world, so has our law passed through all the world also.' 'I am so bold as to say that we are become the teachers of other men.'[1]

In his *Antiquities* Josephus testifies to the variety of Jewish customs in the cities; but the Law has supreme regard for natural justice, and promotes benevolence and friendship to all men, who ought not to consider difference of institutions a sufficient cause of alienation.[2] He aims at reconciliation between the Jews and the Greeks, by removing the unreasonable hatred against the former. The complaints of the Catholic apologists of a pretended irrational hatred against the name Christian, seem to be echoes of these complaints in Josephus.

There is every reason to believe in the substantial truth of Josephus's representations as to the wholesome influence of the Jews throughout the empire. The spirit that breathed in the later prophets was an awakening and renovating spirit. The exaltation of the new or moral law above ritual brought light into dark places. It remains, in great part, historically true that 'salvation is of the Jews.' But they had powerful and jealous rivals for the didactic empire of mankind in the Greeks. The latter seized upon the Old Testament and appropriated its contents in their translation and exegesis, so as to favour their theological views. From Alexandria there dates, about the time of the translation of the Septuagint, a literary

[1] *Contr. Apion*, 2. 11, 40. [2] *Ant.* 18. 6. 8.

warfare of the Greek against the Jew, which called forth the treatise of Josephus against Apion. We observe the like spirit in Justin. Under the new name *Christiani*, it was mainly Greeks who sheltered themselves and carried on their polemic against ancient Judaism. But the true sources of the new Ideas and the religious revolution are largely to be found in that prophetic evangelical literature which furnishes the indispensable materials for Justin's constructions, and in the pure moral teaching, combined with enthusiastic hopes of the 'prophets and apostles' among the saints and elect of the Diaspora.

CHAPTER V.

THE SEAL OF THE NEW COMMUNITY.

WE have seen that our documents show a repudiation of Circumcision as the Sign of Jews and other peoples, marking them out no longer for Divine favour, but for Divine displeasure. But it stands to reason that the ancient and visible $\sigma\phi\rho\alpha\gamma\acute{\iota}\varsigma$ of the former people of God could not thus be abolished, without the substitution of some new seal or sign in its place. Circumcision and the Fasts might be converted from objective rites into subjective states; for the seventh day the eighth might be substituted, with the association of new feelings. But still according to the whole habit of religious thought and of ecclesiastical necessity, there must be some visible pledge of the change, some outward sign of the new inward grace.

Some of our documents speak emphatically of the Seal, and of the sacred necessity for salvation that it should be preserved intact.

A remarkable attempt is made in 'Barnabas,' by the aid of rabbinical ingenuity, to pervert Circumcision itself as first practised by Abraham into a forecast of Jesus and His Cross. He circumcised 318 men. The Greek numeral $\iota\acute{\eta}=18$; and since $\iota\eta=\mathring{\iota}\eta\sigma o\hat{\upsilon}\varsigma$ (Jesus); it follows—things that are equal to the same being equal to one another,—that 18 = Jesus.

So 300=τ', and τ is visibly the Cross.[1] And the writer offers this as a 'rich' instruction to his readers. Abraham practised the rite 'in spirit,' this valuable *Gnosis* having been vouchsafed to him. Tertullian repeats against Marcion, 'The very Greek letter *Tau*, our *T*, is the form of the Cross which he portended should be on our foreheads.' He is followed by Clement of Alexandria and others. The Valentinians, according to Irenæus, saw in the letters $i\eta$ the 'eighteen Aeons.' Where so profound a supernatural sense is shown in reference to trivial things, the reader who enjoys only the guidance of common sense may well despair of making out the real history of Jesus and His Cross. Was Jesus then a Greek, and did the patriarch foresee His Greek name?

We may infer from this writer that the true Seal of the community he represents is the sign of the Cross. And the Cross is further connected with water. The beautiful poem, Ps. I., which sings of the tree planted by the water, points to 'water and the Cross.' The real meaning of the Psalmist is, 'Blessed are they who have hoped on the Cross and gone down into the water.' The time of fruit is the future resurrection, and the unfading leaves the words which shall go out of the mouth of the community. Similarly, the beautiful trees by the river in Ezekiel signify those who have gone down into the water full of sins and filth, have come up bearing fruits in their heart, having the fear and the hope on Jesus in their spirit. There is no allusion to baptism in a Trine name.

With these representations let us compare the allegories of 'Hermas.' In the Building of the

[1] *Barn.* 9. 8.

Tower, stones are placed which 'went up from the pit.' Why? 'It was necessary for them to go up out of the water that they might be made alive; for unless they laid aside the deadness of their life, they could not any other way enter the Kingdom of God. Those too who have fallen asleep have received the Seal of the Son of God. Before a man hears the name of God, he is dead; but when he receives the Seal, he puts off the mortality and receives the life. The Seal then is the Water; into the Water they go down dead, and come up living. To them, then, was preached this Seal, and they used it that they might enter the Kingdom of God.'[1]

Further, the 'forty apostles and teachers,' themselves sealed, passed into the other world, preached the name of the Son of God to the departed, and gave them the Seal of the preaching.[2] The commentators are ignorant as to whence 'Hermas' derived this mysterious legend. We should remember, however, that he lived in a time imbued with the belief in Descents to the Dead, Citations of the Departed, and in sacramental Mysteries, like those of Eleusis, the object of which was the purification of the soul and its deliverance from the burden of the flesh.[3] The baptism of fire is there the sacramental means. The general analogy however is clear between pagan institutes and these new mysteries, as they must be regarded by educated men like Celsus.[4] The yearn-

[1] *Sim.* 9. 16.
[2] See Lucian's allusions to the *nertero-dromoi* and *necrangeloi* in *Peregrinus*.
[3] On σφραγίς and φωτισμός, both borrowed from Greek mysteries, cf. the *signa et monumenta* in Apuleius, *De Magia* 55, and his description of similar Mysteries, with baptisms, illuminations in *Metamorph.* 11.
[4] Cf. Keim, *Celsus Wahres Wort.* p. 27.

ing for the assurance of future weal, and the corresponding need of a symbolic expression and guarantee of it, is common to both systems. We may in passing note that the mission of a plurality of apostles and prophets to the departed prepares the way for the conception of the mission of the individual Christ, according to the analogy in the formation of the legend, elsewhere traceable. In vain we seek to plant our feet on the ground of fact.[1]

Neither in the above passage nor in the rest of the book is there any mystic Cross connected with the Seal. Nor is that Seal termed Baptism, but simply Water. 'On waters the Tower was built, because your life was saved and shall be saved through water.'[2]

Some have received the Seal, but have not kept it intact, but have dissipated it; it may, however, be restored on penitence.[3] In some other passages the Seal in connection with the white raiment and the bearers of the willow branches given by the Angel has a triumphal meaning.[4]

So far it is clear that the Seal is connected with the grace of Regeneration by water; but the absence of any reference to any sacred names invoked shows how far we are here from Catholic Christianity.

Let us turn to a third source. After alluding to the favourite image of the Race and the Crown, the writer of the 'Second Epistle of Clement' asks, What shall he suffer who has broken the rules of the game? 'Of those who have *not kept the seal*, he says, "Their worm shall not die, &c.,"'[5] the answer runs. Again, citing apparently an apocryphal gospel: 'The Lord says in the Gospel, *If ye have not kept the small, who will give you the great?*' &c.

---

[1] See Gebhardt and Harnack, *ad l.*
[2] *Vis.* 3. 3. 5.
[3] *Sim.* 8. 6. 3.
[4] *Ib.* 8. 1 ff.
[5] 2 *Clem.* 7. 6.

He means this: 'Keep the flesh chaste and the seal unspotted, that we may receive eternal life.' In this epistle Baptism is more clearly indicated. 'We, unless we keep the baptism pure and unpolluted, with what confidence shall we enter the Kingdom of God, or who shall be our advocate, unless we be found having works holy and just?' But this is the only place in the epistle where βάπτισμα occurs.

It seems, then, that there was a time when there were communities among whom the Seal and the keeping of the Seal were well known and understood designations of the new life from the dead, apart from any mention of a sacred name or names. We can hardly do other than suppose that Circumcision, which so closely corresponds to the idea of a Seal, lies here in the background.[1] If again the belief underlying Circumcision was that of the Blood-Covenant and the mingling of the soul with the covenantal God—if the like belief underlies the baptism of proselytes, we may perceive that the essential thing in the Sealing is the recognition of a new nature, imparted in the sacramental act of descent into and ascent from the living water. But no distinct theological confession is attached to it; nor can we define the theology or Christology of this writer, so vague are his expressions. If his teaching is Christian it is in that general sense in which Christianity is a *tertium genus* to Judaism and Hellenism. The immediate expectation of the Kingdom of God seems to dominate this writer's mind, and he has no grasp of principles.

It is then to pass a great gulf when we come to the directions to baptize into the name of the Father and

[1] Cf. Lippert, *Christenthum u. Volksgebrauch*, 1882, p. 24 ff.

of the Son and of the Holy Ghost. And here our earliest dated testimony is that of Justin. We have already quoted his words. He does not dwell upon the contrast between death and life, but speaks of a regeneration by washing in water, in the name of the Father of all and Lord God and of our Saviour Jesus Christ and a Holy Spirit. The *Didaché* is more concise: 'Baptize ye *into* the name of the Father and of the Son and of *the* Holy Spirit in living water.' The passage is undated; and we may remark that there is no evidence from the literature of the second century of the dogma of the Personality of the Spirit.

Justin speaks not of any mystic $\sigma\phi\rho\alpha\gamma\iota s$, or Seal. What he affirms is that it is necessary men should not remain children of necessity nor of ignorance, that they should become children of election ($\pi\rho o\alpha\iota\rho\epsilon\sigma\epsilon\omega s$) and of knowledge ($\epsilon\pi\iota\sigma\tau\eta\mu\eta s$), and that they should obtain remission of former sins in the Water. Accordingly, over him who chooses to be born again and has repented of his sins there is named the name of the Father of all and Lord God. This very name alone he invokes, who leads him to be washed to the laver; for a name to (or for) the unutterable God no one can say; if any one should dare to declare there is one, he is mad with the incurable madness.[1] Now this Laver is called Illumination (*Photismos*), because those who learn these things are illuminated in their understanding. 'And on name of Jesus Christ the crucified under Pontius Pilate, and on name of Holy Spirit which through the prophets preached beforehand the whole matter relating to Jesus, he that is illuminated is washed.' We have rendered literally for the English reader; the scholar will examine and draw

[1] *Apol.* i. 61. Here Gnostic influence is traceable.

his own conclusions from the phraseology of the Greek original. To both the one and the other this passage affords matter of extreme astonishment. Why does Justin avoid the words *baptize* and *baptism*? If he had a mandate from the 'apostles' and from the Founder, 'Go and disciple all nations, baptizing them, &c.,' why did he not cite it? He appears in fact to ignore here the religious meaning of the term. Was this a man who knew anything of our New Testament? We cannot but complain of the mischievous sophistry which results from the inattention of scholars to facts like these. All that can be inferred from the passage is that this rite of Washing was of a mystical character, offered to the penitent, but connected with allusions to history and to prophecy quite unintelligible except to the initiated.

Let us turn to the *Trypho*. Here we read of the 'Laver of Penitence' and of the *gnosis* of God, instituted for the transgression of the peoples of God, as Esaias cries out, 'Through it we believed, and do make known that this is that very Baptisma, which alone can purify those who repented it, that is the Water of Life.' Here he means moral purification, as he does when he elsewhere defines it as a spiritual circumcision, or when he says that baptism with a holy spirit does away with the need of 'that baptism'—the useless 'baptism of cisterns,' not to be compared to 'this baptism of life.' But he too has his allegories on waters and trees, rods, staves, and building wood. 'Us, baptized with heaviest sins which we did, through the crucifixion on the tree and through water hallowing, our Christ ransomed, and a house of prayer and worship made.' The wretched style of the language is good enough for the sheer ineptitude of the thinking.

It appears probable that Justin had a positive dislike for the word baptism from its Jewish associations, so that he only uses it in a disparaging sense. Among the Jewish sects he mentions Baptistæ. It seems clear that Justin would spiritualise the external rite, even as he spiritualises circumcision. The Bath is but symbolic of the internal illumination and change; and there is no allusion to the burial of the head in the water, such as we find in Chrysostom, nor to the sign of the burial and resurrection of Christ.[1]

His emphasis lies on the notion of Illumination in connection with the Bath.[2] He opposes (in *Trypho*) Christ and His proselytes, that is the Gentiles, to the Law and its proselytes. If the Law had been able to illuminate the nations and its own adherents, what need of a New Covenant? But Christ has illuminated us His proselytes. The prophecy in Isa. 42. 6 ff. clearly refers to Christ and the illuminated Gentiles, in contrast to the Jews, who are so manifestly both blind and deaf. 'Those who are under illumination,' is a technical phrase for disciples, under instruction; 'those who have been illuminated' are those who have passed through the rite which completes the instruction. They are then led to the Brethren in assembly, prayers are offered, the Kiss is then exchanged, the bread and the Cup of wine and water are partaken of, and the Eucharistia follows.[3]

We are here studying the Protoplasm of a New Religion; that is to say, the old imaginative material which is gradually being shaped into new forms, and assuming new names. As with Circumcision, the mystical Seal, the living waters and the trees, so with the sign of the Cross, the Bath, the Illumination, the

[1] *In Joann.* iii. 5. [2] *Apol.* i. 65. [3] Ibid.

Kiss, the Bread, and the Cup; all are traceable, as we believe, to ideas of the soul and its intercourse with the supernatural, that are essentially as old and as widely diffused as human nature itself. They were abroad in the time of Justin; we need only read in the pages of Apuleius, of Lucian, of Pausanias, to understand how deep was the thirst for covenantal union with the divine. Especially we may point to the mysteries of the suffering Dionysos, who returned from the dead, and to the worship of Asklépios, who was believed supernaturally to heal, and to raise from the dead. It is doubtless because Justin is so well aware of these analogies, and so sensitive as to the polemic use that could be made of them, that he speaks of the Laver in so peculiar a manner. He looked upon the sprinklings, the libations, and the incense applied in heathen rites, upon the baths of purification which prepared the worshippers for entrance to the temples. And having himself traced the Laver of illumination to the inspiration of a prophet (Isa. 61.), he could only account for the similar heathen practices by assuming that 'the dæmons,' had heard of the prophet's preaching, and had accordingly impelled their worshippers to mimic the true Laver![1] In short, Justin, as usual, begs the question in favour of the *Christian* laver, as opposed both to the Laver of the Jewish proselytisers (their Cistern, as he chooses to call it) and to the Laver of the pagans, such as we find it described, with the accompaniments of fasting, solemn mandates, and visions, the robes and the crown, in the initiation of Apuleius.[2] We may account for the confusion of ideas in respect of the Laver from the fact that the rite was universal in the religions of the

[1] *Apol.* i. 62; cf. Tertull. *De Bapt.* 5.   [2] *Met.* lib. xi.

time, and that it was necessary for the apologist of
the Christiani to find some explanation of the efficacy
of the waters which should be distinct from that of
the proselytisers to the Law on the one hand and that
of the heathen on the other. The allusion to the ineffable Name might satisfy both converts of Jewish
and of heathen education ; while the legend of Jesus
Christ crucified under Pontius Pilate and the idea of
the prophetic spirit as the source of all true knowledge
must win their way through the laver and the pre-
paratory 'illumination.' But Justin is silent as to
that supernatural change effected in the waters, of
which Tertullian speaks distinctly. 'When God is
invoked, immediately there comes down from heaven
the Spirit ; He is over the waters, hallowing them from
Himself.'[1] Justin vaguely says that 'for the sake of
men' Christ was baptized and the Dove descended
upon Him, and the fire was kindled in the Jordan.
He needed neither baptism nor the Dove, any more
than He needed to be born or to be baptized.[2]

THE KISS—THE BREAD AND THE CUP—THE EUCHARIST.

Justin tells us, that after prayers in the assembly
on behalf of the newly illuminated and themselves,
they greet one another with a Kiss. As for the mode
of salutation itself, there is nothing more strange in it
as an Oriental custom than the mutual grasp of the

---

[1] *De Bapt.* c. 4.

[2] More definite and instructive are the particulars of Gnostic rites, the ἐπισφράγισμα with oil connected with the sign and mystery of the Cross, as 'Tree of Life,' and the σφραγίς of the Laver, in the 'Acts of Thomas.' To the initiate Christ appears as a torch-bearer. Lipsius, *Die Apokr. Apostelgesch.*, 1883, i. 330 ff.

hands among ourselves in token of friendship. But if we go back to the old underlying idea of the Kiss, it is that of a spiritual covenant or bond, between those whose breath is thus mingled. Similar is the underlying idea of the afflatus by which gifts are communicated, of the Imposition of Hands and of anointing, of the common bread and cup. The rite then of the Kiss may be regarded in some sort as the tautological repetition of the rite of the laver: a new life and the introduction into a new community consequent upon it is signified.[1] The notion of the Seal might also fit the rite of the Kiss. Our view becomes clearer, if we learn to look upon the cumulation of these initiatory rites as the iteration of one leading thought. It seems as if, when once Circumcision was relinquished or converted into a figure of morality, the old objectifying needs of the imagination reached after and found satisfaction in a plurality of symbols, extant in the cults of the time, all expressive of union with the Divine nature.

We know of no older Catholic account of the Eucharistia than that in Justin. He says of the Bread and the Cup of wine and water, 'This food is called among us Eucharistia. No other is allowed to partake of it except he who believes that our teachings are true, and who has bathed in the Bath for the remission of sins and unto regeneration, and is so living as Christ handed down. For not as common bread nor common drink do we receive these. But even as through the logos of God, Jesus Christ our Saviour made flesh had both flesh and blood for our salvation, so the food which has been made *Eucharist* through logos of prayer from Him, out of which our

---

[1] Cf. Lippert, *Christenthum*, p. 128.

blood and flesh by a change are nourished, we have been taught was the flesh and blood of that Jesus made flesh. For the apostles in their *Memorabilia* thus handed down the mandate given them by Jesus. He took a loaf and gave thanks and said, "This is for My memorial, this is My body." The cup in like manner He took, gave thanks and said, "This is My blood," and distributed to them alone.' We leave the obscurities of the passage.[1] They are such as arise from the nature of the case; nor has anything clear resulted from the discussions of Romanists and Protestants, or of Protestants among themselves, in reference to the supposed words of the Founder—except this, that a hopeless confusion of ideas exists upon the subject; and that any simple clue to the meaning of the Eucharist has long been lost.[2] The same remark holds good of the connected subject of the Atonement.

But the historian of Christian origins may by no means neglect the hint repeatedly given by Justin himself as to the origin of the rite of the Loaf and the Cup. With regard to 'the apostles' and their *Memorabilia*, this means nothing more than that the words cited formed part of that floating mass of tradition and of doctrine brought forward at the worship of the First Day of the week, and which was assigned, for want of any ascertained authorship, to the propagandists of the new order of things. And here we may borrow a helpful analogy from our own time. In studying rites or traditions of barbarous tribes which present resemblances so striking and so far-spread to Jewish and Christian institutions—for example, the tradition

---

[1] *Apol.* i. 66.
[2] That the Eucharist was no more than a *spiritual* Sacrifice, like Prayer, cf. Harnack, *Lehrb.* 152, n. 1.

of a Deluge, or the rite of Circumcision, or of the Blood Covenant[1] in general: the first question to be asked by the critic is, Can this rite or tradition be traced to 'the missionaries'? And if in numberless cases this cannot be done; if these ideas and practices are found to be indigenous in the native mind, which often finds in them an argument against rather than in favour of another religion which presents similar features; then we have here a tolerably exact analogy to the state of religious affairs in Justin's time. The rite of the Loaf and the Cup was not an innovation: it was used in the rites of Mithras,[2]—a circumstance which would probably have never been connected with the history of the Christian religion, but for the mention of Justin, and of Tertullian. The circumstance is so embarrassing to Justin's apologetic, that he has no resource but to fall back upon his usual explanation, that dæmons here mimicked the Christian rite. He could not assert a human imitation, since the religion of Mithras was earlier in existence. It is the Apologist himself, then, who in his ignorance of a 'Luke' or a 'Paul,' and of any source but certain anonymous note-books, points the historical inquirer to the mysteries of Mithras, for the origin of the rite in question. It is the controversialist with the Jews who informs them that the tradition of Mithras was that he was born from a rock, and that the place where those who believe in him are initiated was called a cave. Is it not clear, he asks, that this

---

[1] Cf. the recent work of Dr. Trumbull on this subject and that of Gloatz, *Die Spek. Theologie*, &c., which contains a mass of examples from 'savage' tribes.

[2] *Apol.* i. 66. The Cup was of Water. So probably among the Gnostics; see the account of the initiation of Mygdonia in the *Acts of Thomas*, Lipsius, *u. s.* 339.

is an imitation of Daniel's[1] and of Isaiah's[2] words about the stone cut from the mountain, and the just man who dwells among the rocks? No answer of a priest of Mithras[3] is extant to this argument, if such irrationality deserves the name. There must have been men, even in that mystical and muddle-headed time, who must have known that this talk of rocks and caves, of Mithras and Christ, was sheer hallucination, and had no more to do with the question in hand than the proverbial 'talk of oaks and rocks' with the theme of the poet of the Greek Theogony. To Justin, however, it was clear that the words of the prophet concerning the good man, 'Bread shall be given him and his water sure,' were spoken 'of the loaf which our Christ handed down to us to do for a remembrance of His having assumed a body because of those believing on Him, for whom He also became passible; and of the cup which he handed down for us to do in the Eucharist for a remembrance of His blood.'[4]

At the time of Justin it is probable that the religion of Mithras was still a formidable rival with that of 'our Christ' for the spiritual empire of the world. It seems possible, humanly speaking, that Mithras might, but for historical circumstances we are seeking to understand, have filled the aching void in the bosom of Paganism.[5] We can pretend to understand little of the genius and spirit of this religion. Yet the impressive though ænigmatic group of 'Mithras slaying the Bull,' hinting some mystic persuasion concern-

---

[1] 2. 34.   [2] 33. 13 ff.
[3] The origin of the legend about Mithras' birth appears to have been the fact that his worship was held in sacred caves, Porphyr. *De Antr. Nymph.* 6.
[4] *Tryph.* 70.
[5] Cf. Aug. *In Joh.* i. ; *Dis.* 7.

ing death and immortality, seems to have had great power over the imagination of the time.[1] And Justin himself bears witness to moral teachings of his worshippers, so noble and elevated that he concludes they were all imitated from Isaiah. He seems haunted by Mithras.

In the entire absence of historical information (for we need hardly remind our readers that the date and genuineness of the related passages in 'Luke' and 'Paul' are still *sub judice*) the historical inquirer can only infer that the mysterious use of the bread and the cup in the initiation of Christian proselytes was probably imported from the religion of Mithras. It appears that the mysteries of Mithras were analogous to those of Eleusis in many respects: there were purifications and probations for the initiate, who were confirmed by receiving a mark in the forehead, by partaking of bread and of the cup, with which was associated a symbol of the resurrection.[2] The diffusion of the belief in the resurrection must have been in great part due to the Mithriac cult which Plutarch traces from Cilicia into the Roman empire at the time of Pompey's war with the pirates.[3]

On the other hand, Justin finds that the paschal victim was Christ; the blood upon the door-posts foretold His saving blood, of which also the red rope given by the spies to Rahab was the symbol.[4]

But to return. We have seen that the Christiani in their initiation of proselytes made use of forms

---

[1] See a recent article by Mons. J. Réville on Mithras in *Revue de l'Histoire des Religions*, 1885. C. W. King, *The Gnostics*, p. 7 ff.
[2] Tertull. *Præscr. adv. Hær.* c. 40; Windischmann, p. 70 ff.
[3] Cf. Havet, *Le Christianisme et ses Origines*, 3. 490, 4. 76, 116, 113; Hartung, *Rel. u. Myth. der Griech.* 4. 143 ff.; Hausrath, *Zeitgesch.*
[4] *Tryph.* 111.

already long in existence, and which may be shown to be various symbolic expressions of one leading idea—that of introduction into a Covenant with a spiritual being. Circumcision was itself the rudiment of a still older form of the Blood Covenant, in which the mixing of blood and of souls was believed to take place. The offering of the blood in this rite denoted the adherence of the circumcised to a covenant. As Circumcision was spiritualised and explained away, Baptism replaces it and expresses the same thing: a spiritual change, the entrance of a new soul. Whether the baptism is watery or fiery the purport is the same, mortality is exchanged for immortality. It is the Bath of Regeneration—may be defined as a Burial and a Resurrection. In the sacred bath, the candidate receives the descending spirit, or partakes of it. The Kiss betokens the fact of this common participation and the fellowship founded on it. Still more intimately does the sacred Meal express the sacramental union of the worshippers with the divine Spirit, or the 'divine human interunion.'[1] Especially the symbolic cup of blood expresses in another way the radical idea of the Blood Covenant, union of blood, union of souls (according to the old physiology and psychology) through union of blood. This is the most important part of the transaction.[2]

But now with the idea of the Covenant that of the Oath involving solemn imprecation is connected. And if we trace the analogies to the Broken Loaf in ancient religions—especially the dismembered victim which

---

[1] Trumbull, *Blood Covenant.*
[2] See Lippert, *Seelencult.* 61 ff.; *Die Relig.* 48 ff., 292; *Christenthum*, p. 83; H. Clay Trumbull, *The Blood Covenant*, New York, 1885.

sanctioned the Greek *synomosia,* down to the broken platter used in the administration of the oath among the Chinese at the present day—it will be seen what was the real original significance of the *klasma* in the Eucharist. It was doubtless the sign of that oath by which Christians bound themselves according to the so-called letter of Pliny to Trajan. For the blessing of the common bond implies the curse upon the unfaithful who would sever it. Here the passage referring to the first century before Christ, from Sallust, may be adduced in illustration; Catiline, desiring to attach to himself by an oath the accomplices of his crime, caused human blood mixed with wine to circulate in the cups. A solemn imprecation was made, such as takes place in certain religious acts. Then all partook of it.[1] The simple and radical idea is best understood from the rite by which blood-brotherhood is cemented among the tribes of Africa and elsewhere.[2]

An actual mixing of the blood of the parties takes place. The symbolism of the bread and the cup is from this point of view so far clear. But when these symbols were explained as memorial of a historical victim for the sins of mankind, another order of ideas was introduced; and the simpler notions of brotherhood, of communion in a new and immortal life, became confused with those of sacrifice and atonement and its commemoration. To partake of food in the spiritual presence of Christ is one thing, to partake of Christ Himself in the presence of the Father is another; and we see not that theology has ever been able to clear up a confusion which originated with itself. The

---

[1] Catil. 24, cf. *assiratum* for such mixture, Paulus, *Ex Festo,* 16. 12. 29.
[2] See many examples in Gloatz, *Die Spek. Theologie,* &c.

transition from the idea of the sacred Meal to that of the sacrifice in the proper sense is not, however, to be found in Justin.

He is strongly polemical against sacrifices except in the allegorical or spiritual sense,—in the *Dialogue*. He maintains that God of old needed no sacrifices, and that if He ordained them, it was in accommodation to the people and because of their sins. As God receives sacrifices from none except through His priests, the Christians are a priestly race of God; and perfect sacrifices consist in prayers and thanksgivings. These are offered by Christians in the whole world. He refers, in his usual disjointed style, to 'sacrifices through this name (of God) which Jesus the Christ handed down, that is, at the Eucharist of the loaf and the cup.' And again, 'the memorial of their food dry and moist,' when remembrance is made of the passion of Christ, is connected with these only true sacrifices. If he has no clear conception of the meaning of the Eucharist, at all events he is certain that it is not a sacrifice, except in the general sense in which all devout acts are a sacrifice.

The 'pure sacrifice' spoken of in Malachi, an universal sacrifice, is a favourite passage for quotation; but it is construed in the same general sense of worship, not of the unbloody repetition of an atoning sacrifice, as we find it in Cyprian and others. The direction in the *Didaché* is: 'On the *Kyriac* (day) of the Lord, when ye are gathered together, break bread and give thanks, having first confessed your transgressions that your sacrifices may be pure. Let no one who has a dispute with his fellow join you until they be reconciled, that your sacrifice be not profaned. For this is that spoken by the Lord: In every place and time offer Me a pure sacrifice; for I am a great King, saith the Lord, and My name is wondrous among the Gentiles.'

In another part of the same tract an eucharistic form is given, where 'knowledge, faith, and immortality,' 'spiritual food and drink and eternal life,' are named as subjects for thanksgiving after the participation of the bread and the cup. The cup, named first, reminds, as we have seen, of the ' holy vine of David ;' and the broken loaf apparently both of 'life and knowledge,' and of the scattered Ecclesia, to be gathered from the ends of the earth. The entire absence of any reference to the body and blood of Jesus, or of Jesus at all, except in a way that suggests His name has been grafted upon an originally Jewish form, here arrests attention.

The only other passages which teach us anything on this subject are those in the 'Ignatian' epistles. The Ephesians are exhorted frequently to come together for *eucharistia* of God and for glory. Similar exhortations to meeting occur elsewhere ; and we see that the chief object of meeting is said to be thanksgiving and praise. He who absents himself, the writer says, in language meant figuratively, is deprived of the bread of God. In such meetings they 'break one loaf, which is a drug of immortality, an antidote of death, for life in Jesus Christ for ever.'[1] The one sacred meal expresses the union of Christians of a single locality :[2] ' Study to use one Eucharistia ; for one is the flesh of our Lord Jesus Christ, and one cup for oneness of His blood ; one altar, one bishop, with the presbytery and deacons.'

The Smyrnæans are told that some heterodox ones

---

[1] 20. 2 ; cf. *Smyrn.* 7. 1. Repeated by Iren. 4. 18. 5 ; 5. 2. 2.
[2] *Philad.* 4. ; *Smyrn.* 8.

abstain from Eucharistia and Proseuché, because they do not confess that the Eucharistia is the flesh of our Saviour Jesus Christ which suffered for our sins, which in His goodness the Father raised up. It would profit them 'to love' (probably to keep the Agapé), that they too may rise again.[1]

Here is the disclosure of an important change of opinion. Eucharistia, in the general sense, is but the service of Thanksgiving, as Proseuché is prayer. From worship these heterodox did not hold aloof;[2] but they dissented from a dogma we now for the first time find distinctly formulated: '*The Eucharist is the flesh of Jesus Christ.*' The *Didaché* knows nothing of this; and Justin, amidst his mystical vagueness, stops short of so precise a statement. It is a vast advance from the indefinite poetical conception of a spiritual meat and drink symbolised by the bread and the cup of the regular worship, to the definite form of such celestial meat, the 'flesh of Jesus Christ.' And yet such an advance is quite in accord with what we know of the laws of the religious imagination. It begins its quest of new spiritual truth with vague yearnings and conceptions correspondingly vague, of their object; and the object becomes more and more definable under the pressure of the cravings of the congregation, as well as the instincts of its teachers. Among Christian communities of the present day who have adopted Zwinglian views of the Eucharist, which empty the elements of every 'real presence,' the difficulty is often felt to reconcile the mere observance of the rite with the simply memorial view of it. What need of a visible commemoration of that which cannot be forgotten in song, sermon, or prayer? And we see,

---

[1] Zahn. *ad l.*   [2] Cf. Iren. 4. 18. 4.

occasionally a reaction set in towards a 'higher' theory of the sacrament among those who profess the merely commemorative belief.

We are not about to reopen the unending controversies as to the relative priority of the documents under examination. But we may simply point out that there is a natural and logical transition from the idea of food to that of spiritual food, which implies knowledge and faith; and hence again to immortality. It should be remembered how deep in the popular heart, as popular tales and legends still testify, lies the yearning after the healing and reviving drug, the 'water of life' or of 'immortality,' which is efficacious even at the point of death. Such popular lore is a common possession of Greeks and of Jews. The Vine was in its way among the latter a symbol of immortality. And when they with like-minded Hellenes, broke away from the positive institutions, then their life must have been greatly nourished by poetical allegories, as the 'Hermas' bears witness. It is, as we have seen, probably an innovation of thought and a literary interpolation when the name 'Jesus' is inserted in the *Eucharistia* of the *Didaché*, as the mediator of the Vine and of spiritual knowledge. But a much more violent innovation is it when the central idea is narrowed down to 'the flesh of Jesus Christ.'

Poetical conception occupies the borderland between the natural and the supernatural; and insensibly the mind passes over either into dry and unimaginative materialism, or into equally barren superstition. In the Ignatian epistle to the Romans we read, 'I delight not in corruptible food, nor in pleasures of this life. Bread of God I would have, that is, flesh of Jesus Christ, of the seed of David, and drink I would have,

His blood, that is incorruptible love.' This, as the context shows, is allegorical of celestial blessedness of the spiritual fruition of Christ. Yet how easily might such mystical poetry be converted into rigid belief in connection with the participation of the Eucharist. So long as the mind, from its very law, leans upon the material as expressive of the spiritual, there is always danger that the spiritual itself shall be materialised. English dissenters have written eucharistic hymns which would satisfy, so far as language goes, the believers in the 'Real Presence.' It depends on the habits of the imagination whether the 'real presence' is supposed in the elements, or in the mind of the partaker alone.

The only certain trace, however, of difference of opinion, sharply marked enough to cause a split in the communities, is that in reference to the Eucharist conceived as the flesh of Jesus Christ in the Ignatian epistle, combined with the corresponding passage in Irenæus. According to all the evidence, this difference was caused, at an undated but quite late time, by the growing disposition of church doctors to define more precisely the meaning of a rite which had previously among Jews been one of general thanksgiving for spiritual food and drink.

And now to glance back along the road we have recently travelled, and to draw some negative and positive conclusions. The literature belongs to a class of religionists who have not learned to assume the name Christiani, and who appear in fact to shun any general distinctive appellation, but whom, amidst the vagueness of our knowledge of Jewish and Jewish-Christian sects, we may call Hagioi or Saints, or Elect of God. They congregate in *ecclesiæ* at particular places; and they hold the conception of an Ecclesia in a wider sense, comprising the Dispersed through the world. They have broken with the old observances of Judaism, the Sabbath, the fast-days, the Temple and the sacrifices. Circumcision has been spiritualised and replaced by Baptism, which also, according to some of our sources, is the substitute for the sacrifices. The conception of a New People and a New Law published to all the world has dawned upon them. They find in Baptism a mystic seal of this new life; and in the First Day observance, and in the Eucharist, some, at least, find allusions to the same new life, with intimations of resurrection and immortality. Their thought moves with freedom within the confines of prophetic declarations, which are interpreted in favour of the negative and revolutionary views already indicated. And as the prophetic gift is conceived as continuous and still existing, scope is still further given for the efforts of inspired imagination. Allusions are here and there made to an Evangelion, or Good Tidings preached by 'apostles,' derived from the Lord, and to 'teachings' also of unnamed apostles. Negatively, this Evangelion must be understood as the good tidings of release from ceremonial burdens, and positively, as a body of practical precepts, such as those relating to conduct or to forms of prayer.

But we have not yet been able to trace out a historic Founder or Founders of this new order of things. There is no 'Canon,' no New Testament, no body of writings of any kind on a level of authority with the Old Testament. And the probable conclusion is that the religious *movement* we are endeavouring to follow dates from a time even before our era. So far as the obscure history of the Essenes can be made out, their principles so far coincided with those of the Hagioi, that they had renounced the Temple and its sacrifices, probably from the time of the Syrian war. There is no reason to suppose that their spirit died out with the extinction of the sect. On too partial grounds, doubtless, some scholars have sought to find the origin of Jewish 'Christianity' in the sect of the Essenes.[1] Yet the conjecture was perhaps a cast in the right direction. If the most remarkable external peculiarities of Essenism were not destined to survive, its innovating and reformatory spirit, and its simple and lofty morality, are traceable everywhere, mixed with elements of another kind, in the old Christian literature.

We may draw another general inference from the state of thought and feeling exhibited in that literature, namely, that communities which held so lightly by old positive religious institutions, must all the more tenaciously have insisted upon a pure standard of morality amongst its members.

---

[1] See Lucius on this subject.

CHAPTER VI.

MORAL TEACHING AMONG THE HAGIOI—THE 'TWO WAYS'
—COMMANDMENTS OF THE APOSTLES.

UNDER the name of the '*Didaché* or *Didachai* of the Apostles,' a phrase often repeated as if a technical designation, a golden vein of pious and practical teaching was signified, which has been preserved for us, apparently in its simplest and perhaps oldest form in the MS. published by Bryennios:—

'There are two Ways, one of Life and one of Death; but a great difference between the two Ways.'[1]

The writer of 'Barnabas,' after dealing with the question of the Temple, as already noted, passes to 'another *Gnosis* and *Didaché:* there are two Ways of teaching and authority, that of Light and that of Darkness; but there is a great difference between the two Ways.'

This clear popular image of the broad distinction between Right and Wrong, found in slightly varied forms in the older Scriptures, and in the rabbinical writings, must have been familiar to every Jewish child;[2] and the 'Way' must have been proverbially current as a synonym of righteousness, truth, salvation. The 'apostles and all the prophets,' as well as 'The

---

[1] *Didach.* I. I.   [2] Deut. 30. 19; Jer. 21. 8.

Gospel,' proposed these two ways according to Clement of Alexandria.[1] Nevertheless, the saying is never cited twice exactly in the same form; and the variants show that we have to do with a leading thought, and by no means with a rigid and sacrosanct formula of Law. Thus among the 'Mandates' of 'Hermas': 'Do thou trust in right and trust not in wrong; for right has a straight road, but wrong a crooked. Do thou proceed by the straight road and plain, but the crooked leave. For the crooked road has no worn paths, but blind ways and many stumbling-blocks; rough it is and thorny. Hurtful therefore is it to them that walk in it. But those that go by the straight road walk smoothly and without stumbling; it is neither rough nor thorny. Thou seest then that it is more profitable to go by this road. . . . Whosoever from his whole heart turns to the Lord, shall proceed in it.'[2] Another source expands the dualism by the addition of 'two counsels and two practices, two places and two goals.'[3] Another source defines the Way of Life as natural ($\phi v \sigma \iota \kappa \dot{\eta}$), that of Death as 'brought in afterwards, being not according to the mind of God, but from the plot of the alien one.'[4]

There is no proof, it may be remarked in passing, that this 'teaching' of the two Ways was assigned to Jesus until the later half of the second century. It is simply an 'apostolic' and 'prophetic' teaching in that vague and impersonal sense we have already learned to recognise.

Justin does not mention it; but the second Apology which has passed under his name refers to the well-

---

[1] *Strom.* 5. 5. [2] *Mand.* 6. 1.
[3] *Testaments of the Twelve Patriarchs*, Migne 2. 1120.
[4] *Constt. App.* 7. 1.

known story of the Choice of Hercules between Virtue and Vice, which was as familiar to Greek youth as the two Ways to Jewish youth.[1] Where the latter thought of angels of light or of Satan, the former thought of the forms of women, impersonations of the moral opposites. As Jews intermingled with Greeks through the world, doubtless it was a frequent and pleasing discovery, the discovery we all make once in a lifetime, that the virtuous and reverent of every nation follow one religion and one moral code, and may reduce their vital creed to a few short and simple forms.

It is a vital creed that is before us. 'The Way of Life is this: first thou shalt love God who made thee. Second, thy neighbour as thyself. And all things whatsoever thou wouldest not should be done to thee, neither do thou to another.'

The 'Apostolical Constitutions'[2] give: 'First there is the Way of Life; and it is that which also the Law appoints ($\delta\iota\alpha\gamma o\rho\epsilon\acute{u}\epsilon\iota$), to love the Lord thy God from all thy heart and from all thy soul, the One and Only, beside whom there is not another, and thy neighbour as thyself. And everything that thou wouldest not should be done to thee, this thou shall not do unto another.'

The 'Epistle of Barnabas' gives: 'The Way of Light is this: if any one desires to go his road to the determined place, let him study his deeds. The Gnosis then given to you that ye may walk in it is this: Thou shalt love Him that made thee, thou shalt fear Him that fashioned thee, thou shall glorify Him that redeemed thee from death.'

[1] Xen. *Mem.* 2. 1; Cic. *Off.* 1. 32. Cf. Lucian, *Somn.* c. 6; Silius It. *Pun.* 15. 18. [2] Of third or fourth century.

'Thou shalt love thy neighbour beyond thy soul (or life).'[1]

The road is above thought of as leading to a destination, the 'place of glory' or the like, as our own poet sings: 'The path of Duty is the Way to Glory.'[2]

The Golden Rule, as it has been called, of conduct towards one's fellows has been ascribed to many masters—to Confucius, to the Buddhists, to the great Rabbi Hillel in a striking anecdote. Isocrates gives utterance to it.[3] It is a principle of the Stoics. The emperor Alexander Severus got this saying from certain men, Jews or Christians, and loved it as so truly divine, that he ordered it to be written up in the Palatium and on public works.[4] We should do injustice to the simple universality of the thought if we ascribed it to any but an anonymous source. It is an oracle of the human heart, an expression of that nature in which self-regard and sympathy are never divorced, and which identifies in imagination the individual with his kind.

We have cited three sources, one of them indisputably late, yet in none of them is the saying of the 'Way' ascribed to any but the anonymous 'apostles.'

But now we have another document which incidentally illustrates the process of the formation of the narrative Christian legend, in which named teachers gradually took the place of the proverbial *ait's* and *aiunt's*, the 'says he' and 'say they' of ordinary quotation. The 'Ecclesiastical Canons of the Holy Apostles' in use among the Christians of Egypt are issued in the names of John, Matthew, Peter, Andrew,

---

[1] *Barn.* 19. 1, 2, 6.
[2] Cf. 1 *Clem.* 5. 4, 7; Polycp. *ad Philipp.* 9; Ignat. *ad Magn.* 5; *Acta Thecl.* 28; Gebhardt and Harnack.
[3] In *Nicocle.* t. i. 93.   [4] According to 'Lampridius.'

Philip, Simon, James, Nathanael, Thomas, Kephas, Bartholomew and Judas, son of James. The list speaks for itself. Twelve names are made out; but only by a series of gross blunders, if the New Testament is to be followed. Peter and Kephas are made two persons, another pair is formed out of Nathanael, also (according to the fourth gospel) called Bartholomew, Matthias and Paul are ignored, and one James only is known. However, the main point was to secure the 'historical' number; 'facts' must give way to this formative necessity. And as there was a time when the organised communities, looking back to the 'Apostles' as the fountain-head of authority, were no longer satisfied with the constant φησί, 'says he,' of these anonymous teachers, the *numina* became *nomina*, the *nomina persons* of flesh and blood. And thus the pious teaching which had hitherto hovered in the abstract, was distributed in speeches among the Twelve; and each contributes his parcel, to borrow an expression of Dr. John Lightfoot. So John spoke first and said: 'There are two Ways, one of life and one of death, but a great difference between the two Ways. The Way of Life is this: First, thou shalt love God who made thee from thy whole heart, and shalt glorify Him that redeemed thee from death, which is the first commandment. Second, thou shalt love thy neighbour as thyself, which is the second commandment. Upon which things the whole Law hangs and the prophets.' Matthew said: 'All things whatsoever thou wouldest not should befall thee, neither do thou to another.' Then Peter is called upon to utter the *didachê* of these *logoi*,—in other words, to expand in details the moral prohibitions, which he does.

For a later time even than that from which the

originals of these documents date, it must have been reserved to substitute the One Teacher for the artificial Twelve, as they had been substituted for the indistinct Seventy, or a ghostly and undefined plurality of 'Apostles.'

Let us glance at the prohibitions which form the contents of the second *Entolé*, *i.e.*, Commandment or Mandate. Practically they are an expansion of the Law of the Second Table. But it is worth notice that the term 'Law' is not relished by 'Barnabas,' nor apparently by any of our authorities unless with the qualification 'New Law.' The term *Entolé* seems to have prevailed, because it detached the subject from the odious associations of orthodox Judaism, and suffered these universal moral præscripts to appear as a new *Didaché* of the 'apostolic' founders. From this point of view also the idea of the universal proclamation above touched upon is illustrated. It is but another way of saying that these commandments are echoed from the universal conscience of mankind. There is nothing against the supposition, there is everything in its favour, that during the decay of the Jewish state and the relaxation of the rigidity of Jewish rites, the Dispersed, brought into close contact with the nations, discovered in the universal prevalence of the knowledge of moral law evidence of a divine revelation, or in their mode of phantasy, of the preaching of an angel from heaven.

THE 'COMMANDMENTS OF THE APOSTLES,' AND PROPHETS.

It is impossible for a new body of religionists to invent a new morality, whatever may be done by change of rites, by alteration of feast-days, to distinguish themselves from others. Yet it is interesting to observe how the Hagioi, by ascribing the precepts of universal morality to their Apostles, as well as baptism and the new fast-days, contrived to represent their innovation as also a moral one, and the 'Hypocrites' in an unamiable light. We will ask the reader to consider whether the attacks upon the Jews of the Circumcision and of the Law in Tacitus and in Juvenal, and above all in our canonical Gospels, on the ground of their hard-heartedness and misanthropy, do not proceed from the same general cause as the insolent bullying of Justin of Neapolis. Is not one spectacle clear to the historian's view through all the mists of passion,—a people sullenly retiring with dogged loyalty upon themselves and the traditions of their fathers, and whose 'hatred of the human race' the ill-will of their accusers has either imagined or caused? But to return. The additions to the Second Table of the Decalogue here concern us. The love of the neighbour requires abstinence not only from ordinary crimes and vices, but from odious forms of evil well known to have been prevalent in the world which Juvenal scourged and which Seneca, amidst all his frailty, would have allured by persuasive 'verba et voces' to better things. Thus the 'Doctrine of the Apostles' enjoins:

'Thou shalt not corrupt boys.'[1]

The Law made the offence punishable with death; nor could the warning from Sodom be forgotten. Measuring morality amongst any people not by the mere prevalence of particular vices, but by the clearness of conscience which condemns, or the darkness which permits, there can be no question of the superiority here of Jews over Greeks and Romans. So again of

[1] *Did.* 2. 3; Cf. *Barn.* 19. 4; *Constt. App.* 7. 2.

the command: 'Thou shalt not fornicate.' The heathen would recognise no *flagitium* here.[1]

'Thou shalt not play the Mage.' Here too the Law condemned. The extraordinary picture of Simon the Mage in old Christian literature, in which the features are generally borrowed from a world of supernatural intuition, is in effect that of a dæmon who possesses the mind of his worshippers, or of a man in intercourse with dæmons. The whole edifice of heathen religion which rested on the belief in departed spirits and communion with them is here assailed.[2]

'Thou shalt not practise witchcraft' ($\varphi\alpha\rho\mu\alpha\kappa\epsilon\dot{\upsilon}\omega$).

The use of potions, philtres, poisons is prohibited; spells and enchantments. Such figures as that of Medeia, the great sorceress of Corinth, were typical of long-standing belief among the people in their fatal efficacy.

'Thou shalt not procure abortion nor slay the new-born child.'[3]

And here again it is the humane spirit of Jews who believed in Him who 'loved the things He had made and abhorred nothing that He had made,' in 'the Lord, the lover of souls,' which speaks. The 'old inhabitants of His holy land He had destroyed, because they wrought odious works of witchcrafts and wicked sacrifices; the merciless murderers of children, the devourers of man's flesh, the feasts of blood, with the priests out of the midst of their idolatrous crew, the parents that killed with their own hands souls destitute of help.'[4] Here the writer probably mingles views of

---

[1] *Did.* 2. 2; *Barn.* 19. 4; *Constt. App.* 7. 2, 10; *Jud. Petr.* 97. 6.
[2] Cf. the description in Lucian, *Asin.* 11.
[3] *Did.* 2. 2; *Barn.* 19. 5; *Constt. App.* 7. 3; *Jud. Pet.* 97. 7. Cf. Tertull. *Apol.* 9; Clem. *Al. Paed.* 3. 3; Athenag. *Suppl.* 35; Diog. 5. 6. [4] *Wisd.* 12.

the past with the present state of an 'empire stained with the blood of infants.'[1]

Emphatic also are the prohibitions of sins of the tongue, as in all Jewish teaching speech is sacred, involving strict accountability. 'Thou shalt not be froward with the tongue.'[2] 'Thou shalt not forswear thyself, thou shalt not bear false witness, thou shalt not speak evil.'[3] 'The word of God shall not go forth from thee in any impurity.'[4]

The sins of the tongue are traced to the temper.

'Thou shalt not remember ill (bear malice).'[5] 'Thou shalt not be double-minded nor double-tongued, for doubleness of tongue is a snare of death.[6]

Here again we may compare the spirit of the 'Son of Sirach': 'Winnow not with every wind, and go not into every way; for so doth the sinner that hath a double tongue. Be steadfast in thy understanding, and let thy word be the same.'[7]

'Thy speech shall not be false nor vain, but fulfilled by deed.'[8]

Comparison of the *Didaché* with the 'Epistle of Barnabas' shows in general a more expanded expression in the former, and so far points to the 'Epistle' as the earlier document. Nothing can be more strenuous than the exhortations to simplicity and purity of life, alike in thought, word, and deed, in this 'apostolic' literature.

'Thou shalt be simple in heart and rich in spirit; thou shalt not join with those who go in the way of

---

[1] Gibbon, c. 4. [2] *Barn.* 19. 8; 1 *Clem.* 57. 2.
[3] *Did.* 2. 3. [4] *Barn.* 19. 4; *Constt. App.* 7. 3.
[5] Cf. *Testaments of the Twelve Patriarchs*, Zab. 8; *Barn.* 19. 4; Jud. Pet. 97. 9.
[6] *Did.* 2. 4; *Barn.* 19. 7. Cf. *Constt. App.* 7. 4, 13; Jud. Pet. 97. 9.
[7] Ecclesiastic. 5. 9 ff. [8] *Did.* 2. 5; *Constt. App.* 7. 4.

death; thou shalt hate all that is not pleasing to God; thou shalt hate all hypocrisy; thou shalt not desert the commandments of the Lord.'[1]

That meek temper which is sometimes made a reproach against the Jew as if it were the sign of servility, has its admirable aspect, as a temper really inspired by religion. 'Thou shalt not exalt thyself, thou shalt be lowly in all things. Thou shalt not take upon thyself glory.'[2] 'Thou shalt not give to thy soul insolence.' 'Thou shalt be meek, thou shalt be quiet, thou shalt tremble at the words which thou hast heard.' Here is an echo of Isaiah 66. 2.

The manner in which these short sayings occur, loosely as it were shaken together, without strict method, suggest the existence of a collection of proverbial *Memorabilia*, strictly speaking anonymous, and preserved in mind by constant recitation in preaching.

Some of them have a peculiar and characteristic turn, such as the warning against the 'double soul' or mind, whether it refers to prayer, or more generally to future reward and punishment, or to the opposite of simplicity of character.[3]

A happy trust in overruling Providence is expressed in the saying: 'The effects that befall thee receive as good, knowing that without God nothing takes place.'[4] This might be illustrated from the story of him called 'Gam su letofa' ('This too shall be for good') in the Talmud. But no beautiful enforcements of these lessons from the life of birds or flowers, such as we are familiar with in the Sermon on the Mount, occur.

---

[1] *Barn.* 19. 2. Cf. *Did.* 4. 12; *Constt. App.* 7. 14.

[2] *Barn.* 19. 3; *Constt. App.* 7. 8; *Jud. Pet.* 99. 8; 97. 13.

[3] *Did.* 4. 4; *Barn.* 19. 5; *Constt. App.* 7. 11; *Herm. M.* 9. Cf. *Sirac.* 1. 28.

[4] *Barn.* 19. 6; *Did.* 3. 10. Cf. *Sirac.* 2. 4.

Here, too, the duties of the family life and of the household are recognised in a manner which shows the true heart of Judaism. 'Thou shalt not lift thy hand from thy son nor from thy daughter, but from their youth shalt teach the fear of God.'[1] 'Thou shalt be subject to masters (or lords) as a type of God in modesty and fear.' 'Thou shalt not give orders to thy man-servant or maid-servant in bitterness, who hope on the same God, lest thou shouldst not fear God who is over both, because He came not to call according to the person, but to those whom the Spirit prepared.'[2]

'Thou shalt communicate in all things with thy neighbour, and shalt not say there is private property; for if in the incorruptible ye are partakers, how much more in the corruptible.'[3] For the latter sentence, the Apostolical Constitutions have, 'for the common participation has been appointed to all men from God.'

Great emphasis is laid upon almsgiving in these ethical mandates; and it can hardly be denied that something like a 'salvation by works' is taught; at least a salvation apart from faith and knowledge is recognised.

'Be not one that stretches out his hands for receiving but draws them in for giving.'[4] In better Greek Siracides expresses the same thing. But the place which eleemosynary acts hold in reference to the health of the soul and the future judgment may be most accurately understood from the citation of the context.

[1] *Barn.* 19. 5; *Constt. App.* 7. 12; *Did.* 4. 9.
[2] *Barn.* 19. 7; *Const. App.* 7. 13; *Did.* 4. 10.
[3] *Barn.* 19. 8; *Constt. App.* 7. 12; *Jud. Pet.* 100. 16; *Did.* 4. 8; 2 *Clem.* 8. 5.
[4] *Barn.* 19. 9; *Did.* 4. 5; *Constt. App.* 7. 11. Cf. *Sirac.* 4. 31.

'Thou shalt remember the day of judgment night and day, and shalt seek out each day the faces of the Hagioi, either through *logos* labouring, and going to exhort, and meditating to save a soul by the *logos*, or by thy hands thou shalt work for redemption of thy sins. Thou shalt not hesitate to give, nor murmur in giving, but shalt know who is the good recompenser of the reward.'[1]

That the means of redemption from sins is in the above passage either spiritual or eleemosynary service on behalf of others can hardly be doubted. The Apostolical Constitutions quote from Proverbs (16. 6):[2] 'for by alms and faiths ($\pi i \sigma \tau \epsilon \sigma \iota \nu$) sins are purged away.' The teaching of the same book connects almsgiving and the neglect of it with recompense and with punishment.[3] 'If thou hast,' says the *Didaché*, 'thou shalt give with thy hands a ransom for thy sins.' When we compare this with a saying in the 'Testaments of the Twelve Patriarchs,' 'In proportion as a man is pitiful towards his neighbour, will the Lord be pitiful towards him,'[4] and with passages in the Book of Daniel and of Tobit,[5] the strong connection between almsgiving, deliverance from death and the Divine mercy looks us full in the face. The same vein runs through the Talmud. 'The case of the Poor,' said a Sage, 'is left in our hands, that we may thereby acquire merits and forgiveness of sins.'[6] 'Solomon the Wise says: Charity saves from death.'

We are not among those who can delight in the

---

[1] *Barn.* 19. 10; *Did.* 4. 2 ff.; *Constt. App.* 7. 9, 12, 14. 10; *Jud. Pet.* 99 and 100; *Herm. M.* 2.
[2] Cf. 15. 27.   [3] 19. 17, 21. 13.   [4] Zab. 8.   [5] 4. 27, 4. 10.
[6] Cited by E. Deutsch, *Quarterly Review*, No. 246.

artificial oppositions of a *doctrinaire* system of life and morals, or can see in the famous contrast of salvation 'by faith' and 'by works' anything more than a designation of the extremes between which human thought of its very nature oscillates. This Jewish 'teaching' seems fairly to take a *via media*, connecting genuine piety with its genuine expression,—morality, and refusing to hold asunder elements of thought and conduct which all experience shows to be vitally one. We do not find in these proverbial doctrines the heartless notion of salvation by dialectics, or of health of soul derivable from the apprehension of abstract propositions.

These teachings are lofty, and yet not strained beyond the reach of ordinary human nature. The 'yoke of the Lord' is not to be made oppressive; 'if thou canst bear the whole, thou shalt be perfect; but if thou art not able, do what thou canst.'[1] The Levitical directions as to food clean and unclean seem to be slightly touched upon, as if a change of opinion were going on. 'Concerning food bear what thou canst, but against idol-offerings beware exceedingly; for it is a service of dead gods.'[2]

We have then here before us an outline of the moral teaching of Hagioi, apostles, prophets of the Diaspora during the second century. It is more correct thus to speak and think of it than to attempt to define a 'Christian' morality distinct from any that had gone before. If Christian morality be a mode of life called into existence by the genius or will of an individual founder, if its canons be 'These Sayings of Mine,' and its inspiration his example, how is it that atten-

[1] *Did.* 6. 2. Cf. *Barn.* 19. 8.
[2] *Did.* 6. 3. Cf. *Constt. Ap.* 7. 20, 21.

tion is not concentred upon such a Master, especially where the thought of a yoke difficult to bear was in question? In connection with this vein of moral teaching, for which the earliest document appears to be the nineteenth chapter of 'Barnabas,' the name of Jesus is conspicuous by its absence. The 'mandates of the Lord,' the 'name of the Lord,' not to be taken in vain, manifestly bear allusion to God, in the ordinary Old Testament sense.

Yet there is no difficulty in accounting for these facts in accordance with the conclusion already forced upon us by the general evidence. As the time had not yet come when these 'apostolic' teachings were assigned to individually named apostles (the 'Epistle of Barnabas' forms no real exception, internally considered), still less had the time come when they were ascribed to one Authority, the utterances of one Voice. They stand before us on their own intrinsic evidence, utterances of the anonymous Heart of Judaism, breathed upon by the spirit of wisdom and of holiness. Party and sectarian questions seem to be out of place in studying these noble deposits of a nation's life of conscience and in the fear and love of God. Never can one people borrow its modes of feeling about life and its duties and its ways of expressing them from another. But it is always interesting to note the distribution of light and shade, and the different proportions of objects in various moral systems. To us it seems that a profound and simple sense of the good of life, a relish for its natural pleasures, unites with the sense that He who made it must be an all-good and lovable Being, to give the colour of health and soundness to Jewish morality. And the system which deduces everything from the will and positive commandment of a perfect Being must have a great advantage, at least with the multitude, over one which finds law in the nature of the mind itself. That habit of constant reflection which stands more in awe of self-criticism than of any external tribunal, and to which self-approval is the sweetest of all satisfactions, is always rare. And a doctrine which bids men think humbly of their powers and highly of their possibilities, has always been more acceptable and credible than one which places them on a pedestal of self-sufficiency, but knows not how to console them when they fall.

We cannot understand the 'origin of Christianity except by studying the great revival of free intelligence, the vigorous criticism of life and of ancient institutions which was going on from the times immediately preceding our era, and which is represented not only in our anonymous sources, but in the writings of Jews like Philo and Josephus, and in our well-known Greek and Latin authors. Spiritual good was being diffused through the world; all of them in their way bear witness to the consciousness of this, and of the spiritual brotherhood founded upon it. No one will ignore the truth expressed in the fable of the friendship of 'Seneca noster' and Paul. But that truth seems to be, as nearly as we can express it, not that Paul was the teacher of Seneca, nor that Seneca was the teacher of Paul, but that a spiritual brotherhood was established and grew to mighty dimensions during the second century between kindred spirits from Jews and Gentiles. The name of that brotherhood is Christianity, if a name must be found for it. But when we look to the quarter whence the anti-idolatric movement came, whence sprung the love of the Nations, the propagandist zeal for the universal Kingdom of God and the reign of righteousness, must it not still be maintained, and that most gratefully, 'Salvation is of the Jews?' Apart from their Scriptures, the *Christiani*, whom Justin champions, had neither a basis for a creed, nor a code of morality, nor the materials for the construction of a historical genesis of their faith.

To state that the morality of the *Didaché* and of the 'Epistle of Barnabas' is borrowed from the New Testament is to beg an important question, and that in opposition to the *prima facie* evidence. To say that this morality is neither Jewish nor Pagan, but distinctively Christian, is also to assume something about the name Christian, which our previous inquiry does not warrant us in assuming. Nor can we find, amidst many striking coincidences, a probability that Seneca furnished these 'apostles' with their ethical stock. Far more justified, as we believe, on the ground of affinity, of imagery, of style and treatment, is the comparison with the writings of Philo.[1]

'THE LORD'S PRAYER.'

We have been following the traces of a great revolution amongst Jewish communities against hierarchical Judaism. A developed moral sense has revolted from the 'righteousness' of an external *cultus*, and those who carried on this movement, whether they be termed Hagioi, or Ebionites and Nazarenes or Galilæans, were men who had seized upon the essential and the real in the piety and morality of their fathers. The old

---

[1] See the edition of the *Didaché* by Massebieau and his article in 'Le Temoignage,' Feb. 7, 1885, also the edition by Sabatier.

conception of the Law is exchanged for that of the
'Commandments,' or, in other words, moral notions
are transferred from the tables of stone to the fleshly
tables of the Heart. Nor will a literal fulfilment
suffice; there must be an extension of moral require-
ments in the light of a more awakened conscience.
Ideal 'perfection' is never lost sight of. 'The teaching' (of the Apostles) is this: 'Bless them that curse
you and pray for your enemies, and fast for them that
persecute you; for what grace is there if ye love them
that love you; do not the Gentiles also do the same?
But love them that hate you, and ye shall not have an
enemy . . . If any one give thee a blow on the right
cheek, turn to him also the other, and thou shalt be
perfect. If any one press thee to go with him one mile,
go with him two. If any one take away thy cloak, give
him also thy tunic; if any one take from thee what is
thine, ask it not back; for thou canst not.'[1] In that
which follows on the emphatic duty of giving, the
'Will of the Father' is referred to, and 'the Commandment,' but no reference is made to the *dicta* or
the authority of Jesus.[2] And since, where internal
evidence is our sole guide, we must take the simpler
forms of these injunctions to be the earlier, the conclusion is that the Kingdom of God and His righteousness was a conception long formed before the preaching
of it was ascribed to him.

And here the noble Prayer which aspires for the
fulfilment of that Kingdom in the accomplishment of
that Will of the Father, may well engage our attention. Apart from the Gospel of Matthew, we find this
Prayer given in the *Didaché*. As the new fast-days

[1] *Did.* 1. 3 ff.
[2] Cf. *Herm.* 2. 4 ff.; *Constt. App.* 7. 1 ff.

are to be a mark of separation from 'the Hypocrites,' so also the Prayer. It is thus introduced: 'Neither pray as the Hypocrites, but as the Lord commanded in His Gospel.' At the end the direction is added, 'Pray thus thrice a day,' a well-known Jewish practice.[1]

We can find no date for the Prayer but that of Marcion's Gospel, which substitutes for 'Hallowed be Thy Name,' 'let Thy Holy Spirit come upon us.' But, so far as we know, it was always ascribed to 'the Lord' and found in a 'Gospel,' with the exception of the *Didaché*. The question therefore arises. Of what antiquity is the phrase, "The Lord in His Gospel bade,' as compared with the indefinite phrases, 'the commandment of the Gospel,' or 'as ye have it in the Gospel,' or simply 'the commandment?'[2] The student will at once note how far more numerous are the latter modes of expression. And we must conclude as before that the general authority of recognised moral Commandments was the earlier conception, the personal authority the later.

Thus again we are thrown back upon the internal evidence of the Prayer. So viewed, it falls into members and has all the appearance of a Symbol habitually recited and faithfully kept, though with variations, in memory. Its theology is of a simply Jewish cast. 'It excludes every thought of later speculation and Christology, turns *only* to the Father-God of Heaven, and replaces the atoning and ceremonial rites by a fulfilment of the refined moral law. For it connects the remission of guilt with the condition of one's own kindness of heart. No sacrifice can any

---

[1] Dan. 6. 10; Ps. 55. 17.
[2] *Did.* 11. 3, 15. 3, 4.

longer redeem from guilt in the new sense, guilt, that is, against the new moral law. But thus the notion of the Cultus is entirely broken away from its historical basis.'[1]

Whensoever this Prayer came into circulation, its internal evidence concurs with that previously adduced, to prove that those who used it first as a symbol were Jews who had fully adopted the principles of the great revolution against the hierarchical Judaism of the Sanhedrin. The phraseology, the ideas are those of men who believed in the internal fulfilment of the Law and in the spiritual Kingdom of God. The beautiful and sublime description of God as 'the Father in Heaven' is one of the many designations in the Talmud of Him whose real Name is ineffable. 'Every nation has its special guardian angel, its horoscopes, its ruling planets and stars. But there is no planet for Israel. Israel shall look but to Him. There is no mediator between those who are called His children, and their Father which is in Heaven.' 'As long as Israel are looking upwards and humbling their hearts before their Father who is in Heaven, they prevail; if not they fall.'[2]

Since the Prayer occurs only in a few sources and is of origin so obscure, we can only venture to make these general remarks upon it. The strange and novel word ($\dot{\epsilon}\pi\iota o\acute{u}\sigma\iota o\varsigma$) which is found in it, and which continues to exercise the ingenuity of philologists, is said by Origen to have been formed by 'the evangelists.'[3] And as the 'Lord's Prayer' always occurs in an Evangelion, this affords some general clue to its origin.

---

[1] Lippert, *Christenthum*, &c., 175.
[2] E. Deutsch, *Quarterly Review*, No. 246, pp. 457, 460.
[3] *Orat.* c. 27.

What is of most importance to note is that prayer, fasts, almsgiving, the remission of debts, are all organically related in one system of thought. These are the new and spiritual Sacrifices, and on the offering of these the remission of sins and the Divine favour depends.

CHAPTER VII.

THE EVANGELION AND THE EVANGELISTS—THEOLOGY
OF THE HAGIOI.

THE natural course of our inquiry brings us to ask the important question: How is it that the word *Evangelion* and connected words, which glitter in the pages of the New Testament like daisies in a field, appear so sparsely in our so-called 'Apostolic Fathers,' or the 'old Christian literature' generally. The student who approaches these documents with the presumption that he will find in them from first to last references to 'the Gospel' or proclamation of good-tidings of definite and universal import, will be disappointed. And this discovery, if nothing else, should lead to an entire reconsideration of the subject.

'Hermas,' through all his diffuse Mandates, Visions, and Similitudes, never uses the word *Evangelion*, nor has the idea of it in any specific sense. Once he speaks of 'good news' (ἀγγελία ἀγαθή) in connection with the vision of the old woman who becomes young and beautiful:[1] the good news is the 'renovation of the spirit' visibly illustrated by that metamorphosis. He speaks of the 'Kingdom of God,' and of 'the law of the Son of God' and its universal proclamation; but if any allusion to the 'Gospel of Jesus Christ' is here found, it is because the commentators have

[1] *Vis.* 3. 13.

read it into the text, which knows nothing, again, of
'Jesus' or of 'Christ.' For us this silence speaks;
and it remains to be shown in what sense 'Hermas'
is an evangelical or a Christian document at all.

We have already adverted to the two passages in
'Barnabas'[1] where 'the Evangelion' is mentioned,
preached by the superlative sinners chosen out by the
Lord, twelve in number. Its contents were *the
remission of sins and the chastity of the heart.*' This
statement alone is of historical value, consonant as
it is with all that we have learned concerning the
spiritual revolution which was going forward in
Judaism. Under other phraseology, the writer asserts
the principle of that revolution. The Old Testament
of the tables of stone was dashed in pieces, 'in order
that the testament of the beloved Jesus might be
sealed upon our heart in hope of His faith (or, the
faith upon Him).'[2] And Sacrifices and Sabbaths have
been made void, in favour of the 'new law' of our
Lord Jesus Christ. The writer adduces some mystical
'types of Jesus' from the Old Testament or from
tradition, as we have seen. But he betrays no
knowledge whatever of any preaching of Jesus in the
synagogues of Galilee or elsewhere; no knowledge of
John the Baptist or of the *personnel* of the 'apostles.'

Simply and in short, he is aware of a great change
which has passed over the inner landscape, within the
horizons of the ideal; but to translate this change into
even the semblance of a matter-of-fact narrative with
dates of time, place and person, is beyond the resources of his knowledge or invention. One circumstance distinguishes him from 'Hermas'—he has the
idea of 'the beloved Jesus' and His testament and

---

[1] 5. 9, 8. 3.   [2] 4. 8; cf. 14. 5.

little more. In one doubtful passage, he speaks of His having risen on the eighth day, and after manifestation, having ascended into heaven.[1]

And we must again remind ourselves that the 19th chapter of 'Barnabas,' which contains the 'teaching' similar to that of the 'Sermon on the Mount,' quite ignores either 'Jesus' or 'apostles' as its source. Nor is there any 'Paul,' nor any 'Gospel' in the sense in which 'Paul' speaks of it in our 'Pauline epistles.'

In the 'First Epistle of Clement' there is a slight advance out of this ignorance. 'The apostles were sent as *good messengers* to us from the Lord Jesus Christ, Jesus the Christ was sent forth from God.'[2] 'Take up the epistle of the blessed Paul the apostle. What first did he write to you in the beginning of the Evangelion?'[3] This is all. What 'the beginning of the Gospel' means, we must leave to our readers. Once only, in the 'Second Epistle of Clement,' 'the Evangelion' is named, and then to support a saying which is *not* in the Gospel, as we understand it, but from some 'apocryphal Gospel.' The Lord in the Gospel says, 'If ye have not kept the little, who will give you the great, &c.?' And He means by this: 'Keep the flesh chaste and the seal unspotted, that we may receive the eternal life.'

If the reader fails to find satisfaction in these allusions, he will certainly not obtain it from the 'Ignatian epistles.' As to these documents, there are opinions and opinions, for all of which doubtless 'a great deal may be said.' But we are in quest of what can be known, at least negatively, if not positively, from these documents. We can only dig:

[1] 15. 9.   [2] 42. 1.   [3] 47. 1, 2.

we are ashamed to beg; nor will we pretend to find gold in the Ignatian mine which we have first carried thither ourselves. Frankly we must confess that whether as literature or as 'evidence' of anything worth knowing this mine is not worth the intellectual labour which has been attracted to it. The first feature which excites attention in these epistles is the frequent recurrence of the term *Christianos*, also *Christianismos*, and *Joudaismos*, which are startling novelties when compared with the current phraseology of the 'apostolic fathers.' The extraordinary and ridiculous prominence given to the *Episcopos* is another feature. Here there is nothing that will appear historical, nothing vigorously ethical, no practical *Didaché* or *Gnosis* of value, unless to those who are imbued with that reverence for the name and office of bishop which the writer would instil. But on these points we can appeal only to kindred tastes and distastes; and these must count for much, where all the learning lavished upon the object serves only to stimulate doubt as to the reality of the 'martyrdom' and the very person of Ignatius or Egnatius. But this by the way.

What can be made, in point of mere sense, of the fifth chapter of the Epistle to the Philadelphenes? What is 'fleeing to the Evangelion as flesh of Jesus, and to the apostles as presbyterion of the ecclesia? And the prophets also let us love, because they also announced unto the Evangelion, and upon him hoped and him waited for; in whom also they believed and were saved, being in *oneness* of Jesus Christ, Hagioi worthy of wonder and worthy of love, testified by Jesus Christ and numbered together in the Evangelion of the common hope?' What can be made of the following?

'I beseech you to do nothing according to strife, but according to Christomathy. For I have heard some saying, "If I do not find in the *archeia*, in the Evangelion, I do not believe." When I said to them "it is written," they answered me, "that is the question!" (πρόκειται). For me the *archeia* are Jesus Christ, the inviolable *archeia* His cross and death and His resurrection, and the faith that is through Him. In these I would be justified in your prayer.'[1] It is useless to ask for interpretations of such language, the like of which may be heard in the preaching of enthusiasts to-day. From a question of letters and history they will soar into mystic, and from the heights of mystic will look down contemptuously on those who demand the evidence of history and letters. What information is there in the sentence, 'the Evangelion is a perfection of incorruption?'

In another place some deadly teachers are alluded to, who have denied Jesus Christ, who have not been persuaded by the prophecies nor the law of Moses, 'nor even to the present time by the Evangelion, nor our sufferings of those according to a man (κατ'ἄνδρα).'[2] One is ashamed of such illiterate and unmeaning jargon.

Heed should be given 'to the prophets, but especially to the Evangelion, in which the Passion has been manifested to us, and the resurrection has been perfected.'[3] In the few references to 'the Evangelion' in the 'Martyrdom of Polycarp,' the reader will find no further information.

It is not without disgust and even shame that we turn from that 'mass of falsification, interpolation, and

[1] 8. 2; cf. 9. 2. See Zahn, *ad loc.*
[2] *Smyrn.* 5. 2. [3] Ib. 8. 2.

fraud' called the Ignatian literature. Of what avail is it to have learned to appreciate what is correct in letters, and still more what is manly in sentiment and vigorous in thought, if we are to be called upon to regard this congeries of 'wood, hay, and stubble' as constituting the 'immediately outlying buildings' of the 'House of the Lord'?[1]

Not only, as the author of 'Supernatural Religion' with patient toil has shown, are those beautiful books we know as 'the Gospels' unknown till late in the second century; but 'the Gospel' in any sense is seldom referred to, and in nowise so as to hint the existence of a rich narrative or a body of ethical teaching such as we do find current under the name of the 'Apostles,'—their *Didaché*, or their *Memorabilia*. On looking back, and omitting the mystical and muffled references to 'the Gospel,' we can fix upon only one good description of it, that of 'Barnabas.' It is good tidings of remission of sins and a clean heart. This might well correspond to the beautiful passage in Isaiah which speaks of 'good tidings to the meek.' But how can the chasm be filled up between this slight and simple reference to a belief founded upon the nature of the God who delights to pardon on the ground of conversion alone, and the allusions to the cross and passion and resurrection as essential to 'the Gospel,' and the ringing and repeated sound of the word in a passionately exclusive sense in the 'Epistle to the Galatians?' There were not only many literary 'Gospels,' there must have been irreconcilable differences of sentiment as to what the good tidings really consisted in, during the second century. They exist to-day; they seem to arise from

[1] Bishop Lightfoot; Preface to Apostolic Fathers, Pt. II.

organic differences in men; and they have a long theological history behind them. This much we may safely say, that the leaders in the spiritual revolution we have been tracing, the men who emphatically repudiated bloody Sacrifice, and found in prayer, thanksgiving, and alms the true and pure Offering, could hardly have found a place for the atoning blood of Christ in their system. It would have been to build again the things they had destroyed. But it was otherwise with the Hellenes and the mass of the Gentiles.

THEOLOGY OF THE HAGIOI.

Justin Martyr's statement of the Theological confession of the Christiani is as follows. They adore and worship 'the most true God, who is Father of righteousness and temperance and of the other virtues, and is unmixed with evil; and the Son who came from Him and taught us these things, and the host of other good angels, following and made like, and the prophetic spirit.'[1] The passage relating to the angels is obscure; but at least it seems that the angels were closely associated in worship with the Son. Again, Jesus Christ they had learned was 'Son of the very God,' and they held him in a second place, and the prophetic spirit in a third rank. They were accused of madness because they gave a second place after the immutable and eternal God to a crucified man.[2] In other words here was the leading feature of that τελετή which met the observation of Lucian. The latter in particular contemptuously refers to the worship of 'the impaled one' in Palestine.

But the central point in Justin's theology is the

[1] *Apol.* 1. 6.   [2] Ib. 1. 13.

deified Logos, who was the Son of God [with and begotten by the Father before the creation of the world],[1] and whose nature in various ways the apologist seeks to define and to illustrate. He is the Seed from God,[2] or the Spirit,[3] of indivisible substance with the Father, yet numerically distinct.[4] He is related to the Father (some say) as speech which does not lessen the speaker, as fire which does not lessen the kindler.[5] He is the 'first power' after the Father of all and Lord God, and the instrument of Divine operations.[6] He is called Angel, God, Lord, Arch-leader, Wisdom, Son, Glory, Apostle; and these because He is the minister of the Father's Will, and the messenger to men.[7] He, and not the supreme God, appeared to the patriarch and to Moses,—as man and angel, or in the form of fire. With Him Jacob strove.[8] His glory the people at Sinai could not look upon.[9] He moved the prophets; and of his influence Gentile philosophers and legislators partook.[10]

It is evident that we have here the conception of a spirit, analogous to the old Greek conception of a *dæmon*, or the Jewish conception of an angel, who can enter all bodies and assume all forms. And it is important to note that such conceptions, like all which have sprung up and been refined in the schools, lie deep in the popular imagination and religious folk-lore of the nations. That such a being was endued with form, made man and called by a Name,—this idea was congenial enough to both Greek and Jewish intuition. What was novel was the *name* not the

---

[1] *Apol.* 1. 32, 63. Cf. Pseud. Justin, *Apol.* 2. 6; but cf. *Dial.* 62 for the distinction of λογος ἐνδιάθετος and προφορικός, cf. 129.
[2] *Apol.* 1. 32.   [3] *Ib.* 1. 33.   [4] *Tryph.* 56. 128, 129.   [5] *Ib.* 61.
[6] *Apol.* 1. 32, 15, 59, &c.   [7] *Apol.* 1. 63; *Tryph.* 61. 56, 58.
[8] *Ib.* 125.   [9] *Ib.* 127.   [10] *Apol.* 1. 5.

nature of such a being. Justin further mystically states that the Logos declared His name was Jesus, saying, 'My name is in Him.' And Jesus was before called Auses.[1]

We will not here discuss that mode of intuition of the Divine operation in Nature and man which is found in Plato and the neo-Platonists, in Philo and the Alexandrian *apocrypha*, and which gave rise to the grammatically, rhetorically, and metaphysically personified 'Wisdom,' 'Virtue,' 'Reason.' It is perfectly intelligible as the result of an effort to combine in a mythological way the thought of the unknown and ineffable with that of the manifested and known Divine. What arrests attention is the stupendous proposition that the eternal reason or spirit of God became incarnate in Jesus of whom Justin only knows that He was put to death more than a hundred years before his time. It is a tremendous leap from the ideal and subjective to the objective and real. There is no statement in Justin or elsewhere that Jesus asserted Himself to be the Logos, or that the 'Apostles' asserted it of him. Where and when did the statement first originate?

It is to pass into altogether another climate when we turn to the theology of the Hagioi as represented in the 'Shepherd of Hermas.' This is not a dogmatic treatise, but a work of poetic fiction, full of a certain delicate suggestiveness and purity. The book will be better appreciated and take its proper place in literature when it is once recognised that it is neither the work of an 'apostolic father'[2] in any sense commonly

[1] *Tryph.* 75.
[2] In the course of the second century it was connected with an 'apostolic' Hermas, Rom. 16. 14. On this process of naming anonymous writings, see Harnack, *Hdb.* 278, n. 2.

given to that term, nor yet of a Christian, if by that name we recognise one who owned 'Christ' and 'Jesus.' For these words do not occur in the book. And if for this reason only, we must say that the interpreters and commentators who have approached the book under the impression that a 'Christology' is to be found in it, have fallen into the greatest illusions, and have obscured rather than elucidated the text.

The book speaks throughout of 'God' and of 'the Lord' (ὁ θεός and ὁ κύριος), also of 'the Spirit' in the manner usual in Jewish writings. Nor can we find any departure from the monotheistic conception.

In the last part of the book alone, the Similitude, a new and peculiar figure, appears amidst the scenery. It is 'the Son of God.' A master of a vineyard has selected a faithful and beloved slave, and has intrusted to him the care of the vineyard, on departing to a foreign land. On his return he finds the vineyard in fair order, and calling his son and heir and his friends who were his counsellors, he announces that he will make the faithful slave joint-heir with his son. Presently he calls a feast, and sends to the slave many dishes from his table. The slave took what was sufficient for himself, and distributed the rest among his fellow-slaves. His conduct gives universal pleasure; and all are delighted that the slave should become joint-heir with the son.

The parable is told to illustrate and emphasise the duty of fasting, in the refined spiritual sense, from evil thoughts and words, and of charity closely joined with it. This much is clear. And if we had not a word more, we might fairly conclude that the parable teaches, and was designed to teach, the acceptableness of the

Gentile proselytes along with the genuine Israelite sons to God, on condition of their offering those spiritual sacrifices which are required by the 'New Law.' 'If you observe fasting, as I have commanded you, your sacrifice will be acceptable to God, and this fasting will be written down; and the service thus performed is noble and sacred and acceptable to the Lord. These things, therefore, shall you thus observe with your children and all your house, and in observing them you will be blessed; and as many as hear these words and observe them shall be blessed; and whatsoever they shall ask of the Lord they shall receive.'

Unfortunately, a reluctant and hopelessly confused attempt to explain the details of the imagery follows. And thus, as usual, the parable is spoiled. The slave is said to be the Son of God; the dishes sent him are the commandments given to the people through the Son (!). And then, again, the Son of God is not in the form of a slave, but in great power and might; and He has the people given to Him, who are represented by the vineyard. 'He Himself purged away their sins, having suffered many trials and undergone many labours, for no one is able to dig without labour and toil (!). He Himself having purged away the sins of the people, showed them the paths of life by giving them the law which He received from His Father.' The slave now becomes an allegory of the flesh inhabited by the spirit, and remaining pure. Enough! The simplicity of the parable has been hopelessly tampered with. Old stories may be charged with old morals and with simple lessons: they break down beneath the weight of theological mysticism. The passage betrays the sense of this in an amusing manner. It is an example of the funest influence upon the beauties of

L

poetic literature of minds prepossesed with fixed ideas. But in passing we may note the idea of the pre-existent spirit, holy, made to dwell in an appointed or chosen body. This resembles the idea of the Sheckinah which the rabbins said rested on the head of every Israelite before the people fell into sin. The craving to give individuality and historic personality to strong general belief may well account for the idea of the descent of the spirit into the womb of the actual mother or the body of the actual son, which is, however, entirely remote from this book. Its delicate and fugitive dreams are suddenly transformed into flesh and blood and life-likeness as we open the 'Gospels' we possess. We dare not use words like 'impossible' or 'inconceivable;' but we will say that it is in the last degree improbable that this writer had before him any tradition that either the 'Son of God' or 'the Spirit' or 'the Logos' had become incarnate in 'Jesus' or in a 'Christ.'

In another parable, that of the tree aforementioned, the tree is interpreted as 'the law of God—that is, the Son of God—proclaimed to the ends of the earth;' the people under its shadow have heard and believed on Him. 'And the great and glorious angel Michael is he who has authority over this people and governs them; for this is he who gave them his law into the hearts of believers; he superintends them to whom he gave it, to see if they have kept the same.'

With regard to the proposition 'this law is the Son of God,' we must leave it as it stands: it has no possible logical connection with such propositions as 'Christ is the new lawgiver,' or 'an eternal and final law' in Justin or elsewhere.[1] Nor can we admit any impor-

---

[1] See references in Gebh. and Harn. *ad l. Sim.* 8. 3.

tation of 'the historical person of the Son of God' (Zahn) into the place.

But Michael, the Guardian Angel of Israel, who figures so strongly in Jewish apocalyptic literature, and in the Talmud, here appears to coincide in his functions with the 'Son of God.'[1] The law seems to be spoken of as Michael's ($a\dot{v}\tau o\hat{v}$, prob. = $\dot{\epsilon}av\tau o\hat{v}$). The ideas of the guardian angels among the Jews, to be compared with the Persian *Yazatas* and *Fravashis*, date from post-exilian times their influence. The origin of these shapes may distinctly be traced to the need of the imagination to find a link between the Divine Being, mysterious and ineffable, and the world of matter. And Persia seems to have contributed Mithras to their number. 'There is a distinct foreshadowing of the Gnostic Demiurgos to be found in the Talmud. What with Plato were the Ideas, with Philo the Logos, with the Kabbalists the 'world of Aziluth,' what the Gnostics called more emphatically the Sophia or Dynamis, and Plotinus the Nous, that the Talmudical authors call Metatron.'[2] It is this profuse and many named impersonation of a ruling idea of the times which impresses upon us the necessity and the extension of the belief. Whether we meet with the 'Son of God' or with Michael we are still in an ideal, never to be confounded with a historical world.

But to return. In the Tower of a later Similitude the old rock and the gate freshly cut are interpreted as the 'Son of God.' 'He is elder than the whole creation, so that He became fellow-deviser of the creation to His Father; for this reason He is old. And

[1] Dan. 10. 13, 21, 12. 1; Apoc. 12. 7; Jud. 9; Henoch 9. 1. c. 20; *Assumpt. Mos.* 10. 2; *Anab. Jes.* 9, 23, and further in Gebh. and Harn. *ad l.*   [2] *Quarterly Review*, No. 246, p. 456.

because in the last days of the consummation He became manifest, the gate was new, that those about to be saved through it may enter into the kingdom of God.'[1] The Tower itself is the Ecclesia. Further, the condition of entering the kingdom of God is 'receiving His holy name,' and this is not distinguished from the 'name of His beloved Son,' who is repeatedly called the 'gate.' And this son is imaged as a man lofty in stature, so that he overtops the tower, and he is accompanied by six men who wrought on the tower. The maidens who keep the tower run forward and kiss him; and he proceeds to test the stones. The six men are six Angels, and the maidens are 'powers' of the Son of God, in other words, impersonations of virtues, which must be borne by all who bear the name of the Son of God. He himself bears the names of those virgins. The imagery of this allegorical poetry is clear enough when we revert to the Seven Angelic Princes of the Talmud, whose names and functions correspond, as nearly as can be, to their Persian prototypes [2] (the *Amesha-Çpeñtas*), who on their own part have been discovered to be merely allegorical names for God's supreme qualities.[3]

It is noteworthy that the Son of God is a man of lofty stature, like angels in general. He blends the human and the divine in a way that ever captivates the religious imagination. And here further comparison leads to the identification of the Son of God with 'the holy spirit,' with the angel Michael, with 'the glorious' or 'the august angel,' with the

---

[1] 9. 12. I ff.

[2] The ranks and classes of the angels appear to have been a reflection from the Persian court. Chagiga, fol. 12 b; cf. Pirké de R. Eliezer, c. iv.; Wuensche, *Beiträge*, 212.

[3] Deutsch, in *Quarterly Review, ubi s.*

'angel of the Lord,' with the 'prince of the archangels,' with 'the holy angels.'[1] The figure of the youth of lofty stature more eminent than the multitude of them that praise the Lord appears also in the fifth book of Esdras.[2] We see no more accuracy in describing 'Hermas,' as a 'Christian' book than in so describing Esdras or Henoch.

It is a remarkable example of the blinding effect of habit upon the judgment that scholars should, in the face of the plain facts of the book, persist in identifying this glorious angel or Son of God with Jesus Christ. If the writer meant Jesus why did he not say so? Nothing is more familiar, for example, than the image of the Rock and the Gate elsewhere as applied to Jesus. 'Hegesippus' speaks of the 'gate of Jesus,' the 'gate of Jesus within the cross.'[3] 'I am the gate,' Jesus is represented as saying in the fourth of our Gospels. The representation in 'Hermas' must be earlier than, or if not earlier, quite independent of the sources which identify Jesus with the Son of God.

Studied apart from bewildering assumptions of its Christian character, 'Hermas' is an engaging book; and it throws much light upon those lofty if vague dreams of an universal kingdom and Ecclesia, of an arch-angelic Son of God and His preaching to the nations, which haunted the Jewish imagination of the time, and which were gradually assumed to have historic reality as their source. To a religious world saturated with such dreams, and no more accustomed to discriminate imagination from historic truth than

---

[1] See *Vis.* 5. 2, note, in Gebh. and Harnack.
[2] V. Esr. 2. 43.
[3] Eus. *H. E.* 2. 23. 8, 12; Ignat. *ad Phil.* 9. 1; 1 Clem. 48. 4, &c.

the religious world of to-day, it must have appeared in course of time that the preaching had an earthly beginning and that the preacher was of angelic nature. But how a name and a date was found for such a preacher remains as yet unexplained. We should note in passing from 'Hermas,' that there is no hint of the 'Son of God' having suffered an ignominious death or having risen again.

We pass to the 'Epistle of Barnabas.' This is distinguished from 'Hermas' by the fact that it distinctly names Jesus and *Christos*. But there is no distinct account of a theological Trias, nor any attempt to give precision to the various divine names used in the book.

We read of 'the covenant of the beloved Jesus' sealed upon the hearts. We find several strange 'Gnostic' or rather Haggadic interpretations of the Old Testament, and of rabbinical writings as referring to Jesus. Thus when Moses says, 'Enter the good land,' &c. (Ex. 33. 1, 3), 'the gnosis' explains: 'Hope on Jesus who is to be manifested to you in flesh. For man is suffering earth, because from the face of the earth the plasis of Adam was formed.'

We have already seen how a 'type of Jesus' is found in the goat Azazel of the rabbinic tractate Joma.[1] The goat under the curse, bearing a strip of purple wool on its head, meant that 'they shall see Him on that day having the purple robe round His flesh, and shall say, Is not this He whom we once crucified, setting Him at naught and spitting on Him and goading Him? Truly this is He who then declared Himself to be Son of God.'[2] The author reads a double interpretation into the rabbinic tradition:

---

[1] vi. 3-6.   [2] 7. 7-10.

there are thorns pointing to the thorny crown of Jesus, and the wool among the thorns points to the suffering Ecclesia. But the wool has already done duty for the robe of the triumphant Jesus. 'So saith He (Jesus), they who desire to see Me and to lay hold of My kingdom, ought afflicted and suffering to receive Me.' There is no quotation here, no allusion to any of our New Testament documents. It is rather one of many examples of the manner in which dream sayings are ascribed to a being made of the stuff of dreams. So in another rabbinical tradition, 'the calf is Jesus.' And according to a Greek reading of Ps. 96. 10, 'the kingdom of Jesus is on wood (or, a Tree).'[1]

We have already seen how by garbling two passages in Genesis (17. 26 f. and 14. 14), and by unfolding another 'gnosis' of the 'three letters,' the Greek T is made to signify the Cross, and the numeral $ιη$ Jesus. If Tertullian and Clement of Alexandria follow these precious interpretations, while the Valentinians find in the $ιη'$ eighteen Aeons, this only shows how possessed were men's minds by such hallucinations. But fancies so absurd do not captivate intelligences otherwise acute, except where there is an absence of close and first-hand acquaintance with the subject-matter. It could only have been in utter ignorance of a 'historical Jesus,' such as He who is present to all our imaginations, that men snatched at evidence of this far-fetched kind.

Had there been a picture living on amidst the most sacred treasures of memory from the time of Pilate, of a beloved Crucified one, what need to hunt for the Cross in writings where it is not to be found?

[1] 8. 5. Cf. Justin, *Dial.*, 73; Tert. *adv. Marc.* 3. 19; *adv. Jud.* 10.

The writer would find it in the fourth book of Esdras, he would find it in Exodus,—in the extended hands of Moses in prayer! and in the extended hands of Jehovah to His people in Isaiah 65. 2! Another 'type of Jesus' was the serpent made by Moses.

But perhaps the most important passage is that which seems to tell us that the very name of Jesus was assumed from a mystical discovery in the Old Testament. 'What says again Moses to Jesus son of Navé, putting upon Him this name, prophet as he was, that alone the whole people might hear that the Father manifests all things concerning the Son Jesus? Moses then says to Jesus son of Navé, putting on him this name, when he sent him as spy of the land: Take a book in thy hands and write what the Lord saith, that the Son of God will dig up from its roots the whole house of Amalek in the last days. Behold again Jesus, not Son of man but Son of God, but by a type manifested in flesh. Since then they will say that Christ is son of David, David himself prophesies, fearing and understanding the error of the sinners, The Lord said to my Lord, sit on My right hand until I make Thy foes the footstool of Thy feet.[1] And again Esaias says thus:[2] The Lord said to Christ my Lord, whose right hand I held, that nations should listen before Him, and I will break asunder the strength of kings. See how David calls Him Lord and Son of God.'

'He was manifested that they (the Jews) might be consummated in sins, and we through the heir might receive the covenant of the Lord Jesus.'[3]

The designation 'the Lord' is sometimes contrasted with 'God,' sometimes is itself used for God.

---

[1] 12. 8 ff. [2] For Κύρῳ in LXX. Isa. 45. 1. [3] 14. 5.

'If the Lord endured to suffer for our soul, being Lord of all the world, to whom God said from the foundation of the world, Let us make man according to our image and our likeness, how then did He endure to suffer at the hand of men? Learn. The prophets, having the grace from Him, prophesied unto Him. And He, that He might make void death and show the resurrection from the dead,—because it behoved Him to be manifested in flesh,—endured, that to the fathers also He might give the promise, and Himself preparing for Himself the new people might show forth, being on the earth, that Himself having made the resurrection, He will judge.' The thought of a 'manifestation in flesh'[1] for the end of suffering recurs. Even the 'dwelling in us' is coupled with this manifestation in flesh as an end; which shows that the conception of a spiritual being who can assume visible form, and can take possession of the mind of prophet or believer, is meant.

Theological ideas can never be properly appreciated until we relate them to the profound passions to which they give expression. The sense is everywhere in these writings that a great change has occurred in the minds of men; which change can only be referred to personal causes, and ultimately to a divine drama, enacted partly in the councils of eternity, partly in the theatre of earth and time. If a new people and a new law exists it *must have been* divinely ordained from the first; it *must have been foretold* by the all-knowing 'Spirit' through the prophets. A divine agent, a Son of God, and no mere Son of David, must have executed the divine will. He must have been manifested 'in flesh' to the gaze of men that they might believe, and

[1] 6. 7, 9, 14.

that the wickedness of those who had rejected the prophets of old might be consummated. He must have suffered as a scapegoat in the flesh; as a spiritual being he could not die. He must have been manifested after death and have ascended. He lives again in all who have received the baptismal seal, and is the pledge of their immortality. Such is the implicit reasoning of this and related documents. And from this point of view it seems sufficiently clear how from the mine of the Old Testament and the rabbinical writings materials were gradually collected out of which the Construction of that life manifested in the flesh gradually assumed distincter and yet distincter outline at the close of the second century in the person of Jesus. If this conclusion astonishes the reader, it is because he has not given due attention to the study of the religious imagination in general, and especially to its feats in the plastic use of Scripture as they are exhibited on almost every page of this old literature. It appears that the Jesus (*i.e.*, Joshua) of the Old Testament was for these students not a historical person to be understood in relation to his own times, but a prophet by name and by deeds whose name was changed that the future Son of God might be manifested. Another source says: 'Now Jesus, Nave's son, before called Auses: Him the Holy Spirit joined as associate to Himself by name.' Amalek, on the other hand, really signified the 'old serpent.'[1] If it cannot be denied with good reason that 'Barnabas' is anterior to our Gospels, then we see not how it can be disputed that the real origin of the name Jesus, as applied to the 'Son of God' who

---

[1] Carm. *adv. Marc.* 3. 67. Cf. Justin, *Dial.* 75. 49, 106, 113, 132; Tertull. *adv. Marc.* 3. 16; *adv. Jud.* 9; Lactant, *Instt. Div.* 4. 17; Euseb. *H. E.* 1. 3, 4.

came in flesh, is to be found in the Haggadistic exegesis of passages in Exodus and in Numbers. When we name the Haggadah, or popular and poetic exposition of Scripture, we name that which was the great instrument in the early propagation of Christian ideas among those who held the Old Testament to be infallible. The Haggadah has been called 'the fostering and teaching mother of Christianity; and by means of it the Christian doctrinal writings gained their overmastering charm, which subsists to the present day. It is Jewish spirit, old wine in new bottles. The New Testament is a highly successful Midrasch for Christian ends.'[1]

In the so-called 'First Epistle of Clement'[2] the tension of the teaching is ethical rather than theological; or theological examples are brought in to illustrate and enforce moral duties, such as hospitality, meekness, and humility. Thus we read: 'The Christ is of the lowly-minded, not of those who lift themselves up above His flock. The sceptre of the majesty of God, our Lord Jesus Christ, came not in boast of pride and haughtiness, though able; but lowly-minded, even as the Holy Spirit spake concerning Him.' Then follows the citation of Isa. 53. 1–12, also of Ps. 22. 7–9, in part from the LXX.

Obviously, the writer thought of the pre-existence of Christ, whether as 'angel' or 'son;' but upon so poetical a passage no precise definition can be pressed.

In a later chapter we read: 'This is the Way, beloved, in which we find our salvation Jesus Christ, the high-priest of our offering, the patron ($\pi\rho o\sigma\tau \acute{a}\tau\eta\nu$)

---

[1] Leop. Stein, *Die Schrift des Lebens*, Th. ii. p. 281, 1877.
[2] We must remind our readers of the unknown date and interpolated character of this epistle. *Supernat. Rel.*, I. 222.

and helper of our weakness.' We must warn our readers against the assumption, on the ground of similarities of phraseology, that the writer was acquainted with our 'Epistle to the Hebrews.' The internal evidence is against this. The writer thinks only of the high-priestly mediation of Christ in reference to the spiritual offerings of prayer and to intercession on behalf of men in their weakness. He has not a word to connect that high-priestly office of Christ with His death.[1] The 'way' is the pure moral way on which we dwelt above, the 'way of truth' described in the preceding chapter. And the doctrine is, that by good works and a life conformed to the divine will men are rendered worthy of the mediation of Christ. And when He is called 'our salvation,' this bears no allusion to a vicarious death. The idea is the general one, of 'the salvation of the Lord,' as it occurs in Jewish books.[2]

But the proposition, Christ is High-priest—apart from all connection with a vicarious death—is important, as pointing to that ideal sphere from which such conceptions alone were drawn. It is one of the forms by which men trained in the old institutions made clear to themselves the idea of the Intermediary between God and men, the 'Gate of the Father,'[3] as He is elsewhere called, or the Gate alone, as we have seen in 'Hermas.' All this is plainly poetry, national poetry; and it is only necessary to advert to the Talmudic conceptions of the ministry of angels, particularly to the idea of Sandalphon (said to be another form of Elias), who presents the prayers of the faithful

---

[1] Ritschl. *Altkath. K.*, ed. ii., p. 279; Lipsius, *De Clem. Ro.*, p. 89.

[2] *Testam. Dan.* 5; *Sym.* 7; *Juda*, 22; *Benjam.* 9. 10.

[3] I *Clem.* 48. Cf. Ign. *ad Phil.* 9; 12; Test. *Rub.* 6; *Sym.* 7.

before the throne of God, that we may feel at home amidst this scenery, and relish its beauty. It seems to us there is a great and gaping chasm between the idea of such an intercessory High-priest, the bearer of spiritual offerings, and the confused representations of the 'Epistle to the Hebrews,' where the priest is also the victim, or the representation of Justin, 'Christ a *crucified* High-priest.'[1]

In the same chapter a highly mystic poetic description of the same being follows: 'Through Him we gaze into the heights of heaven. Through Him we behold as in a mirror His spotless and surpassing visage. By Him were opened the eyes of our heart. By Him our senseless and darkened understanding blossoms out into His marvellous light. By Him the Lord willed that of the immortal Gnosis we should taste. Who being the splendour of His majesty, is by so much greater than angels as a more distinguished name He has inherited.' Again, there is no proof of a citation from the Epistle to the Hebrews, from whose words our author slightly departs. All that is proved is a coincidence of ideas. All that can be inferred is that we have here the effort after a Christology which shall mark off the celestial Mediator from the ranks of those beings to whom by nature and functions He is so nearly allied. And we note also the dithyrambic character of the above passage. Its imagery is the stuff of which our adoring hymns are still constructed. It can only be properly appreciated when we listen to the still music of ecstatic emotion by which it is accompanied. Its object is a being conceived as ever majestic in His nature, however He may have voluntarily stooped from His height for men's sakes. The author proceeds to

[1] *Dial.* 116.

cite Ps. 104. 4 on the nature of angels, Ps. 2. 7 on the distinct nature of the Son, also Ps. 110. 1 on His session at the right hand of God.

It should be remarked that it was no innovation to find in the 'Son' of the second Psalm the Messias. Many rabbins so interpreted it.[1] But no orthodox Jew could think of the 'Son of God' as a personality who in any *material* sense proceeded from God. The angels themselves, the *Beni Elohim*, or 'sons of God,' were beings standing near to Him, by Him created, His privy councillors in the government of the world. Concerning the Anointed Himself the opinions of the rabbins appears to have been somewhat uncertain;[2] nor could they venture on any opinion for which a semblance of support was not derivable from the letter of Scripture. Son of David and Son of Man were the preferred designations. On Dan. 3. 25, where Nebuchadnezzar speaks of a 'Son of God,' a Talmudic tractate says: An angel came down and smote him on the mouth, saying, Order thy words! God has no Son. Nebuchadnezzar then amended his speech, 'His angel, not His Son.'[3]

So far as the 'First Epistle of Clement' is concerned, Christ is not the second person of a divine Trias, but a glorious potentate, patron, and leader of the faithful. He is not a vicarious victim, but one who has manifested a lowly mind in spite of His sceptred majesty. There is no traceable history from which these ideas are taken; but the ideas themselves belong to the sacred dream-life of Jewish phantasy, are read into the Psalms, and are ready to be transformed into

---

[1] Sueca, fol. 52 a ; Wuensche, *Beiträge*, p. 344.
[2] Ib. 301.
[3] Talm. *Jerus. Schabt.* c. vi. ; Wuensche, p. 376.

retrospective legend, of the actual existence of which in any detail there is no sign as yet.

Later in the epistle (c. 42) Christ is subject to and sent by God to preach the good tidings. When Tertullian says, 'We walk in that rule, which the Church from the apostles, the apostles from Christ, Christ from God handed down,'[1] he was speaking of a past which was more obscure to him than it ought to be to us. It is the statement of a man who is the first to emerge distinctly to our view ont of the shades of the second century; and little indeed is the information he can give. He is a declaimer; and his declamation means only that 'the apostles,' the nebulous missionaries we have so often encountered, were the first imagined authors of the spiritual revolution, that their authority was derived from an ideal Messias, as his from God. In other words, the *à priori* of Tertullian as of Justin of Neapolis is and must be *à posteriori* for us. To the standpoint of the close of the second century and the imaginary perspective into the twilight past thence gazed upon, we are forced, by the sheer pressure of negative evidence, again and again to return.

Twice in this Epistle, the Resurrection of Christ is mentioned. In the first of these passages, He is raised from the dead as the first-fruits of the general resurrection of the beloved. In the second, His resurrection is the means of conveying full certainty to the minds of the apostles, before they went forth on their mission of announcing the kingdom of God. But (as Ritschl remarks) there is no hint of the idea of 'the reciprocity of the death and the resurrection of Christ as the foundation of a specifically new relation of believers to God.' The writer has no notion that

[1] *De Præscr.* 37.

'the believer, solely on the ground of Christ's resurrection, bears a new principle of life, from which the necessity of the moral walk proceeds.'[1]

The writer brings in the 'blood of Christ,' not as the ground of 'justification,' but as having been shed for men's salvation, and as having set the 'grace of repentance' before all the world. And in the favourite allegory of Rahab and the spies, the scarlet thread hung from the house signified redemption through 'the blood of the Lord' for all who have faith and hope in God.[2] Christ is said because of love to have given His blood for us, by the will of God, 'His flesh for our flesh and His soul for our souls.' This illustrates the praise of Love.

The idea of the Person of Christ shows some advance in distinctness upon that of the angelic Son of God in 'Hermas' or the Jesus of 'Barnabas.' The name and title are more fully given; the preciousness of the redeeming blood is recognised, and the worth of the resurrection of Christ as evidence. But the writer shows no acquaintance with our Gospels, nor with the 'Pauline epistles,' with whose teaching his own is not to be confounded for a moment. But one who introduces the sublime example of a glorious, divine, and kingly Son, self-humbled, suffering death in love, and raised again, not for the purpose of theological dogmatic teaching, but to enforce simple piety, charity, humility and repentance, must have been writing to those before whose minds that example had long shone. The epistle must be of quite late origin; and yet it has none of those not-to-be-forgotten sayings concerning the motive of the ransoming death, placed in our Gospels in the mouth of Jesus. What the

---

[1] *Altk. K.* 280 ff. 1 Clem. 24, 42.
[2] 12. 7; cf. 21. 6, 49. 6; Lipsius, 74, ff.

epistle puts into his mouth is not to be found in our Gospels.¹

Of the 'Second Epistle of Clement' much the same may be said. It puts into the mouth of Jesus sayings entirely strange to our ears. And as to its Christology, this, as in the first epistle, is subordinated to its earnest ethical strain of exhortation. What gives solemnity to these exhortations is that sense of impending resurrection and judgment which is so marked in the Jewish doctrine of life outside Sadducæism. 'Let not any of you say that this flesh is not judged, nor rises again. Know! In what were ye saved, in what did ye receive sight, if not while ye were in this flesh? We must therefore guard the flesh as God's temple. For in what manner ye were called in the flesh, ye shall also come in the flesh.'² We can hardly perhaps understand the full force of this grave and even awful passage until we compare it with the general beliefs of Greeks and Romans in the disembodiment of the spirit, yet in the necessity of the due burial of the body, as its partner in destiny; and in the relative annihilation of the spirit consequent on the destruction of the body. These beliefs are still widespread, and deeply rooted. Again the general in belief becomes the individual in retrospection; and we discern the necessity, the 'must have been' in the resurrection of Christ—a process of thought so openly laid bare in the fifteenth chapter of 1st Corinthians in the New Testament.

'If Christ the Lord who saved us, being indeed at

[1] The student may compare Harnack's section *Der Glaube an Jesus Christus, Hdb. d. Dogmgesch*, 128 ff. Unfortunately he neglects the undated character of the evidence, and finds 'Jesus' and 'Christ' in Hermas. But he sufficiently shows the vagueness of the allusions. It is not clear, as he assumes, that ὁ κύριος = Jesus.

[2] 2 *Clem.* 9. 1 ff.

first a spirit, became flesh and thus called us: so also we in this flesh shall receive the reward. Let us therefore love one another, that we may all come into the kingdom of God.'

Nothing seems more momentous than this passage with reference to the formation of the *logos* of the Christ actually and not merely docetically risen in the flesh. If we may assume that there always has been and that there is a strong repugnance to the idea of a material resurrection on the part of refined and thoughtful minds, we need not wonder at the strong opposition of the 'Gnostics' to the same. They said it must be understood in an allegorical sense of the knowledge of the true God.[1] Others (like the African chief interrogated by Sir S. Baker) said it was 'past already'—their children were a resurrection of themselves.[2]

The evidence of the Talmud shows how profoundly the idea of the resurrection and of the day underlay the whole thought of duty, and how powerfully it must have invigorated the moral conscience.[3] In discussions on the subject, Greeks, Romans, Sadducees, Samaritans, Essenes appear as assailants of the dogma; in defence of which arguments are taken, now from the Bible, now from Nature, now from the laws of reason,—just as in our early Christian or hagiographic literature.

Here then was an irreconcileable conflict of belief, which led inevitably to irreconcilable constructions of the past suffering and triumph of the Christ. Had there been during the second century recognised 'witnesses of the resurrection' in the physical sense

---

[1] Iren. 2. 31. 2, 5. 31. 1.; Tert. *De Resurr. Carn.* 2 and 19.
[2] *Act. Thecl.* 14.   [3] See Wuensche, *Beiträge*, 258.

to whom appeal could have been made, we should have heard of them. We have abundance of *à priori* argument, but witnesses are not forthcoming, in the sense which proof demands. The question is one of belief, from which the facts were to be inferred, not of facts on which the beliefs were to be built.

Therefore those who on general grounds thought the idea of a material resurrection illusory, yet held to the tradition of a suffering and returning Christ, were forced upon some Docetic explanation. What had taken place in the theatre of believing imagination had not necessarily taken place in the theatre of ordinary perception. The resurrection occurred in the place where all events of true grandeur and beauty befall,—the human spirit itself. But those who had been trained to recognise in a fleshly resurrection the guarantee of all future felicity for the good and of punishment for the wicked, felt that if the reality of the physical resurrection of the Son of God were denied, the whole fabric of faith and hope sunk into ruins. No one who has ever known the sorrow of the soul which discovers that it is impotent to make its own deepest persuasions of destiny an evidence to others of unlike temperament, but must sympathise with such feelings. But there is a good in such disappointments, if they teach at last the lesson that those hopeful persuasions which spring up as the fruit of a life of duty, bring a comfort to the possessor and it may be to others, none the less because they are denied the instrument of language and of thought to make them clear.

To-day intelligent men are not to be convinced of the physical resurrection by rabbinical arguments from texts, nor yet by false analogies from the seed-corn, which a mere savage or a child can refute, nor from the story of the phœnix, or of the mice in Egypt half flesh, half earth, and again all flesh, nor yet from the fortunes of the embryo.[1] And as for *à priori* principles, where Plato has failed to convince, another will hardly succeed. But it is needless to speak of the resistance of modern reason to a dogma which seems nowhere actively and earnestly forced upon its notice. It was otherwise among Jews of rabbinical training at the beginning of our era. The resurrection of the body was a necessary part of the system of theological and moral ideas. And this being so, as these ideas gradually shaped themselves into the form of a personal history, it was an equal necessity of belief that the Christ had risen again. That which has happened since in the theological world was happening then. Men do not willingly correct their assumptions by an appeal to history, its testimonies, and its silences; they prefer to cling to their assumptions in the sphere of phantasy, and to beg a history which shall afford them confirmation. If their *à priori's* are denied, their history falls with them to the ground. We simply shut our eyes to the evidence which looks us full in the face, if we fail to recognise that the 'apostolic' preaching of the risen Christ was from the first a theological manifesto. Had it been the announcement of a fact, certified from the first by eyewitnesses, nothing could have dispensed with the necessity of the continued reference to those witnesses. It is the silence of our literature on this point which speaks. Even if we include the New Testament books, the narratives and statements there made, apart from the fact that they occur in dateless and anonymous books, unknown till late in the second century, cannot carry persuasion except to the minds

---

[1] Sanhedrin, fol. 92 a.

of those with whom the Resurrection is a foregone conclusion. Had the personal resurrection of Christ been believed on historic grounds during the second century, no one would have been so rash as to assert that it rested on the ground of a general Belief. What is clear beyond dispute is that the idea of the general resurrection is organically connected in belief with the particular resurrection of the Christ; and the latter is a logical deduction from the former, standing or falling with it. To dwell at length upon the point seems to be a disrespect to the judgment and information of the reader.

Where the modern apologists fall into hopeless sophistry in dealing with 'evidences of Christianity,' is that they are either ignorant of or suppress their knowledge of certain elementary facts of human passion and imagination. The force of human imagination has not decayed since the first two centuries; but it now works under the restraint of changed habits. We cling not less passionately to our ideals; we believe they have been partly realised in human lives, and will be realised again. But the ideal of a resurrection and a recompense in the flesh is not, so far as we know, a fixed or dominant ideal of our time. Hence the narratives of personal resurrections present, as we believe, one of the greatest difficulties of belief among all classes. There was a time when among large classes they were matter of easy and almost matter of course belief, because they fell in with impressions concerning the ghostly world that were the heritage of ages, the lore of childhood and of maturity. In short, the whole mass of Jewish, Greek, Roman spiritual lore, the writings of Haggadists, of logographers, of poets, of calendarists and hagiographers down to the tellers of folk-tales by the winter fireside, form one vast monument of the powers of human imagination and belief. Thousands of miraculous tales have been cast as pictures upon the blank and void of the past from the *camera* of the people's phantasy, which have no less and no more certification as 'fact' than the tales of Elias and of the Messiah in the Talmud. 'Facts' are to be found in overwhelming profusion in the newspapers and blue-books of to-day; and they are sobering and saddening. Images, fancies, teem like the products of a tropical clime in the literature of antiquity; they are brilliant, awful, inspiring. Facts are very scarce yonder; and learning finds that in trying to 'add to their number,' it is but increasing the stock of fancy. The study of antiquity must be barren or perverted which does not see these 'evidences,' and which persists in bringing the prosaic habits of an English jurist into the investigation of the fluid dream-life of impassioned and poetic times. We must have shared that life or we cannot understand how ghosts acquired flesh and blood, and visions of the ideal Humanity were caught and fixed as fact by the genius of literature.

In brief. Whether we turn to the books of Palestinian or of Alexandrian Jews, or to the speculations of Greek and Roman Stoics, amidst an absolute dearth of facts, there is a captivating wealth of that precious ideal life of the human breast and brain which alone imparts undying charm to letters. The forms of mediate beings which here appear upon the stage of a supernatural theatre play a majestic part as interpreters between the Ineffable and Humanity. So long as we remain at a proper distance from them, they command us, because they are expressions of remoter truths. Only when we come too near, when we rudely question them and criticise them as if they were allied to earth and matter, the spell departs, the illusion vanishes, and we pass from the refined poetical mood to its opposite. These delicate creatures transform themselves, under treatment so rude, into the unpleasing puppets of theological wrangling. The ordinary theologian makes havoc among truly sacred objects, because he does not know his distance from them and the reserved behaviour required in their presence. The shapes of Wisdom, of the Logos, of the Sheckinah, of the Pneuma, are all metaphysical kindred of the Son or Messias; the imagination incessantly plays between the abstract and the concrete representation; but if its movements be arrested, all its poetic vitality ceases. The fluid hardens, the poetic personification becomes the person or hypostasis.

It is only by a historic accident that the Sophia of Siracides has not been in theology personified, and made a historical daughter of God. She describes herself as coming out of the mouth of the Most High and covering the earth as a mist. She is an universal presence; in the waves of the sea, and in all the earth, and in every people and nation she obtained a possession. But especially the Creator gave her a commandment, 'Tabernacle in Jacob, let thine inheritance be in Israel!'

'He created me in the beginning before the world, and I shall never fail. In the holy tabernacle I served before Him, and so was I established in Zion. Likewise in the holy city He gave me rest, and in Jerusalem was my power, and I took root in an honourable people, even in the portion of the Lord's inheritance.'

'I am the Mother of fair love and fear, and knowledge and holy hope. I, therefore, being eternal, am given to all my children which are named of Him.'

'He that obeyeth Me shall never be confounded, and they that work by Me shall not do amiss. All these things are the book of the covenant of the most high God, even the law which Moses commanded for a heritage unto the sons of Jacob.'

'I will yet make doctrine to shine as the morning, and will send forth her light afar off. I will pour out doctrine as prophecy, and leave it to all ages for ever!'[1]

It should be noted how strongly the expressions 'rest' (שרה) and 'tabernacle' are connected in Jewish poetry with the Sheckinah. 'Before the Israelites sinned, the Sheckinah rested upon each one of them.'[2] Rabbi Chalephtha ben Dosa of Capernaum said, 'Between two persons who converse on religious matters, the Sheckinah rests.'[3]

So far Sophia and the Sheckinah in their misty or cloudy shape of indefinable intuition are at one. But no one who feels what poetry is will seek to convert these images into historical facts, or be disposed to inquire after the birthplace of Sophia, or after the Person on whom the Sheckinah was seen to rest.

In the book of Baruch we read of Sophia: 'Who hath gone up into heaven and taken her and brought her down from the clouds? Who hath gone over the sea and found her, and will bring her for pure gold? No man knoweth her way, nor thinketh of her path. But He that knoweth all things knoweth her, and hath

---

[1] *Sirac.* c. 24.
[2] *Sota.* fol. 3 b.   [3] *Aboth.* 3. 7.

found her out with His understanding.' ... 'This is our God, and there shall none other be accounted of in comparison of Him. He hath found out all the way of knowledge, and hath given it unto Jacob His servant, and to Israel His beloved. Afterwards did He show himself upon earth, and conversed with men.'[1]

Clearly, where the belief in past epiphanies of the Divine lived so strong in the heart of Israel, the hope of future manifestations was a necessary consequence. 'My hope is in the Eternal that He will save you, and joy is come unto me from the Holy One, because of the mercy which shall soon come unto you from the Eternal, our Saviour.'[2]

In the book of Wisdom, Sophia is the breath or vapour of the power of God, and a pure forth-flowing of the glory of the Almighty, the brightness ($\dot{\alpha}\pi\alpha\acute{\nu}\gamma\alpha\sigma\mu\alpha$) of the everlasting light, the unspotted mirror of the energy of God, and image of His goodness.[3] Here are images which might be, and actually were, later associated with the Son or the Spirit in canonical books.

Sophia, 'though she is one, can do all things; abiding in herself she makes all things new, and through ages, passing into holy souls, she makes friends of God and prophets. God loves nothing except him that dwells with wisdom!'[4]

All this has the charm of truth and of beauty. Well may the writer speak of himself as a lover of Sophia desirous to wed her to himself. What in every age is the quest of Truth to the impassioned heart, but the quest of the Bride of our souls?

'She glorifies her noble birth, having a joint life

---

[1] *Bar.* 3. 29 ff.   [2] Ib. 4. 22.   [3] *Wisd.* 7. 25.   [4] Ib. vv. 27 f.

with God, and the Lord of all loved her. For she is the Mystis of the knowledge of God and chooser of His deeds.'

The writer (probably in the reign of Caligula) was acquainted with the moral philosophy of the Greeks, and doubtless saw the parallel to his own conception in the allegory of Athena, the majestic and sapient daughter born from the brain of Zeus. Like Athena Erganitis, Sophia is an all-productive artist, or Technitis.[1] She too was present when God made the world.

Change but the name or sex, and the like position and functions are assigned to 'the Spirit.' 'Who knew Thy counsel, unless Thou gavest Sophia, and sent Thy Holy Spirit from the highest places? And thus were made straight the paths of those upon earth, and the things pleasing to Thee men were taught, and by wisdom were saved.'

So again in like parallelism, the Logos of God is placed side by side with His Sophia. God 'made all things by His Logos, and by His Sophia made man.' Here, we might almost say, an Apollo appears beside his glorious sister. And, indeed, we know not how the lore of Apollo in Greek religion can be understood except by reference to the same process in the imagination by which a predicate of deity gradually becomes a dramatic person, capable of epiphany in the human form and again of aphany into the spiritual world.

Again, we see how the destroying angel may be identified with the Logos of God, all-powerful, sent down from heaven to slay the first-born of Egypt.[2]

Philo hovers between the Greek Ideas and the

---

[1] 7. 21, 8. 5.   [2] 18. 15 f.

Jewish Angels. His Logoi and his Logos are Ideas which lend themselves, with equal readiness as Sophia, to personification.[1] As with Plato, so with him, it seems unworthy of the Supreme that He should personally appear on earth, or that the sensuous and transitory world should proceed immediately from Him. Hence the necessity of these mediatorial entities, under various names, now masculine, now feminine (ἀρεταί, προσρήσεις), which might, under the concentration of personal predicates upon them, easily acquire the value of persons and agents in popular acceptation.[2]

The Logos is the Image of God, after which He formed the world, especially mankind; He is the Ideal Man,[3] the eldest, first-begotten Son of God before the world, who 'fashioned its form in imitation of the ways of the Father, looking to His archetypal patterns.' Or God made use of the Logos as an Organ[4] and so made the world, and He is still the rudder as it were by which God steers the universe.[5] Or, He is the divine Law of the world, which holds all parts of the physical and moral together, and keeps them in order.[6] The Logos is the principle of wisdom and virtue for the human race, the heavenly manna which God rains down upon all spirits. He is the bearer of divine revelation to the chosen people, the subject of the theophanies of the Old Testament, in which aspect He is called Angel or Archangel. As the rational principle of the soul and of prophetic inspiration, he is Pneuma, Spirit.[7]

[1] Dähne, *Philo*, I. 202.   [2] Ib. 241.
[3] *De Confus. ling.* 427 ff. M. ; ib. 414 M.
[4] *Leg. Alleg.* 2. 79.
[5] *De Migrat. Abh.* 437 M.
[6] *De Plant. Noe.* 342 M.; *De Opif. Mundi*, 34 M. ; *De Agric.* 308 M.
[7] Dähne, I. 301, 387.

He is Supplicator and Paraclete on behalf of men, Mediator between them and God.[1]

In a relative, not in the highest and strictest sense, the Logos may be called God, *i.e.*, a God (the article being omitted), or the second God.[2] The reader will note how nearly this approaches to the language of Justin Martyr.

Similar is the conception of the Messias and of the Sheckinah in the Talmud, and of the אדם קדמון or primitive man, the first and only begotten of God. The name of the Messias is among the seven things created before the world. King Messias, like Jacob, is made first-born of God.[3]

---

[1] *Quis. Rer. Div. Her.* 501 M. ; *De Vit. Mos.* 3. 155 M.
[2] *De Somn.* 655 M. ; Euseb. *P. E.* 7. 13.
[3] Wuensche, *Beiträge*, 499 f.

CHAPTER VIII.

THE IDEAL AMONG JEWS AND GENTILES.

IT seems needless to pursue these illustrations further. That tacit alliance between the professors of Jewish and of Hellenic wisdom which had been slowly cementing since the conquests of Alexander, and the evidence of which is in both Philo and the Talmud, that joint sowing of the seed of the Ideal in the world by the teachers of the Academy and the Porch, and of the rabbinical schools and the synagogues, seems to be the great source of the great Christian Ideal. Whether the Jew or the Greek had most to do in the formation of that Ideal is a question that cannot be answered by generalities. The New Testament being excepted from our inquiry, we find in the most valuable of our early documents that the Jewish idiom of language and thought everywhere characterises them. We recognise the Ideal in the Jewish form of it: a glorious angelic being who has come and proclaimed the law to the whole world, and who has commissioned certain unknown 'Apostles' for the same work; whence the consequent duty of repentance, and good works in expectation of an approaching end and a day of judgment. Slight and vague are the references to Jesus or to Christ, or to an unnamed 'Lord' to whom sayings are ascribed, sometimes strange in themselves, and wholly without proof of historic authenticity. Every student must read and consider the effect of these writings as a whole; and then he will see that a chasm separates them from any objective fact that can be known. It seems wholly impossible to reconcile their silence even with the bare knowledge which Tacitus and Justin seem to possess of the event in the reign of Tiberius.

The question which presses for solution is, Where and how did the abstract belief in the Logos, the Pneuma, the Messias or the Son of God become connected with the belief in a historical Jesus? For the view of Strauss that the New Testament writers did not aim at speculation on the Divine nature, but sought to give adequate expression to that which they thought they had found in Jesus,[1]—rests upon the assumption that Jesus was a character historically known, which is the question at issue.

This much is clear. Even as the writers of the Old Testament represented to themselves the beginnings of the Law and the Prophets under the form of theophanies, ministries of angels, magnificent poetic figures of Moses and Elias, and the inheritance of the Twelve Tribes under the legend of Joshua and Rahab,—so the religious revolutionists of the second century may well have found a substruction or poetic origin of the movement in an analogous theophany far back in the reign of Tiberius. But the idea of a *suffering* and *risen* divine being is not included in the Jewish conception of a theophany; and we cannot find it, whether in Philo, the apocrypha, or the rabbins.

An idea, however, which is common to Jews, Greeks, and Romans, nay to the universal human heart, is that

[1] *Glaubensl.* § 30.

suffering not only purifies the sufferer, but tends to the redemption of the world. The wise man is a ransom for the worthless:[1] this thought is in Philo. The rabbins taught: sufferings purify men, and he who assumes them with love and patience, brings salvation (יְשׁוּעָה) to the world.[2] As for the Greeks, the thought of the voluntary sacrifice of youths and maidens for the public weal, the λύτρον of the one for the many, imparts undying pathos and poetic charm to many of their patriotic legends.[3]

Above all and most distinctly this Ideal is exhibited in the writings of Seneca, who represents that Stoical communion in which, rather than in the Jewish Diaspora, a scholar of bold and original views, sees the source of the 'Christianity' of the New Testament. The ideal Person of the Stoics is the 'wise man.' When Plutarch caricatures them as men who hold that if a solitary wise man in any place only stretches out his finger in a rational manner, all wise men on the whole earth derive advantage therefrom, he in effect pays a tribute to the grandeur of their social conceptions. On this passage Bruno Bauer remarks: 'The popular philosopher of the second century was not aware that the Stoical Union was a mystical fellowship of Saints, to whose treasury of grace the works of their members belonged; a fellowship in which a master could not think and speak without imparting a fruitful stimulus to the whole. This Union had helpers and spiritual assistants, before whom the worldly potentates and sensuous images of the gods lost their

---

[1] I. 187, M. πᾶς σοφὸς λύτρον ἐστὶ τοῦ φαύλου.
[2] Taanith, fol. 8 a.; Berachoth, fol. 5 a.; Wuensche on Luke 24. 26.
[3] Apollod. 3. 6. 7; 15. 4. Cf. Soph. *O. C.* 498; Athenæ. 13. 692; Paus. 4. 9. 4; Ovid. *Met.* 8. 483; *Fasti,* 6. 101, &c.

importance. It had its proper ideal in the Wise Man, unattainable indeed in his perfection, who hovers in the distance, but gives the norm, after which the seekers have to strive.' The monarchic head was the object of their aspiration.[1]

Seneca says: 'We should choose out some good man, and keep him ever before our eyes that we may live as in his sight and do all things as if he were looking on. This Epicurus teaches: he gave to us a guard and a pædagogue, and not without reason. A great many sins would be taken out of the way, if a witness were to stand by the would-be sinners. Let the soul have some one to reverence; by whose authority he may hallow even his innocent nature. O happy he who corrects not only appearances, but also thoughts! Happy he who can so revere some one, as to compose and order himself in accordance with his memory. He who can so revere another, will quickly be himself an object of reverence. Choose Cato, or if he be too rigid, choose Lælius. Choose him whose life and speech has pleased thee, setting before thee his soul and countenance. Point him out to thyself ever, whether as guardian or example. We need, I say, some one after whom our manners may be ruled. You will not correct evil except by a Rule.'[2]

'Could we look into the soul of a good man,' he exclaims, ' oh how fair a face, how holy, how splendid and gentle an effulgence! Here justice, there fortitude; here temperance and prudence shine.' The 'Wisdom of Solomon' says of Sophia, the mate of the soul, 'She teacheth temperance and prudence, justice and forti-

---

[1] *Christus und die Cäsaren*, 1879, p. 43. Cf. Havet, *Le Christianisime*, 4. 410, 2. 263 ff.; Harnack, *Hdb. d. Dogmgesch*, 80 ff.
[2] *Ep.* 11.

tude; which are such things as men can have nothing more profitable in their life.' 'Moreover,' continues Seneca, 'frugality, and continence, and temper (*tolerantia*), and liberty, and pleasantness, and, wondrous to say, that rare thing in human nature, humanity, would be seen to have poured their fine splendour upon him. Then thoughtfulness, then elegance, and of those qualities magnanimity most eminent; how much, good gods! of beauty, how much of weight and gravity would have been added! how much influence joined with grace! None would call him amiable, and deny him the description venerable. If any should see this appearance, more lofty and shining than is wont to be beheld in humanity, must he not fall back in amazement as if he had come in the way of a deity, and pray in silence that he may not have sinned in beholding! But then the kindliness of the expression beckons to him, he is drawn forward, he must adore and supplicate. He long contemplates that lofty figure, beyond the stature that you are wont to behold—that form elate, the eyes gleaming with mild yet living fire. At last he must, in fear and amazement, utter the well-known words of our Virgil:

"O quam te memorem virgo ! namque haud tibi vultus
Mortalis, nec vox hominem sonat.
Sis felix nostrumque leves quemcumque laborem."

'She will appear, she will relieve our toil, if we resolve to worship her. But she is worshipped not with the fat of slain bulls nor with offerings of gold and silver, but with a pious and upright disposition. No one, I say, but would glow with passion for her, could we but behold her. But now our gaze is daunted by excessive splendour, or is hampered with the darkness.'[1]

Seneca was a true poet; his dream-power is of the highest order. And, what is germane to our present subject, nothing ravishes him more than the contrast of his glorious spiritual ideal with conditions and circumstances of shame or suffering. 'If we will free the eye of the mind from impediments, we shall be able to behold virtue, though she is shattered in body, though she fronts poverty, though lowliness and infamy lie in her path. We shall discern, I say, that beauty, though in sordid wrappings,' even as its opposite, in spite of the false light of honour and power that may beat upon it. To be crucified, fettered, maimed, to offer oneself as a sacrifice; these are marks of the virtuous men, who toil for the great common weal of humanity.[2] 'If you see a man unterrified by dangers, untouched by desires, happy in adversity, calm in the midst of storms, looking down upon men from higher ground, from a level upon the gods, do you not feel veneration for him? Will you not say, This thing is too great and lofty to be believed like to this little body in which it is? A divine power has descended thither: an excellent soul under government, that passes over all things as if too small, smiling at all that we fear and desire, is stirred by heavenly power. So great a thing cannot stand without the aid of deity. For the most part it is yonder whence it came down. Even as the rays of the sun touch the earth, but are there whence they are sent; so a great and sacred soul, for this end sent down that we might more nearly apprehend divine things, converses indeed with us, but cleaves to its origin.

[1] *Ep.* 115.   [2] *De Provid.* c. 5. Cf. *De Benef.* 4. 22.

Thence it depends; thither it looks and strives; is present among ours as if of nobler nature.'[1] In the same epistle the indwelling of God—what God is uncertain—in the breast of every good man, is taught. 'God is near to thee, is with thee, is within thee. A sacred spirit has His seat within us, the observer and guardian of our evil and good; He treats us, according as He is treated by us. There is no good man without God.[2]

Seneca appears to be so engrossed with his ideal wise man that he can hardly allow him to be a mere product of the imagination, however rare so extraordinary an appearance may have been.[3] Cato in part realised this ideal. And the hope should be cherished of the future manifestation of this exalted form. 'There is some one whom nothing can conquer, one against whom fate has no power. This is according to the commonwealth of the human race.'[4]

It is clear that the Stoics, as represented by Seneca, were powerful fellow-workers in that great spiritual revolution which we have been tracing on the Jewish side. He who so powerfully preaches the truth of the indwelling God, sees that the conception of a law of external ordinances must give place to that of the inner law of love, written on the heart. The first article of religion is belief in the gods. Secondly, to render to them their majesty, to render goodness, without which there is no majesty. They who preside over the world, who guide the universe as their own, who discharge the protectorship of the human race, have an occasional care for individuals. They neither

---

[1] *Ep.* 41. Cf. *ad Marc.* 22.   [2] Cf. *Ep.* 83. 1.
[3] *Constant. Sap.* 7 and 14; *Ep.* 67.
[4] *Constant. Sap.* 19. "The longing for redemption and divine help is clearer in Seneca than in the Christian philosopher Min. Felix."—Harnack, u. s. 85, n. 1.

inflict nor suffer evil. But they chastise some and restrain, and inflict punishment, and sometimes punish under the form of evil. 'Dost thou desire to propitiate the gods? Be good. He that imitates them, worships them enough. The second question is, how we should behave to men. What is our way of dealing with this? What precepts do we give? To spare human blood? A small thing not to injure the man you ought to profit! A great praise forsooth, if man is kind to man! Shall we teach the duty of stretching out a hand to the shipwrecked, showing the way to the wanderer, dividing one's loaf with the hungry? When shall I say all that is to be done and avoided? Briefly this formula of human duty I can deliver: All this that thou seest in which divine and human things are included, is one. Members we are of a great body. Nature made us akin, for she produced us from the same source and for the same ends. She implanted in us mutual love, and made us sociable. She composed the equal and just. According to her constitution it is more wretched to hurt than to be injured. According to her command, assisting hands have been furnished. Let the verse be in your heart and in your mouth:

"Homo sum, humani nihil a me alienum puto."[1]

We may observe in passing that Plutarch, who satirises the Stoics, has some very similar teaching on the duty of 'Brotherly Love' (*philadelphia*), which also presents in parts a very close analogy to the ethical teaching of the New Testament. But while the close coincidence of the thought and even of the language of the philosophers with that of the New

[1] *Ep.* 95. Cf. *De Ira*, 1. 13.

Testament should be fully recognised, and the fair historical inferences be drawn that the philosophers did much to form the Christians: on the other hand, the fine differences in sentiment and in the mode of intuition should be equally considered. The life-ideal determines the theology; but the life-ideal itself is determined by the belief in the possibilities of human nature. And in general, it will not be denied that the Stoic has a lofty confidence in human nature which distinguishes him from both the Jewish moralist and the Epicurean. What we understand by the Christian ideal seems, according to the fine criticism of Pascal, to occupy an intermediate position between that of the Stoic and of the Epicurean, in this respect.

No one, however, can busy himself with the rich volume of Seneca's moral teaching, comparing it with the New Testament, and holding aloof the unhappy polemics of the apologists, without perceiving how much we owe to the joint spiritual efforts of inspired Romans, Greeks, and Jews. The Christianity of the Heart that all good men love is here. Citing Hecaton, Seneca says, *Si vis amari, ama*. This is the innoxious *amatorium* or philtre. 'For what purpose do I make a friend? That I may have one for whom I may die, one whom I may follow into exile, to whose death I may oppose and spend my own.'[1] 'Thou shalt love thy neighbour beyond thine own soul,' says the 'Epistle of Barnabas.'[2]

But to return to the specifically theological question. Not only did Seneca and his fellow-labourers, by their enthusiastic elaboration of the ideal of goodness and wisdom prepare the way for the belief in an actual Incarnation: on the other hand, their lax and

---

[1] *Ep.* 9.   [2] 19. 5. Cf. 1. 4, 4. 6.

latitudinarian theology offered no resistance to that new theology destined to be gradually shaped into the dogma of the Trias or Trinity.

Seneca represents the like reaction against the poetic and popular conception of Jove to that which went on among the Gnostics against the wrathful God of the Old Testament. He sought to explain the anthropomorphic pictures in the poets as the result of 'poetic licence.' They believed, he says, in the same Jove that we believe in, the guardian and ruler of the universe, a soul and spirit, the lord and artificer of this mundane work. Every name is suitable to Him. 'You would call Him fate? you will not err. He is the Cause of Causes; on Him all things are hung. You would say that He is Providence? You will say rightly. For He it is, by whose counsel this world is provided for, that it may go unshaken on its course, and unfold its acts. You would call Him Nature? You will not sin. It is He, from whom all things have sprung, by whose spirit we live. You will call Him the world? You will not be deceived. For Himself is the whole you see, He is whole and enters into His parts; He sustains Himself by His own force. The Etruscans thought the same; and therefore said that bolts were sent by Jove, because nothing goes on without Him.'[1]

This is not a historical account of Roman religion, which can only be understood, as we apprehend, by reference to the local and tribal principle, according to which each deity was once held by his community to be the universal god, operating alike in Nature and in human life. Here national barriers are broken down, Jove is no longer fixed in his Capitoline seat,

[1] *Nat. Qu.* 2. 45.

but becomes the universal lord of Nature and of man. The universalism of the Roman confronts the universalism of the Jew. The one speaks of Providence, and gives a noble word to our theological thesaurus. The other thinks, according to the habit of his imagination, of a divine law published to the whole world by angelic mediation. But the refined Deism or Pantheism of Seneca could not be an acceptable creed among the vulgus; and without constant regard to the instincts of the vulgus the growth of religious communities can at no period be understood. The religious and moral views of Seneca and those parts of the New Testament which correspond to them are still comparatively unpopular. His books are beloved in the study and by the unworldly recluse. He condescends too little to ordinary flesh and blood, which still must have its ideals presented in flesh and blood, if they are to be owned at all. Pale and ghostly, cold and unattractive to ordinary minds, as we apprehend, must seem his Ideal in comparison with the vivid Messianic form of the New Testament. Nearer is the comparison with Philo and the Alexandrians, with their Logos and their Sophia, as mediators between the human and the divine. But as yet we have not found the ideal of *the* Mediator brought down to *terra firma*, and indelibly marked with the traces of suffering, not to speak of penal suffering, which is central in Christian conception after the second century. When Bruno Bauer remarks that 'the later combination of the Oriental and the Occidental, of the Jew and the Roman, of Philo and Seneca, of the Logos of Heracleitus and the Stoical Wise Man produced the animated Form, which was sought for on both sides,' he seems too much to ignore the great classical passages in the later 'Isaiah,' which give the first distinct sketch of that form. We know of no class of men during the second century who looked upon Seneca as a prophet, and assumed that his forecasts must by supernatural necessity have been fulfilled. But this we do know, that the nameless 'apostles and prophets' of the time did so think of the current 'Scriptures' of their own people. There were trained minds among Jewish scholars, doubtless, who could distinguish between ideal painting and historical description or forecast; but the teachers who were listened to then, as in every time, were the men who could assure their disciples that every picture in sacred poetry was drawn from the life, seen by the telescopic vision of the inspired writer.

THE SUFFERING MESSIAH.

Although the idea that great suffering purifies and refines the mind, and has redeeming efficacy upon others, may be said to belong to universal religion, and need not have been excluded from the Jewish ideal of the Messiah, the cursed death upon the tree was certainly abhorrent to that ideal. The words put into the mouth of Tryphon the Jew illustrate this feeling.[1]

It is important, therefore, to inquire what light our early literature, apart from the New Testament, throws upon this subject.

In 'Barnabas,' as we have seen, the theoretic necessity is that the 'Son of God' should have come in the flesh, that He might consummate the sins of the persecutors of the prophets, that He might abolish death, and show forth the resurrection.

In proof he cites prophets and psalms: the ideas,

---

[1] Justin M., *Dial.* 80 ff., 96 ff.

under this imperious necessity of thought, are equivalent to historic facts. But his citations are vague reminiscences, as it seems, of prophetic fragments. 'When they shall strike their own shepherd, the sheep of the fold shall perish.' This means: the 'blow of his flesh' is from those persecutors.[1] The Son of God willed to suffer; and it was necessary that He should suffer, that He might suffer on wood! By a similar senseless jumble of texts, or fragments of them, from the LXX., the writer seeks to prove that it had been predicted that the 'Son of God' should be put to death, not with the sword, but by crucifixion.[2]

It would have been strange, indeed, if the writer had not used for his purpose the great ideal of the 'Servant of the Lord' in the Prophet Isaiah. The writer maintains that in Isa. 53. 'some things are written for Israel, some for us,' meaning that he and his fellow-religionists alone understand the true sense of this Scripture. It is that 'the Lord endured to deliver His flesh to destruction, that by the remission of sins we might be sanctified, which is in the blood of His sprinkling.' Here he does not speak of the 'servant of the Lord;' but elsewhere he reads this title ($\pi\alpha\hat{\imath}s$) into a passage where it does not exist, Isa. 50. 8.[3] Again he says, 'The Spirit of the Lord prophesies: who is he who would live for ever? *by hearing let him hear the voice of my servant.*'[4] The latter words are not to be found in the Bible.

Where we have to deal with a reckless inaccuracy of this kind, creating evidence where it does not exist, the only course is to note the recurrence of the fixed

---

[1] 12. 6. Cf. Isa. 53. 5; Zech. 13. 7.   [2] 5. 12 ff.
[3] 6. 1. See the references for $\pi\alpha\hat{\imath}s$ in Gebh. and Harn.'s note.
[4] 9. 2.

ideas in favour of which such feats were performed. One of these is the voluntary *endurance* of the ideal sufferer.[1] The word runs through some documents probably of about the same date. 'Jesus Christ *endured* to suffer;'[2] He '*endured* for our sins even unto death;' to '*endure* to suffer all things.'[3]

One might say that *Hypomoné, patience*, implying constancy and hope, is a cardinal virtue of Jewish saintdom. 'The Lord is good to them that call upon Him in patience,' says the Psalter of Solomon, which dates shortly after the death of Pompey, and contains the first formal expression of Messianism.[4] It is a book of the Hagioi, who look forward to dwelling in Jerusalem under their king, 'the Christ of the Lord,' or 'Anointed Lord.' Well, therefore, to the Messianists might their expected Head be the impersonation of steadfastness in suffering, crowned by a glorious issue. For if the two things were constantly connected in thought, even as cause and effect,—courage with patience and the realisation of long hopes,—this connection must be necessarily transferred to the personal ideal. The Messiah, as the servant in Isa. 53., must reflect the character of suffering Israel itself. But we can hardly suppose, from anything that is known of the Messianic ideal of the Jews, that the idea of a Messiah suffering actual death[5] could have gained much ground among them until the days of horror and despair which followed upon the defeat of Barcochebas, the flight to Bettar, the abandonment of the holy city to the Romans, and the 'abomination of desolation;'

---

[1] $\dot{\upsilon}\pi o\mu\acute{e}\nu\omega$, 5. 5, 6.   [2] 2 *Clem.* 1. 2.

[3] Polycp. *ad Phil.* 1. 2; J. Martyr, *Dial.* 121.

[4] Hilgenf. *Messias Jud.* 1869; A. Carrière, *De Psalt. Sal.* 1870.

[5] Cf. Edersheim, *Life of Jesus*, 1. 164 f.: 'all is indistinct, incoherent.'

when the illusions respecting the king in Jerusalem must have passed away. Nay (to quote Havet), 'le regne de Jehova était fini.'[1]

It is to the time immediately following that we must, according to all indications, refer the ignorant and insolent polemic of such men as the author of 'Barnabas' against Jewish rites and institutions, and the rise of the 'scandal of the Cross.' The old enmity of Greeks and Jews was intensified by the fact that the latter had now to deal with foes of their own household. Men of Jewish blood and education must have conspired to cast the odium of the murder of the Messiah and His accursed death upon the ancestors of the afflicted race. Hate can cement and idealise as well as love; and it seems that we can only understand how the Cross should have become the symbol on the one hand of indelible shame, a stone of stumbling and a rock of offence, on the other of immortal love, in the light of this principle. We who from childhood have been wont to revere the Cross as the sign of salvation by divine love, rather than as the monument of human blindness and hate, must in the light of the evidence reverse this view. For it must be repeated, we know nothing earlier respecting the fact or the dogma of the Cross than the Cabbalistic absurdities of 'Barnabas,' and the unproven statements and sophistries of Justin of Neapolis. No rational exegesis can find the Cross in the Old Testament. And it is to us at least inconceivable that had these writers possessed the accounts that we possess of the crucifixion, they would not have used them, when in search of taunts and reproaches to hurl at the Jews. If the account in 'Barnabas' of the Cross is our

[1] *Le Christianisme*, 3. 329.

oldest, then it proves negatively that a historical crucifixion was by our oldest source belonging to the 'New People' ignored; and positively that it was sought to make it historical by absurd and reckless perversions of Scriptures and rabbinical traditions. The probable explanation of the theory of a crucified Jesus is the use of the sign upon the forehead at baptism and on other occasions,[1] and this seems to have been derived from the religion of Mithras.[2] Incredible as it seems at first sight to modern habits of thought that from such a hint a historic construction should have been raised, it will not so appear to those who have once familiarised themselves with the fictitious and baseless reasoning of these documents. The habit of the time, the only resource from the anguish of doubt, was on both sides Belief. The Rabbi Akiba, the inspiring genius of the Barcocheban insurrection, was a great teacher of faith. The faith in the promises to the fathers and the election of Israel is now confronted by the faith of the New People in their destiny as the true heirs of the promise. It was the greatest religious crisis the world has witnessed. Both parties had but one court of appeal,—the Scriptures and the traditions of the elders. The rabbins, the Haggadists, and Cabbalists had forged a two-edged weapon of exegesis which was turned against their own bosoms. The educated world is now waking up to

---

[1] Tert. *De Coron. mil.* 3; *De Præscr. H.* 40.

[2] The whole subject of the archæology of the Cross would need to be examined here, J. Lipsius, *De Cruce.* But it is at least clear that the mystic efficacy of the *Signaculum* made on the Brow so habitually, doubtless as aversive of evil spirits, was the immediate cause of the ascendency of the Cross over Christian imagination. The Cross in connection with the σφραγίς in Baptism among the Gnostics, R. A. Lipsius, *Die Apocryph. Acten.*

understand by what false means the New People or *Christiani* contrived to push their way in the second century. And surely the solemn lesson arises out of those studies that the partial and passionate perversion of literature to our own ends, or in favour of our own belief, is one of the gravest offences we can commit against the cause of humanity, and is certain sooner or later to be avenged. We cannot but figure to ourselves the mute indignation with which sound Jewish scholars must have listened to such sophistries as those of 'Barnabas' and 'Justin;' and yet they must have felt something akin to remorse when they reflected that this very spirit of solemn trifling about sacred things had been nurtured in their own schools. The best of the 'Gospel' finds an echo in the Talmud; but the worst of the apologetic characteristics among the Christiani find also their reflection in that medley.

We dwell upon the dogma of the suffering Christos because it seems clear that here is the indication of the great crisis of the second century. The new people, no longer adhering to the old prophetic doctrine of remission of sins in the mercy of God, conditioned by repentance and good works, are beginning to proclaim that remission is by blood, the blood of one who fell a crucified victim to Jewish hate. We must again remind our readers that this dogma is not to be found in the *Didaché* and parallel documents, which we have termed documents of the Hagioi; and can but generally infer that the fading away of beloved Jewish appellations like 'saints and elect' before the name *Christiani* was coincident with the rise of this new doctrine of a vicarious Messiah, or rather *Christos*, whose identification with the Messiah of the Jews appears to have been never other than artificial, and of mere verbal suggestion. The descended, dying, rising, ascending god belongs rather to Hellenic and Persian intuition and belief.

THE BLOOD OF CHRIST.

Let us turn to the 'Epistles of Clement.' (1. 7. 3.)

On the duty of Repentance the writer says, 'Let us attend to what is good, pleasing, and acceptable in the sight of Him who made us.' And in the next sentence but one, 'From generation to generation the Lord granted a place of repentance to those willing to be converted to Him.' The examples of Noah and Jonah are cited. But after the first exhortation the following is thrust in: *'Let us gaze steadfastly at the Blood of Christ, and see how precious it is to God and His Father, because poured out for our salvation it brought to all the world grace of repentance.'* This has nothing to do with the context, as the reader who consults the tenor of the epistle may easily satisfy himself. It is a piece of new cloth on an old garment.

The same remark applies to 12. 7, where to the story of Rahab as an example of faith and hospitality is added the absurdity that *the scarlet thread signified redemption through the blood of the Lord for them that believe and hope in God.* 'Ye see, beloved, there was not only faith but prophecy in the woman.' The patch is as glaring as in the former case.

In c. 21, amidst the gentle precepts of humility, with similar irrelevance the exhortation occurs, 'Let us reverence the Lord Jesus Christ, whose blood was given for us.' In c. 49, amidst praises of Love as a virtue which unites men to God, covers a multitude of sins, perfects the elect, the statement occurs, *'On account of the love He bore us, Jesus Christ our Lord gave His blood for us by the will of God; His flesh for our flesh, and His soul for our souls.'*

In the very next chapter we read: 'Blessed are we, beloved, if we keep the commandments of God in the harmony of love; that so *through love our sins may be forgiven us.*' Citing Ps. 32. 1, 2, 'This blessedness cometh upon those who have been chosen by God through Jesus Christ our Lord.' And again in c. 52 : 'The Lord of all stands in need of nothing, and desires nothing of any one but that confession be made to Him.' We pretend to no faculty of 'higher criticism,' but only to ordinary judgment. And it seems clear to us that the doctrine of a merciful Father in heaven who desires only the repentance of the sinner belongs to an entirely different theology from that which insists on a vicarious victim as required by Him. Modern theologians have never been able to reconcile in one system, the Scriptures which look in these opposite directions; and the whole theory of vicarious atonement is unintelligible until it is recognised that the offering is made to a devilish infernal being, until we adopt the explanation in Basil and Origen of the sacrifice of Christ as a ransom paid to the devil. This is the old belief of Greek religions; and nothing can be more alien to the spirit of the refined piety of the Jewish Hagioi. He who desires not the death of a sinner, but rather that he should turn to Him and live, could never be thought of as exacting the flesh and soul of an innocent victim on the sinner's behalf, or as bestowing the grace of repentance through the contemplation of the precious Blood. That those who love much are forgiven much is a beautiful thought, true to those primary intuitions in the light of which the Divine can alone be truly conceived. They 'perform a saintlike sorrow; pay down more penitence than do trespass;' they may 'forget their evil; do as the Heavens have done, forgive themselves.'

We leave it to the judgment of readers who have studied the epistle as a whole, whether the passages relating to the Blood of Christ are not foreign to the tenor of its general teaching.

In the second chapter we have a strange passage which speaks of the 'sufferings of God'[1] being before their eyes. This may be compared with the 'suffering of God' and the 'blood of God' in the 'Ignatian' epistles, and in some of the Greek apologists.[2] No one writer who had any due sense of the value of terms could thus have spoken of one whom he was to speak of in the same epistle as chosen of God, sent of God, high-priest and protector of men.[3] Here again are the traces of patching, due to polemical theology. To speak of the sufferings of Christ as the sufferings of God, to insist that Christ must be thought of as of God;[4] to say that He was 'sent as God,'[5] or as artificer and demiurge, not as angel or ruler: these things savour of the fourth century rather than the second—in other words, of a Hellenic theology.[6]

We have hitherto been engaged with conceptions of the 'Son of God' or of 'the Lord,' or of 'the beloved Jesus,' much too poor and lowly for the upholders of the new 'Theology of Christ.' With reference to this theology, the commentators on 2 Clem. I. I remark that it is not clear whether a merely Ebionite theology, or one that is Gnostic, Ebionite, or modalistic Ebionite,

---

[1] αὐτοῦ, ver. 1.
[2] Ad Rom. 6; ad Eph. 1; Melito, Fragm. VII.; Tatian c. Græc. 13.
[3] Chaps. 42, 58.   [4] 2 Clem. I. I.
[5] Diogn. 7. 4.   [6] Ib. 7. 2.

is opposed; but that this is certain, the theology in question existed in the Church of Corinth as well as among certain hæretics.[1]

The Ebionites, and those we have spoken of generally as the Hagioi, must have felt that to think too highly of the Son of God, to make Him equal with God, was to infringe upon the ineffable Majesty, was to commit blasphemy. Greek theologians had no such scruples. According to Pausanias, a contemporary witness, in the happy days of yore gods were born from mortals; and gods might and did suffer, according to strong popular belief. The Hero was the blessed Departed, and the Hero might be raised to the rank of deity, in recognition of his sufferings and trials for the human race. There was nothing in Greek or Roman theology to hinder, all to favour the assumption of an ideal Christus into the popular pantheon. Later history shows how facile the process was. But to educated Jewish piety such a process of deification must have seemed precisely the same kind of process by which the Cæsars were raised to deity. The transition from the idea of a suffering Servant or Son of God to a suffering Anointed seems great; greater still to the idea of an Anointed who is a vicarious victim; greatest of all to the idea of a suffering God, the Judge of the world. The latter is developed Greek *Christianism* as opposed to *Judaism* or Ebionæism, or the teaching of the Hagioi, apostles and prophets of the second century.

We need only advert in passing to the distasteful mysticism of the 'Ignatian' epistles, where the blood of Christ is spoken of as if identical with 'love' and 'grace.' Here the words *Christianismos* and *Judaismos*

[1] Gebh. and Harn., *ad l.*

appear: words apparently of later origin than the second century.

THE RESURRECTION OF THE DEAD AND THE END OF THE WORLD.

The references to the risen Christ are slight in our early literature; and an emphasis is not laid upon the fact equal to that laid upon the Cross and the sufferings. As we have seen, there is no organic connection between the life of the believer and the resurrection of Christ; but He is firstfruits of the general resurrection, by logical consequence from that belief. The belief itself appears to have come from Persian Mazdeism more than from any other source;[1] even as the Messianic ideas in the Talmud are strongly coloured by Persian influences.[2] The idea of a Messiah, or Anointed of Jehovah, is in the Psalms; but not the idea of a risen Messiah. Indeed the passages in the Old Testament, which in any sense contemplate a future revival, are so few and slight that the Pharisees in conflict with the Sadducees were constrained to resort to general analogies in defence of the belief.[3]

The belief of the Mages, with whom some Greek writers associated the Jews as their descendants,[4] was that men should live again and be immortal in a new era; to be ushered in by the glorious Çaoshyant, slayer of dæmons. Then should the dead arise. We have seen how Justin Martyr is haunted by the analogy of the Mithraic initiations to the Lord's Supper, and by the idea of the Cave. So does Tertullian seem haunted by the *Imago Resurrectionis* in the religion

---

[1] Darmesteter, *Ormazd et Ahriman*, 1877, pp. 226, 328.
[2] Wuensche, *Neue Beiträge*, 301.   [3] Ib. 258.
[4] Theopomp. in Diog. Lart. *Proœm.* 6. 9; Plut. *Is. et Os.* 370.

of Mithras, who 'signs his soldiers on the brow' (apparently in the *lavacrum*) and 'celebrates the oblation of the bread.'[1]

It is well known that the resurrection of the dead was also an Egyptian belief. In Greece Asklépios was said to have raised many famous heroes from the dead. But in all cases a select resurrection seems alone to have been meant, of saints or heroes; and the event belonged to that imaginative distance in past or future where all marvels become credible. The persuasion itself seems to have rested on the still more impassioned persuasion of the approach of the 'world to come,' in the language of the rabbins, of the 'golden age' in that of Gentile poetry.[2]

'Let grace come, and let this world pass away,'[3] is an Eucharistic prayer of the Hagioi; and it is the expectation of the end which imparts solemnity to moral exhortations. But this expectation of the approaching dissolution of the present world or age was not confined to the saints of the Dispersion. Lucretius had given warning that at any moment it might be seen tumbling in ruin: might fortune avert (he exclaims) this event in his time![4] A single day should give up all to destruction. On that day, echoes Ovid, the songs of the sublime Lucretius will perish. The time would come when sea and earth and sky would be set aflame, when the massive framework of things would be dissolved.[5]

Destruction will not be long delayed, says Seneca, who thinks that the world will perish by an irruption

---

[1] *Præscr.* 40; cf. Havet, *Le Christianisme* 4. 116; Orelli, 2352, 6041.
[2] Cf. Wuensche on Matt. 16. 28, and Luke 20. 36 ff.
[3] *Didaché*, 10. 6.   [4] 5. 91 ff.
[5] *Amores* I. 15, 23; *Met.* I. 256. Cf. Lucan, I. 79; Manil. 2. 807.

of waters. When the human race has perished, and that of beasts, the waters will again be absorbed, the sea will retire within its bounds, and the ancient order will be recalled. Human beings born under better auspices, and innocent of crime, will be given to the lands. Yet this innocence will not endure long. Wickedness quickly steals in; virtue is hard to find, it yearns for a guide and leader; while faults are learned without a teacher.[1]

A century later, Tertullian says, 'We pray for the delay of the end,'[2] in the assembly and congregation. During the second century, then, the tension of the hopes and fears connected with the expected end must have been extreme; and a corresponding pessimism coloured men's views of the present world. A spirit of renunciation in reference to transitory things, a longing to be delivered from the fetters of mortality, and from 'this present evil world,' pervaded not only the minds of the saints and elect, but of those who had imbibed the wisdom of the Greeks. When men are satisfied with the course of things, with life as it is, the soul seems to slumber, and to lose the proper sense of her divine dignity. When the outward world wearies and disappoints, the inner world of imagination opens in all its splendour and promise, and offers to the soul conquests of which it can be robbed by no chance nor change. We have but to imagine ourselves possessed for a moment by similar beliefs, to understand how what we commonly call the real world faded into the dim background for the early believers, and how the foreground of contemplation was occupied by the persons of a divine drama in course of enactment in celestial places.

CHAPTER IX.

THE GNOSTIC THEOLOGY [1]—THE 'APOSTLE OF THE HAERETICS.'

THE distinguished teachers who pass under the general name of Gnostics, known to us as they are almost exclusively through the bitter attacks of narrow-minded ecclesiasts, must have exerted a deep and abiding influence upon the forming belief of the second century. Stones, as the proverb runs, are never thrown but at the fruit-laden tree; and the evidence of Irenæus and Tertullian's polemic goes to show that these men were of powerful and glowing genius, who knew how to give satisfaction to the thirst for knowledge which the Ecclesia failed to supply.[2] The hierarchy has always aimed at keeping the congregation in a state of childlike simplicity, and has shown jealousy of the disturbing element of intellect. We know not how to account for the extreme irritation manifested against confessedly eminent men like Marcion, except by referring to their superior reach and audacity of speculation. Those who imbibed their spirit could hardly be content with that mere practice of faith, humility, and virtue in general, together with strict obedience to

[1] Cf. Harnack, *Hdb. d. Dogmgesch.*, 1886, p. 162.
[2] See the testimony of Jerome, *Comm. in Osce*, 2. 10, p. 106, cited by Harn. 163.

their ecclesiastical superiors, which is recommended in our early literature, especially in 'Ignatius.'

We glance only at the leading features of the Christian Gnosis; it must be remembered that early in the second century the Gnostics shared the name of *Christiani*, as Justin bears witness, and were teachers of the new Revelation long before him.[1]

The great romance of Simon Magus arrests attention as a fanciful effort on the part of the enemies of the sect of Simonians to explain its rise. Justin Martyr refers his activity to Rome during Claudius' reign, about a hundred years before the time of his writing, and ignorantly confuses him with Semo Sancus, as we have seen. The whole account of him is a manifest myth, in which, as usual, general ideas are represented in a personal and dramatic manner. Justin saw in Simon Magus and his disciple Menander, both of Samaria, a land of mixed Jewish and heathen population,[2] a rival to the Christ, among others who said they were gods, or sons of Jove. The Helena who followed him and who had been a prostitute, according to the tale, really represents the soul and its humiliation.[3] When it is stated that Simon called her his first *Ennoia* or Intuition,[4] we see how the allegory breaks down and reveals the bare *idea* which was the foundation of the whole tale. The soul, an emanation of Deity, confined to earth and to a mortal form, be-

---

[1] *Apol.* I. 26. Also *Orig. c. Cels.* 5.

[2] On the Synkretism of Jewish, Babylonian, Persian, Syrian, Hellenic religions out of which the Universal and Absolute Religion arose. Cf. Harnack, 178 f. We hold, on the evidence, that Christianity was this religion.

[3] Iren. I. 23. 2 ; Hippol. *Philos.* 6. 14. Cf. Bauer, *Christus*, 311.

[4] Cf. the similar scoff at the *Pronoia* or Providentia of the Stoics, as an 'old woman,' in Cic. *N. D.* I.

comes in poetry a beautiful woman detained in a brothel, not without hope of deliverance by the wooer or bridegroom. It is this pathos of the Soul which imparts so peculiar a charm to the old tale of Amor and Psyché, and kindred popular tales, where the betrothed, owing to the commission of some unwitting fault, is forsaken by the husband, wanders about in search of him, and is finally reunited to him. Helena of Troy is perhaps an example of a similar spiritual tale used for purposes of historical fiction. Stesichorus gave a 'docetic' explanation of her flight to Troy; it was only her *eidôlon* which went thither. When tale-telling is carried too far, we need to be reminded, as the simple folk say at the close of a feerie, 'I was not there nor you neither, so you need not believe it.' It is one of the worst perversions of the poem or the ideal story when it is made to pass for historic fact, with person and place and specious accessories, as in the polemical romance of Simon Magus. In its developed form in the 'Clementines,' it is Paul who is said to be attacked under the mask of Simon, and Peter is his antagonist.[1] Justin knows nothing of Paul, but he names Marcion immediately after Simon and Menander; and it is in connection with Marcion that we hear for the first time of Paul, whose name has come down to us as the representative of the great anti-Judaistic or anti-nomian movement in early Christianity. It may suggest itself for inquiry whether the Thecla with whom Paul is associated in the 'Acts of Paul and Thecla' is not in some sort a repetition of the Helena of Simon.'[2]

---

[1] See *Supernat. Relig.* 6th ed. p. 34. But more probably Marcion is aimed at, Loman, *Quæst. Paul. Theol. Tijdsch.* 1883.

[2] Also perhaps Philumené, the associate of Apelles. Cf. Tertull.

About the Gnostics in general our earliest informant is Irenæus (c. 140–202), a determined opponent of the Hellenic spirit; especially of that polytheism or relative monotheism which under new names the Gnostics were bringing back. They represented the religious revolution as a war of gods: the god of the Jews or Demiurge (Creator) being lowered in rank and distinguished from the supreme and true or 'good' God.[1] The secret spring of this innovation we can but trace to Hellenic jealousy of the Jews and their Law and Prophets, and to a passionate recalcitration against its impositions, whether circumcision or the ascetic regulations for the proselytes of the Gate. To establish a rival theology, to claim the true knowledge of the Supreme as their own, to invent a new category of mediatorial beings or Aeons: all this was to supersede the Old Testament and to claim the spiritual empire for the Greeks. And it still remains a moot question whether the forms of Christian dogma at the end of the second century owed more to the Gnosis of imaginative Greeks, or to the Midrasch of imaginative Hebrews. The cultus, on the other hand, had its origin in Hellenic, combined with Persian and Syrian forms.

According to Irenæus, the Nicolaitans and their successor Cerinthus (c. 115) must have been busy from the beginning of that century in their work of exalting the new religion over Judaism. What was the new

De Bapt. 17, on the author who wrote *Amore Pauli.* On the 'holy sisters of Marcion,' Tert. *Adv. M.* 5. 8; Iren. 1. 13, 5. 6 (Marcus and the deacon's wife).

[1] The Greek and Platonist character of the Gnosis is strongly emphasised by Joel, *Blicke*, 1. 101–170. On its practical side, as a Mystery related to the ancient Mysteries, Koffmane, *Die Gnosis*, &c., 1881; Weingarten, *Hist. Zeitschr.*, 1881, 461 f.

religion? Here for the first time, as far as we can discover, the figure of 'Jesus of Nazareth, son of Joseph and Mary,' *not* of a virgin, comes into view. He was not Christ; but Christ, one of the Aeons or emanations of the Divine Being, which together constituted His Pleroma or fulness, was caused to descend on Jesus at His baptism in the form of a dove. Through the mouth of Jesus, the Aeon Christ proclaimed the true God; but quitted Him before His death, and had no part in His passion or resurrection.[1] It was, then, a *doctrine* of the true God which Cerinthus set store by; and it was as inconsistent with his theory of a celestial being that he should suffer, or should even be born, as in the case of the analogous emanations in the system of Philo. The descent of a spiritual being into the first Teacher at His baptism appears to have been the oldest mode of conceiving of the beginning of the Gospel; and it is itself, perhaps, an inference from the belief in the entrance of the new soul in baptism. That Jesus was the son of Joseph and Mary appears also to have been the old belief.[2] The centre of activity of Nicolaos and of Cerinthus was probably Antioch; while Antioch is connected with Samaria through Saturninus, who was said to have been under the influence of Simon and Menander, the Samaritans.[3] Cerdo the Syrian was under similar influences.[4]

In all these teachers the doctrine of the unbeginning and unknowable God, the Creator of angels or Aeons, ministerial and mediatorial powers, excluded the supremacy of the God of the Jews, and not only His supre-

[1] Iren. 1. 26; Hippol. 7. 33.
[2] In Carpocrates' system, Iren. 1. 25. 5. On Carpocrates' son, Epiphanes, whose *apotheosis* was celebrated by the Kephallenians, Clem. Alex. *Strom.* 3. 2. 5.
[3] Iren. 1. 23, 24.   [4] Iren. 1. 27. Cf. Hippol. 7. 37.

macy but His goodness. He was 'just,' not in the modern sense of the word, but in the old sense of the arbitrariness, of the right founded on possession, of local deities. And consistently with that Persian dualism which governs these conceptions, and which recognised the dominion and works of Satan in marriage and procreation, it was hardly possible to find a place for the Demiurge except in the category of evil beings. The redemption of the soul from its fallen earthly state, the recovery of its pre-existent blessedness, was the governing thought in these systems; and it appears, especially in the system of Carpocrates, that Jesus was honoured in company with Greek philosophers as one of the typical examples of the upward striving soul in its resistance to the powers of the present evil world;[1] even as the descent of a divine power upon Jesus is typical of the descent of a like power upon chosen souls.[2] In the system of Basilides, Christ, so far from being the Messias of the Jews, was the firstborn Nous of the unbegotten Father, and His mission was to deliver the faithful from subjection to the ruling powers of this world. To believe in 'the crucified one' was still to be under the dominion of those powers. The Nous did not endure to be crucified: Simon of Cyrene, transfigured, was substituted in his stead; or the crucifixion was illusory. This elation of mind toward the spiritual, this disdain of the senses, characterises all the Gnostics. Puffed up in the possession of *gnosis*, they disparaged mere *pistis* or faith, and denied the necessity of works to salvation.[3] They carried on

[1] Iren. I. 25. 6. 'A likeness of Christ was made by Pilate.' We shall see reason to believe that it was through the Gnostics the tradition of Pilate was preserved.

[2] Iren. I. 24. 3 f.

[3] Men are saved by grace, and actions are indifferent. Iren. I. 23. 3.

the old Mysteries in a more refined form; for the Mysteries aimed at the purification of the soul from the fleshly nature as a condition of future blessedness; and initiation had the efficacy of a sacrament. The rites practised by some of the Gnostics and termed by their opponents magic,[1] and the promise to their followers of immortality, indicate the continuance of the old secret rites over which Pausanias draws the veil of reverential silence, but which we know from his and other contemporary testimony, continued to exert a purifying influence upon the general conscience. From this point of view, indeed, it may be said that the Gnostics, sharing the universalistic aspirations of the time, sought to establish a new Mystery and a new Revelation, in which new names were engrafted upon the old Hellenic basis.[2]

The name Sôtér or Saviour,[3] so frequently predicated of the old Hellenic gods, is given in the system of Valentinus to Jesus, also called Christ and Logos and the great high-priest. He is the common fruit of the Pleroma or complement of Aeons, the leading ogdoad, or the four pairs,—Nous, Alétheia, Bathos, Sigé, Logos, Zoé, Anthropos, Ecclesia. These attempts at a logical structure under the forms of persons and generation remind of the old theogony.[4] From the last-named pair proceeds Sophia, who in solitary impotence gives birth to an abortion (ἔκτρωμα). This seems a

---

[1] The charge of magic was brought against Jesus. Justin, *Dial.* 69. Cf. *Celsus in Orig.* 2. 50. 51; Clem. *Recog.* 1. 58.

[2] Cf. the *Pistis Sophia*, Köstlin, *Theol. Jahrb.* 1854; Baur, *Gesch. d. Christl. K.* 1. 205; Lippert, *Christen-thum*, 105.

[3] The Saviour—for they do not call him Lord—did no work in public for thirty years, thus setting forth the mystery of the thirty Aeons, Iren. 1. 1. 3, 1. 2. 6.

[4] Irenæus dwells on this, 2. 14.

confession of the inadequacy of philosophy. But from the first pair proceed Christ and the Holy Spirit, and Christ gives form to the abortion of Sophia.

The Sôtér Jesus is sent by the Pleroma to deliver the wandering Sophia Achamoth, in her sadness, fear, and perplexity. Here is the same idea at bottom as that of the Helena of Simon, or rather of the Jesus of Simon's teaching. These tales may be regarded as 'Parables for the multitude,'[1] rather than as Dogmata in the Gnostic teaching, which aimed above all at an Ascetic and a Life. But not to confuse ourselves amidst these allegorical dream-theorems, the governing thought is still that of the opposition of the pneumatic or higher life in man to the lower, the hylic or material and the psychic life. And this, theologically and dramatically, is the opposition of the Saviour Jesus in whom all the Pleroma of the true God and Father dwells, to the Demiurge Jehovah. The soul is lost in the embrace of matter and longs for redemption and return to the spiritual, its pre-existent state. And this redemption is accomplished by the revelation of the mystery, hidden from the natural man, to the psychic in man, that he may become a pneumatic man.[2] According to this old tripartite psychology, the lower natures are from the Demiurge, the pneumatic is from Sophia. Jesus was psychic until His baptism, when the Sôtér descended on Him.[3] So Heracleon taught. The law and the prophets partake of the inferior nature of the Lawgiver, the Demiurge; and He deceived men when He asserted, I am God and there is none other!

It is impossible not to feel that the Aeonian poem

---

[1] See the instructive passage from Galen in Gieseler, *K. Gesch.* I. I, 4th ed. p. 167, cited by Harnack, *Hdb.* 170.
[2] Iren. I. 6.   [3] Cf. Baur, *Die Christl. Gnosis*, 123 ff.

of Valentinus was the epic of a great revolution in the minds of men, bearing as little relation to actual history as Milton's great epic. The facts of a hundred years before Valentinus we cannot find conveyed by any continuous tradition: merely the belief that a drama in the celestial places had found about that date a *dénouement* in Galilee and Judæa, the tragical end of which was explained away as an illusion. The real 'Gospel,' the contents of which brought redemption to souls alike fettered in Judaism and in Paganism, was in the Gnosis itself.[1] It seems that we have here a refined Hellenism contending for spiritual empire with that refined Judaism of the Diaspora,—that religion of love and good works and faith in no Antinomian sense which inspires the literature of the saints and elect and brethren under 'apostolic' direction. In the face of such phænomena, it can hardly be maintained that 'Christianity,' which still contains implicitly these oppositions in itself, is the product, in any exclusive sense, of either the Jewish or the Hellenic spirit.

We need to bear in mind that our information concerning Valentinus is mainly inferential from that which is said concerning his followers towards the close of the second century; nor must we confuse the subject, by wrongly ascribing to the master a knowledge of our canonical Gospels only possible to the followers. There is no evidence that Valentinus owned any authoritative written tradition; there is evidence that he appealed to the *viva vox*, the 'living voice of Truth' alone, and rejected even the tradition of the 'apostles

---

[1] The remarkable point of affinity between the Gnosis of 'Barnabas' and of these rejecters of the Old Testament is that both seek to evolve 'facts' from the world of imagination.

and elders.'[1] He was independent both of Scripture and Tradition. His followers claimed for their writings the designation of the 'Gospel of Truth,' implying that the other writings which passed as Evangelia of the Apostles at their time, did not contain 'the Truth.'[2] Hippolytus says that Valentinus was rather a Pythagorean and a Platonist than a Christian:[3] not from 'the Gospels' did he derive his system. The Catholics, then, and the Gnostics at the close of the century, meant two different things by the term 'Gospel.' For the former it was a developed or developing narrative of the life of Jesus, His crucifixion and resurrection; for the latter, a poetico-philosophic system, in which the new religion was defined as a redemption from the present world and from the restrictions of the old covenant, and in which the very facts presented in the current narrative were explained as allegorical of 'the Truth' in their own system.[4]

We have seen how exceedingly slight and vague are the uses of the word *Evangelion* in Barnabas, Clement, and Ignatius; how in Justin it occurs only in one probably interpolated place to denote 'Memoirs of the Apostles.' It must be inferred, not only that the *books* we call Gospels, but the very *name* Gospel, came only into current and controversial use about the time of Irenæus. And by the Gospel the Catholics and the Gnostics meant two diametrically opposite things. The latter have the advantage, in that they gave both a more precise and a more comprehensive theological definition to the contents of the good message. So far as we can trace the opposition, it

---

[1] Iren. 3. 2. 1 f.   [2] Ib. 3. 11. 9.   [3] 6. 29; cf. 6. 21.
[4] The Twelve Apostles, a type of the Aeons, Christ's Baptism and suffering twelve months later; the woman with the issue of blood, &c. Iren. 2. 21 ff.

had meant,—for the adherents of the Law and the Prophets, remission of sins, conditional upon the keeping of the moral commandments; for the Gnostics, the complete redemption of the soul alone, by emancipation from its lower and terrestrial life, and from all moral obligations.

It is worth notice, that according to Clement of Alexandria, Valentinus claimed for his teacher Theodas, a disciple of 'Paul,' as Basilides claimed Glaucias, the interpreter of 'Peter.'[1] The Marcionites said that Paul only knew the truth. When the writings we have in our hands, came into acceptation in the communities as Evangelia, it must have seemed to these transcendentalists—we are speaking of the followers of the earlier Gnostics—who had found in the new religion 'the Gnosis of supra-mundane matters,'[2] that its grand epical character had been dwarfed into a series of tales, by much the same process that Euémerus had applied to the ancient gods of Greece. In both cases, spiritual and transcendent beings had been reduced to the proportions of humanity, and brought down to a life in flesh and blood. That a god might appear in the guise of humanity and again vanish was the old belief of the Greeks. Even he might be born of mortals, as in the happier time to which Pausanias looks back. But there was a vast difference between an apparitional and an actual suffering life in the flesh. And where men agreed only in the main fact of an incarnation or an apparition in the distant past, there was room for the most conflicting opinions as to the mode of that appearance, and the contents of the message.

---

[1] *Strom.* 7. 17, § 106; Iren. 3. 13.
[2] Hippolyt. 7. 25.

Nothing can be more fascinating than the figure of Marcion, whose activity at Rome (c. 139-159) produced an impression so lasting and so widespread. He too is said to have followed the line of 'Paul,' whom all indications point out as the arch-Gnostic or Antinomian from this time forward. Our witnesses from the end of the second century, Irenæus[1] and Tertullian,[2] tell us that Marcion upheld the teaching of 'Paul' alone in opposition to the other apostles, who mixed up legal matters with the Gospel. Here for the first time we hear of that solitary apostle whose idea has so long filled the imagination of Christendom. Marcion (or rather the Marcionites) had a written Evangelion; and there is no evidence of his having mutilated our Luke's Gospel, as he is charged with doing in the inverted reasoning of Irenæus and Tertullian, who condemn the earlier narrative because it does not conform to the later ones.[3]

Marcion was eager to establish the antithesis of the Law and the Gospel as he understood it; and Tertullian calls his teaching 'the Gospel according to the Antitheses,' wherein he would separate his own Christ from the Creator, as of another God, and alien from the Law and Prophets.[4] However, Tertullian says that Marcion retained of the Gospel enough for his own refutation. In the pleasant polemic of Tertullian, Marcion and his followers are 'dogs;' and proverbially we know how 'dogs' are to be reasoned with. To the modern reader, however, it may appear that Tertullian, with all his eloquence and wit, might

---

[1] 3. 12. 12, 13. 1.   [2] *Adv. Marc.* 4. 2. 3.
[3] *Supernatural Religion*, p. 80 ff., 90 ff.
[4] *Adv. Marc.* 4. 1.

have chosen a better occasion for their display than in attacking an eminent teacher of confessed ascetic virtue, who had passed away, as if he were still living, and from whose retaliation he was safe. The ghost of Marcion seems to rise in silent dignity of rebuke before us as we read. His criticisms upon the Old Testament, his repugnance to its coarser anthropomorphic representations of the Divine, anticipated the reflections of modern times. A Gospel which came to announce that the Law was still in force, or even that a New Law of less burdensome restrictions was introduced, was to him no good tidings at all. Under the ignorance of an authoritative Rule of faith which prevailed at his time, when life was not to be shaped in accordance with a given creed, but the creed was to be shaped in harmony with the aspirations of the life, the abolition of carnal ordinances was necessarily the negative side of that Deliverance, of which the positive was the acquisition of perfect spiritual freedom. The Antinomian movement was but the tendency we have noticed in the early 'apostolic' literature pushed to an extreme. The Gnostics were the most ardent and thorough-going reformers, only too logical in the application of their principles. The emancipation of the mind from all positive præscription can only lead in the end, as the reformers of the fifteenth century found, to social dissoluteness.[1]

As the free Jewish communities of the Diaspora found it necessary to build their life on the basis of apostolic Mandates, on the broad distinction of the 'Two Ways,' so ultimately the Catholics found it

[1] The charges of Irenæus and Tertullian against the Gnostic brethren and sisters may be taken *cum grano*.

necessary to unite reverence for the Decalogue with faith in One in whom the Law had found its ideal consummation. But if a spiritual movement can only be understood from its logical extremes, then the Gnostic movement reveals the force and the extent of the Innovation of the second century. The Christ (Chrestos, Chreistos) of the Gnostics is neither son of David, nor angel or archangel of Jehovah; he is, in effect, a 'new god,' in that relative sense in which the Greek held the conception of a known god, in contrast to him who ever remained essentially unknown.[1]

Marcion's 'Gospel' was rather a theological manifesto than a historical or quasi-historical narrative. It was called the 'Gospel of the Lord;' and the fact that it bore no author's name is rather a proof of its early origin than the reverse.[2] It was when controversy demanded definite authenticity for statements, that men began to discover the names of individual apostles or evangelists which remain unknown so late as Justin Martyr. And this anonymous Gospel opened with the statement that

'In the fifteenth year of Tiberius Cæsar, Jesus came down to Capernaum, a city of Galilee.'[3]

What was meant was that Jesus, or the *Soter*, the celestial spirit of the Gnostic system, the offspring of the Pleroma, descended from heaven at that epoch. 'Your Lord, that better god,' says Tertullian, 'loved man so well (man the work of "our God") that for his sake he endured to descend from the third heaven into these poverty-stricken elements, and for his sake

---

[1] The reference to 'Christ as God' in Pliny's letter probably refers to Gnostic views.

[2] *Adv. Marc.* 4. 2. Cf. *Supernatural Religion*, p. 141.

[3] Tertullian, *Adv. Marc.* 4. 7. Cf. Iren. 1. 27. 2: He 'came into Judæa.'

was crucified in this little cell of the Creator even.'[1] He had his own condition, his own world, and his own heaven. He was revealed in the twelfth year of Tiberius Cæsar; Tertullian is writing in the fifteenth of Severus; and he says in criticism of the opinion of that better world, that its substance has not hitherto been discovered, as it ought to have been, along with its Lord and Author.[2] Again, 'In the fifteenth year of Tiberius, Christ Jesus deigned to emanate from heaven, a salutary Spirit,' according to the ' Gospel ' of Marcion. Now as 115 years $6\frac{1}{2}$ months intervene between Tiberius and Antoninus Pius, in whose reign Marcion lived, Tertullian suggests that the God of Marcion's revelation had nothing in common with the God revealed by Christ in Tiberius' reign; the former is a new theological birth of the Antonine period.[3] It is throughout no question of history. If Tertullian could have said, 'You have no evidence of what occurred in Tiberius' reign,' he would have cut the ground from under his own feet; he had before him Luke's Gospel, which referred to the same year of that reign. But if the modern inquirer, stepping in between these contending parties, asks, Where is the evidence of any divine appearance and suffering in Tiberius' reign? Tertullian, and the Marcionites, like Justin of Neapolis, and others, have nothing but the bare record of undated books or floating tradition to which to refer in reply. Here and there it seems as if we were about to come upon something of a more historical character, but it fades away, as we seek to grasp it. Tertullian looks back to 'the time of the apostles ' as one of a pure Theology; and in the existing churches ' of apostolic census ' the Christianity

[1] *Adv. Marc.* I. 14.   [2] Ibid. 15.   [3] Ibid. 19.

is that which holds to 'the Creator' in opposition to Marcion. The churches which hold to Marcion's Gospel, on the other hand, are stigmatised as late and spurious. But these assertions prove nothing; for Tertullian *knows* scarce more of individual 'apostles' than did Justin; and his notion of a sacred deposit kept in the churches of the apostles from the beginning is borrowed from the realm of imagination. He says that the apostles one after another clearly affirmed that Christ belonged to no other God than the Creator; and that there was no mention of a second God before 'Marcion's scandal.' He adds that this is easily proved from an examination of the apostolic and the hæretical churches, there is a 'subversion of the rule' where the opinion is of later date. Yet he passes from the point without offering any proof, which, had it been forthcoming, would have rendered his laborious *à priori* polemic unnecessary. His eloquent treatise in truth throughout thinly disguises a deep embarrassment. He had to deal with a sect which taught a Christ of their own, a Jesus of their own, evolved not out of the Old Testament Scriptures, but out of their own philosophic or poetic consciousness. He can only assert that this doctrine was a novelty dating from about fifty years before his time. He probably believed this; for he was of those who could not make out the features of the Christ at all, except from the Old Testament prophecies. But he could not prove that his 'John' and 'Matthew,' his 'Luke' and 'Mark,' were men who had been commissioned by Christ to publish the Gospel; he simply begs the point, as he begs priority for them, against analogy, over the anonymous Gospel of Marcion.

It remains an enigma why Marcion and the Gnostics should have adopted the name Christus at all to designate the celestial emanation of the good God, who had little or nothing in common with the Messiah of the Jews. One is tempted to suppose a misunderstanding, and to conjecture that *Chrestus*, 'the good one' (as in Suetonius), was the original name. However, Jesus was the name with which Marcion's Gospel opened. Yet if it was adopted as the name of their ideal 'Salvation' from the Hebrew *Jeschua*, perhaps no other explanation need be sought.[1] Tertullian claims that Jesus as a name is suitable to the Christ of the Creator, or God of the Old Testament, because the Son of Man has His name changed to Joshua (Jesus) on becoming the successor of Moses—in short, He was 'consecrated with the figure of the Lord's own Name.' He shares the notions of 'Barnabas' and Justin, and offers further, by his use of Old Testament prophecies and narratives, more examples of that licence and often absurdity of exegesis by which the suffering and cross of Jesus are found foreshadowed and made a historic necessity.

It remains to this day a problem whether what Tertullian calls 'my Gospel,' 'my Christ,' 'my Jesus,' or the Gospel according to the Marcionites, which denied the prophetic foreshadowing of their Jesus, was the earlier conception in the world. The subject seems hopelessly obscure; and perhaps no other conclusion can be reached, save the general one, that ecclesiastical Christianity from the time of Tertullian took the form of a compromise between the impassioned ideal of Gnostic innovation, which met the yearnings of Hellenic and Roman mystics, and the positive intuitions of the Jewish spirit. The possession of the

---

[1] For the arithmetical symbolism in 'Ιησοῦς, and ישו, 'the Lord who contains heaven and earth.'—Iren. I. 14. 4, 2. 24. I f.

Old Testament Scriptures was to the majority too precious a thing to be surrendered in favour of the overstrained ascetic and fascinating, but fatiguing dreams of the innovators. Moreover, the sense that the religious life of humanity is continuous, that the relatively new is still to be traced in the old, that it is still by 'law' as well as by 'grace' that men must live, makes itself felt with the development of new communities, after the first excitement of change has passed away. Without admitting the sharp opposition between the new Ideal and the old, men contented themselves with transfiguring the Scriptures of the Old Testament by making it a repository of types of Jesus. The question will again and again recur, whether men who busied themselves with such phantasies, had any grasp of an actual life once lived among men at all? Jesus is more real to imagination now than He was at the end of the new century.

On looking back, we see that the movement called Gnosticism was probably the first impetus of the great revolution. Taking our stand with Justin of Neapolis and Irenæus, we revert to Rome in the time of Claudius,[1] and see dimly the figure of Simon Magus through an exaggerating and distorting mist of fancy, as the first teacher of the redemption of the soul from its worldly bondage. Later comes the kindred ascetic teaching of Seneca;[2] later still that of Hellenic missionaries, if we may so call them, men imbued with the spirit of Plato and of Heracleitus, called to shed

---

[1] If there is no reason for disputing this date (cf. Renan, *L'Antechrist*), then the Samaritan was *the earliest known teacher of the new Religion*.

[2] The passage on the soul struggling against the weight of the flesh towards its native heights, *ad Marc.* 22, strongly resembles Gnostic teaching.

the glamour of the world of poetic contemplation, joined with ascetic renunciation, upon weary spirits. Jewish proselytising ardour was at this time chilled; it had done its work for the world. A new kindling of the imagination was needed; and this was supplied by the Gnostics. Men were intoxicated with a new found liberty and redemption. Again the wave rolled back; and Christianity reverted to those ways of mediation and compromise in the world of thought which it always holds in the Ecclesia, until some new flight of imagination in the region of Gnosis, or Speculation as we call it, disturbs the prevailing dulness, and rouses polemists from their dogmatic slumbers. The history of the second century shows that what rests upon the basis of imagination, may be rudely shaken and threatened with overthrow by a new and more vigorous effort of imagination. The poetic gift is necessary and at the same time dangerous to all established institutions, which owe their permanence to the need of repose, and must look for their reform to the need of activity in the human mind.

With reluctance we pass from Marcion and his compeers. The loss of their writings is strange and irreparable. Knowing them only through their antagonists, whose thought they enriched, we are impressed by their energy as social and moral revolutionists, and by consequence as theological liberators. It was they who seized upon the idea of Redemption by revelation in a distincter and more absolute sense than any of their contemporaries; it was they who gave to the world the idea of celestial saviours, and of the Saviour. They carried forward the teaching of the old Mysteries of which Isocrates said that they imparted 'good hopes for all time,' and of which Cicero said that men learned thereby to live well and to die happily. Their esoteric doctrine must have aimed at the purification of the soul to which their ascetic, doubtless pushed to an extreme, corresponded. They could not believe in a resurrection of the body, from which as from a prison the soul yearned to be free;[1] nor in the continuance of the rule of the Demiurge, the Author of a world so full of evil, and Himself of so mixed a character as He was reflected in the Old Testament pages. Their antipathy to the Law and the Prophets probably had a deeper root in national antipathy, which perhaps finds its explanation in their connection with Samaria[2] and Galilee, the one the home of Simon, the other the region where it was believed that the Saviour had descended in the reign of Tiberius. Whether a historic fact lay behind this ideal descent, or whether it was the historic 'substruction' of a system, supported by astrological calculation, must remain perhaps unknown.

We who consider the problem of Christian origins to be the ascertainment of the *men* who guided and gave shape to a great popular innovation (as Celsus says the movement was), see in the preachers of the Gnosis the most powerful spirits among those who passed as Christiani or as Galilæi in the second century. Before the time of Irenæus and Tertullian we know not where else to look for such men. Justin of

---

[1] Iren. I. 23. 5: the disciples of Menander, baptized into Him, die no more. For comparison with the Mysteries of Eleusis, Tert. *adv. Valent.* I. They too are a Hæresis of Attic superstition!

[2] For the study of Samaritan Synkretism, Harnack, *u. s.*; Freudenthal, *Hellenist. Stud.*, 1875, 2. I. 2; Hilgenfeld, *Ketzergesch.* 1884, 149 ff.; Kessler, art. *Manichäismus, Real. Encyc. f. Prot. Theol.*, 2d ed. Cf. Deutsch art. *Samaria* in Smith's Bible Dictionary. The refinements of the Samaritan Pentateuch, the Dove symbol, are points to be noted. Cf. also Lucian, *De Dea Syr.*, and Selden's treatise.

Neapolis admits that the followers of Simon Magus and of Marcion are *Christiani*, while he denounces them and boastingly seeks to arrogate the name with the system of belief built on the anti-Gnostic premises of the infallible truth of 'the Prophets,' to himself and his fellows. In a fragment ascribed to him by Irenæus, he says he would not believe 'the Lord Himself' if He declared another God beside the Demiurge; and he complains in the *Trypho* of 'blasphemies against the God of Abraham, the God of Isaac, and the God of Jacob.' Justin himself has been weaned from Hellenic wisdom by the study of the prophets. When we consider the near coincidence in point of time between Justin's address to the Romans and the stated arrival of Cerdo the Syrian at Rome, and the excommunication of Marcion (c. 140) it will appear that we here touch an epoch in the revolution. The loftier influence of the Gnostic and his spiritual kinsman Seneca is coming to an end in the great metropolis and spiritual workshop of the world; and popular Hebraism is to resume its power in a new form. Hebraism, according to an ingenious writer of our time, is 'the tendency and powers that carry us toward doing,' Hellenism 'the tendency and powers that carry us towards perceiving and knowing,' (*Gnosis*).[1] If so, Hebraism and Hellenism remain from this epoch blended, now in mechanical combination, now in chemic union. The writings of the New Testament bear witness to this phenomenon. And it is still a question whether 'Paul,' that figure which suddenly starts up in Gnostic company at the middle of the second century more 'hebraises,' or more 'hellenises,' or whether so-called 'Paulinism' be not a heterogeneous mixture of con-

---

[1] M. Arnold, *Culture and Anarchy* 143, *St. Paul* xxxiii.

servatism and innovation; whether the current portraits of this latest 'apostle' do not present variations irreconcilable with the hypothesis of a historic individual.

Havet thus sums up the results of his able work: 'From the earliest years of our era, there were Jews established at many points of the empire. They formed an association which penetrated everywhere, and everywhere exerted their influence on the Roman world, at the same time remaining strange to it and independent of it. Around them were Judaisers, who shared their belief. In particular, they expected an Anointed or Christ, who was to descend from heaven to open the kingdom of God of the Jews, in place of the Romans.

'About the beginning of the principate of Claudius,[1] the rumour spread that this Christ was come, that it was Jesus, crucified under Tiberius; that He had risen, and was about in turn to raise all the just departed, to reunite them in an eternal life to those who were still living, and to cause sinners to disappear. It was difficult to believe, but it flattered all the passions of a suffering and irritated multitude. At first the "good news" was murmured in the ear, then was repeated aloud.[2] Some believed at once; others perhaps only half believed. But, as they were all united in the same wishes, they were delighted to profess the same hopes, the very expression of which was a rallying signal, and a menace or at least defiance addressed to their masters. With faith in the Christ and the resurrection, the worship of one God and aversion from *idols* was adopted, the idols which had already gained so many proselytes to Judaism. On the other hand, in

---

[1] Cf. vol. 4. 225. Havet has neglected the Gnostic movement.
[2] See the opening of the Clem. *Recognitions*.

the name of Christ they rid themselves of all that was vexatious in Judaism, beginning with circumcision. The new faith thus gained upon non-Judaising Gentiles; and this refined Judaism was refined more and more, as it spread among them and became penetrated by the Hellenic philosophy. The two movements became in time confounded. The Christians, who had at first found place within the bounds of Jewish associations, enlarged these bounds according to their usage, and themselves constituted a more extended association. The Church, by title of spiritual power, organised itself in the very bosom of the empire, and substituted itself for the old order, at once insensibly and surely. This work once begun, it was pursued without interruption, with an ever-increasing energy. All the forces which concurred to destroy the Roman empire (and from Cæsar's time it was felt to be menaced) concurred also to aggrandise Christianism. There was the obstacle of persecution; but tardy, intermittent, irresolute, and impotent, persecution only harassed the movement that it fought, sufficiently to render it irresistible.'[1]

It remains for consideration whether the Jesus thus connected with Christ was not an ideal of Gnostic origin in that time of Claudius to which the arch-Gnostic Simon is referred. The Clementine romance seems to preserve very faithfully the features of the conflict between the new Jewish Messianism, the belief in the ideal Prophet, the simple moral preaching of 'the Truth' by Barnabas in Rome, amidst the laughing and captious Greeks.[2] And when the scene is transferred to Cæsarea, and Peter is represented in full polemic with the wizard Simon, we find the reflection

[1] *Le Christianisme*, 4. 485; cf. Harnack, *Theol. Lit. Zeitung.* 1885.
[2] Clem. *Recog.* 1. 6 ff.

of long-existing sentiments, by which the older Messianic conception in its ethical form of 'the Prophet' raised up to instruct mankind in righteousness and the way of life is opposed to the usurpation of the new and greater God. It is commonly taken for granted, on the ground of coincidences, not to be mistaken, that Paul is aimed at under the mask of the wizard. Nothing is more illusive than such coincidences in this imaginative world. Another explanation suggests itself more in accordance with the facts. We cannot find Paul in Justin, unless we determine beforehand that he must be there. But we do find Marcion, with whom Paul is connected later by Tertullian in a way that arrests attention. Distinguishing what Tertullian *says* (and he will say anything) from what he *knows*, it is clear that he knows certain epistles ascribed to Paul, which he ventures not to reject, and which give colour to the Marcionite views. As to these epistles being in Marcion's 'Canon,' this seems to be a mere fancy of modern Canon-worshippers, quite anachronistic. The probability is that Paulus, the Roman-named 'little one,' is a modification of the extravagant ideal of the wizard, and that if the author of the 'Homilies' names not Paul, it is because he does not know of him. The 'Homilies' admit that 'Simon' came to the Gentiles first,[1] and that his influence had been great.

THE 'APOSTLE OF THE HÆRETICS.'

It is clear that Tertullian has no liking for Paul. 'About that third heaven,' he says, 'we will see, should we come further to the discussion of your apostle.'[2] He hints that Paul's censure of Peter and the other

[1] 2. 17, 18. [2] *Adv. M.* I. 15; cf. *Præscr.* II. 24.

apostles for their Judaistic leanings was inconsistent with his own after-practice—'all things to all men.' He calls him the 'hæretics' apostle.'

Tertullian preferred the account of Paul in the 'Acts of the Apostles,' which, however, was generally repudiated by his contemporaries, as it seems.[1] The account in the Epistle to the Galatians was received as authentic, and Tertullian is constrained to deal with it. He makes upon us the impression that he would have gladly set aside 'Galatians,' and retained the doubtful 'Acts,' if this had not been too daring a defiance of current opinion. He is glad to use 'Galatians' to support the credit of 'Acts:' the former speaks of a conversion of a persecutor to an apostle; so does the latter.[2] But the glaring contradiction of the two narratives must have been infinitely more embarrassing to Tertullian than at any subsequent time when reverence for 'the Canon' numbed men's perceptions of the discrepancies of different writings included under it.

He goes as far as he dares in suggesting doubts about Paul and his apostleship. To those who reject 'Acts' he says, 'Who is that Paul of yours' (the supposed author of 'Galatians')? What was he before he was an apostle, and how did he become one?'[3] Everything has a beginning except God. He desiderates the origin of the apostle from Marcion.[4] In general a believer for believing's sake, as Tertullian is, here he protests against rashness; he assumes the air of a bold sceptic. A man is affirmed to be an apostle who is not to be found in the *album* of the apostles in the Gospel. 'And then I hear that he was chosen by the Lord

---

[1] *Præscr. II.* 22, 23. [2] *Adv. M.* 5. 2.
[3] *Præscr. II.* 23. [4] *Adv. M.* 5. 1.

already resting in the heavens. It seems to me a want of forethought, as it were, that Christ did not know beforehand that he was necessary to Him, but that when the office of the apostolate had been already ordained, and they had been dismissed to their labours, He thought Paul must be added, 'and this by an inrush, not by foresight—by necessity, so to say, not by freewill.' Tertullian, who tramples down the 'hæretics,' *i.e.*, the dissenters of the time, vies with them in freedom when his apostolic-ecclesiastic theory seems endangered. He goes on, in his witty way, to challenge the 'Pontic shipmaster' (Marcion),—whether he has never taken smuggled or illicit goods on board his small craft; whether he has never thrown overboard or tampered with a freight. If he is too cautious and faithful in God's affairs for that, will he inform us under what bill of lading he took up the Apostle Paul—who stamped him with his title, who forwarded him to Marcion, who handed him on board, so that he may be landed in confidence, and not be proved the property of one who has brought forward 'all the instruments of his apostleship.' The arrogant temper of Tertullian takes particular offence at the pretensions of the writer of 'Galatians' to be an apostle 'not from men nor by man, but by Jesus Christ.' 'Anybody may make a self-profession, but the authority of a second person is required to confirm it; one *scribes*, another *subscribes*; one seals, another enters the record. A man cannot both profess and witness to himself. Besides, we read that many would come and say, I am Christ; and if a liar could say this, how much more might not a liar declare himself to be an apostle of Christ!' Excellent critical principles: only the application of them to the question of the origin of the Apostolate in general would have disconcerted the assurance of Tertullian.[1]

However, he is willing to accept Paul, as approved. On what grounds of authentication? Where is his voucher? Will our readers believe it! The proofs of Paul, as of Christ, are 'from the instrument of the Creator,' *i.e.* the Old Testament. Paul was promised to Tertullian from of yore in the Book of Genesis, according to the Seventy![2] Jacob says, 'Benjamin, a ravening wolf, in the morning, shall devour hitherto, and at evening shall give food' (Gen. 49. 27). Here Paul of the tribe of Benjamin, in early life the persecutor, in declining years the pastor of Christ's sheep and teacher of nations, is foreseen. King Saul, in his relations to David, is another type of Paul, as David himself of Jesus. Such are the 'sacraments of figures' combined with the 'Acts' (which Marcion 'must not deny') that convince Tertullian.

He denies Paul, then? No, he defends him and 'expels Marcion from the defence of him.' In other words, he fights with Marcion for the true portrait of Paul, who must in some way be found to belong to the Creator and His Instrument, the Old Testament, and the prophetic spirit,—a Tertullianic Paul, in short, and not a Marcionite Paul, the apostle of 'the other Christ,' the teacher of a strange and new God. It does not lie within our scope to examine the genuineness of the Epistle to the Galatians and the other three Epistles which have been assented to almost unanimously as works of Paul until our day,—as it seems

---

[1] Neither the authenticity of 'Galatians' nor its early date can be proved from Irenæus, Clement Alex., and Tertullian; and if not from them, not at all. See Bp. Lightfoot, *Galat.* p. 56 ff.

[2] Jacob as the 'younger son' addresses his youngest. All this is apt for the youngest apostle.

from sheer *inertia* and weariness of questions. But this inertia must be shaken off.[1] The Jewish scholar, Joel, had remarked, without questioning the current view about Paul, that we do not hear of him until the time of Marcion. Professor A. D. Loman shortly after published his *Quæstiones Paulinæ*,[2] in which, with admirable temper, he has re-opened inquiry into the origin of 'Paulus canonicus' and connected matters. The same critic has honourably made amends to the late Bruno Bauer for the injurious treatment he has received at the hands of some theologians. The latter writer has swept the horizons of early Christianity with a piercing and comprehensive glance; and while he pehaps too much depreciates the Hebrew factor in the new religion, has given only a due place to the influence of the Roman Stoics and of the Hellenic philosophy, which through Plato, Heracleitus, through Philo, and again through the Gnostics, streamed in upon the educated mind of the self-renewing world. In the Flavian period was cemented the alliance between the Hellenic philosophy and the Law and Prophets. At the close of the reign of Trajan, the Antinomian and Antitempelian movement breaks out, and continues under the teaching of the historical Gnostics from Cerinthus down to Marcion and his followers through the whole of the second century. Of this movement Paul is the last ideal expression. We can find no proof of his historic reality. The 'Acts of Paul and Thecla,' which contain a sketch of his personal appearance, are declared by Tertullian to be the work of an Asian presbyter and a fiction. Tertullian himself, while expressing the most audacious doubts as to Paul, turns the writings ascribed to him to the account

---

[1] *Blicke*, &c. [2] *Theol Tijdschr.*, 1883, 1886.

of Catholicism, and endeavour to force the Paul of the 'Acts of the Apostles' upon his contemporaries. In the absence of historical evidence, that from the ideal world is strong: Paul is the ideal Benjamin or the Saul of the latter times, the converted persecutor of the fold. Tertullian be our witness!

Alternately Peter and Paul act as foils to each other. The impressive prominence given to the 'lord Peter' in the Clementines, and his antagonism to the arch-Gnostic, the picture of Barnabas as first missionary to Rome, surrounded by jesting Greeks, can be traced to the creative activity of Ebionite feeling and motive. The 'Preaching of Peter' has for its burden 'the Prophet,' who has come to teach his brethren not the abrogation of the Law, but the Law in a new and simpler form; and he vehemently resists the Gnostic innovation, in alliance with James. We have nothing but learned guesswork to help us to the date and original form of this romance. But one thing remains clear. If the writer had heard of *Paulus apostolus* he disdained to own him, and deliberately identified him with Simon Magus. If he had not heard of Paulus, then we must conclude that this name was of quite late origin.

But the Catholics made both figures 'their own,' as Tertullian would say. After the Gnostic innovation had spent its force, the two great figures remained to represent two opposite tendencies in the religious life and the harmony of them.[1] Peter stands for the positive, the legal, the institutional, Paul for the original and the free, the inward and innovating spirit in religion. So long as men's minds are swayed

---

[1] B. Bauer, *Christus*, 384.

between these extremes, and the conditions of the second century repeat themselves anew, the quarrel and the reconciliation of the apostolic Pair will always be felt to be in the symbolical sense, historical and moral.

CHAPTER X.

THE CRITICS AND THE APOLOGETES OF CHRISTIANITY.

AND now we hasten to our close, believing that an answer to the question proposed to us at the outset has already been answered, in a general sense, in the mind of every thoughtful reader who has gone with us. But to gain a distincter view of the object of inquiry, let us now contemplate it in the light of contemporary criticism and defence. We have already referred to the general silence observed by the Greek and Roman writers on the Christiani. To Trajan and Hadrian's time belongs possibly Plutarch's old age : he is silent. So is Florus, the historian in Hadrian's reign. So is Epictetus, the Stoic, with the exception of a passing allusion to the habitual recklessness of the interests of this world shown by the ' Galilæi,'[1] who cannot certainly be identified with Christians. But if the earlier home of the *Superstitio* or innovating cultus was Bithynia and Pontus and other parts of Asia Minor, if Tacitus himself betrays no knowledge of it until after the original letter of his friend Pliny from Asia Minor, the general ignorance or indifference of the educated world may be explained.

We pass to the reign of Marcus Aurelius (161–180),[2]

[1] Arriani *Comm. Epict.*, 4. 7. 2.

[2] We need only refer in passing to the emperor's Meditations. They have long been recognised as *essentially* Christian in the best sense.

during which Pausanias wrote his most valuable *Periegesis* of Hellas. It is a book worthy of deep study. It yields the best insight into the contemporary and the ancient religious beliefs and rites of Hellas; it is written by a man whose simple piety and patient habits of inquiry command respect. Pausanias knew Asia Minor as well as Hellas, and the silence of so curious a traveller upon the subject of our investigation is to us a convincing proof that the new religion had made no noise either in Corinth, or Athens, or in Asia during his time.

We come to Lucian. He was a native of Commagene in Syria; he practised as an advocate at Antioch, where 'the disciples were first called *Christiani*;' he travelled in Greece, Italy, and Gaul. About 160–165, apparently, he was at Olympia in Elis, the scene of the self-immolation of his 'Peregrinus Proteus.' What does this tract teach us as to the Christiani? They are described ironically as possessed of 'the marvellous Wisdom' (τὴν θαυμαστὴν σοφίαν) which Peregrinus learned 'in the regions of Palestine' by associating with their 'priests and men of letters.' Soon he addressed them as 'children,' being their sole 'prophet and thiasarch and synagogeus and everything.' Now he interpreted and made plain, now he wrote many books himself. The Christiani esteemed him as a god, held him to be a lawgiver, and entitled him *Prostates*.[1]

As for the Christians, they still worship 'that Great One,' the man who was impaled in Palestine, because he introduced this new rite (τελετήν) into existence.

Cf. M. Arnold, *Essays in Crit.* It remains to consider whether they are not *historically* so—*i.e.*, whether they were not used by writers of the New Testament Books. B. Bauer, *Christus*, 319 ff.

[1] Cyril gives the title to Peter and Paul. Cat. 6.

After this, Peregrinus Proteus was apprehended and cast into prison. And this circumstance contributed greatly to his subsequent reputation, and to the miraculous and vainglorious notoriety which he was passionately fond of. So when he was bound, the Christians took the matter to heart, and did all in their power to rescue him. As this was impossible, they zealously rendered other services. At daybreak old women, certain widows and orphan children, were seen waiting by the prison. The officials of the Christians slept within along with him, corrupting the gaolers. Various meals were brought in; they held their sacred discourses, and the noble Peregrinus—for so he was still called—was named a new Socrates by them.

Nay, even from the cities in Asia, some were sent by the community of the Christians, to help and encourage and comfort the gentleman (τ. ἄνδρα). When a thing of this kind becomes public, it is wonderful how in a short time they lavish their goods. So Peregrinus enjoyed a great revenue from their contributions: for the wretches have persuaded themselves they shall be entirely immortal and live for ever, and consequently despise death, and give themselves over in numbers. Moreover, the first lawgiver persuaded them that they were all brothers, whenever they once transgress and deny the Hellenic gods and do reverence to that impaled Sophist and live according to his laws. So they despise all alike, and have a common property, receiving such [?] without any valid security. If, then, they are approached by any wizard (γόης) and trickster who knows how to manage matters, forthwith he is enriched in a short time, and laughs at the simpletons.

However, Peregrinus was released by the then ruler of Syria, a man who delighted in philosophy, who perceived the folly of the prisoner, and would not suffer him to acquire the glory of a voluntary death; who did not think him even worth punishing.

Then the knave dons the sordid mantle and takes the staff in full tragic style, and appears in the public assembly of the Parians; tells them he has given up to the public the goods of his 'blessed father.' Thereupon the mob of poor fellows whose pockets had been emptied in distributions, bawlingly salute him as 'a philosopher, a *philopatris*, a zealot of Diogenes and Krates!' Pursued by his enemies, who accuse him of the murder of his father, he escapes stoning, and wanders again, ungrudgingly furnished with supplies by the Christians, until he is deprived of their maintenance because of some sin against them: 'he was seen, I fancy, eating something forbidden (τῶν ἀπορρήτων αὐτοῖς) them.'

Then we find him in Egypt practising 'the marvellous *askésis*' of an obscene character. Beaten and fleeing, he sails to Italy, and, so soon as he disembarks, begins a rude tirade against everybody, especially the emperor, knowing him to be a most mild and gentle spirit. The emperor cared little for his blasphemies; and did not think well to punish a man under the semblance of a philosopher, for words, especially one who had made a trade of abuse. His consideration, however, grew in private life; and when he was driven out, his 'boldness of speech and extreme freedom' was on everybody's tongue; and he was associated with Musonius and Dion and Epictetus, and others of the like condition.

Finally, after making disturbances in Elis, he immolates himself in the flames, calling upon the dæmons of his maternal and paternal line to receive him with good will.

The picture of 'Proteus' is one thing, that of the Christians another. The latter are thought of by Lucian apparently as numerous in Palestine—a wide designation—and in Asia Minor. They are evidently, in his opinion, of the most ignorant and credulous character, having no real basis for their belief, and possessed by a passionate desire to exchange mortality for immortality. This was not peculiar to them: we read not infrequently of religious suicide in the sacred myths of Hellas. There probably were epidemics of this brain sickness which the popular religion did nothing to restrain. If the allusion to the wondrous 'Sophia' points, as it almost certainly does, to the Gnostic creed, and to 'Pauline' associations, then the Christians of whom Lucian knew held as a main article of that creed the redemption of the soul from the prison-house of the body and the evil of the world, whose material goods they were ready to squander upon any clever scoundrel who knew how to play upon their imagination and touch the tender chords of their religious feeling. As we have seen, respectable *hagiographic* documents like 'Hermas' and the *Didaché* confirm in general the truth of Lucian's delineation.[1] The eating of meat offered to idols may well have been a part of Gnostic 'liberty:' we know what resistance was offered to it by the opposite party, down to a time later than Lucian. It was the man 'who had Gnosis' who alone ventured to sit at meat in the idol's temple.

It seems from Lucian's account that a man might readily exchange the garb of the Christian leader for that of the Cynic preacher without exciting the jealousy of the new religionists. Lucian dislikes these bawling

[1] *Mand.* 11. 1 ; *Didaché* 11., and cf. especially *Orig. c. Cels.* 7. 9 and 11.

friars, the Cynics, their ostentatious poverty, and their declamation against wealth. Yet this popular ascetic appears to have formed a part of the early Gospel; and the poor Parians were here apparently at one in feeling in this matter with the Christians of Asia and Syria, who formed so important a brotherhood according to Lucian. Moreover, the Cynics, according to Epictetus, had a lofty conception of their mission: he gives us the portrait, and admits that it is caricatured by many of the staff and wallet.

The true Cynic is a messenger from Zeus to men concerning good and evil.[2] He must not attempt so great a business without God, otherwise he is an object of Divine wrath. It is not the wallet and the staff and the trick of abuse, and the rebuke of luxury, that make the Cynic. It is the character of self-control, and the open and free bearing that needs no concealment, which befits the tutor and pædagogue of the public. The body is nothing to him; death may come when it will; he may be exiled, but cannot be deprived of communication with God. He is a king and a shepherd, and weeps when any of his sheep are seized by the wolf.

Good lies in the soul alone, in the part which is free. God has sent One to show how the poor and naked and outcast may be happy. The Cynic, without wife, children, without coat, with only earth and heaven and one sorry cloke, is the true king and lord in his freedom and his contentedness. A fine trait of his character is that he will endure to be beaten like an ass, yet love those who beat him, as the father and brother of all. He will not roar out, 'O Cæsar, am I to suffer such things in breach of your peace? Let

[2] *Discourses*, 3. 22. 3. ff.

us go before the proconsul.' He invokes none other than Him who hath deputed him and whom he serves (Zeus). Whatever he suffers Zeus doth it to exercise him.

As to marriage, in the present state of things, like that of an army prepared for battle, the Cynic should be without distraction,[1] entirely attentive to the service of God, at liberty to walk about among mankind, not tied down to vulgar duties, not entangled in relations, which, if he transgresses, he will no longer keep the character of a wise and good man, and which, if he observes, there is an end of him as the messenger and spy and herald of the gods. Those who oversee all mankind confer a greater benefit upon the world than those who leave two or three snivelling children. All men are the Cynic's sons, all women his daughters. He rebukes those whom he meets as a father, a brother, a minister of the common parent, Zeus. His commonwealth is the world.

Epictetus is at the same time severe upon the greedy Dogs that Cynics are now; upon their great jaws, their abusive tongue and brawny arm. Unless his ruling faculty be purer than the Sun, the Cynic must necessarily be a common cheat and rascal.

This order of preachers was in course of debasement. But the reader will observe how strong is the spiritual likeness between the ideal Cynic and the ideal 'apostle' or 'prophet' of the Diaspora, and the counterfeits of each. It is but reasonable to suppose that where both were aiming at a common moral ideal with a common monotheistic belief, the influence of good men among the Cynics was considerable upon the freer spirits of the new communities. The Stoical

---

[1] ἀπερίσπαστον, the word in 1 Cor. 7. 35. Cf. 2 Tim. 2. 4.

and Cynical street-preacher of morality, the ἀρεταλόγοι, their long beards at which mischievous boys were wont to pluck, the staff with which they chastised these impertinences, had been popular figures since the days of Horace.[1] They were doing the work among the vulgar that Cornutus, Persius, Seneca and Epictetus were doing among the *gens du monde;* they were arousing and stimulating the general conscience, they were labouring for the regeneration of the world.[2] When we look at the line of the teachers and fathers and exemplars of this communion, and recall the energy and the simplicity of their unworldly life and precepts, when we contrast all this with the aims and spirit of such as Justin of Neapolis, of Irenæus and Tertullian, their imperious ecclesiasticism, their anxiety about everything except the one thing needful, their ferocious polemic against freedom, we cannot doubt that the boastful *Christiani* reaped where they had not sown, and gathered where they had not strawed, that they were the inheritors of the fruits of a great reformation of which Cynics and Stoics were the pioneers.[3]

But to return to Lucian and his romance of 'Proteus.' The question arises whether the author has drawn any of the traits of his portrait from any actual Christian apostle of the time. The suggestion of Zahn (followed by Bishop Lightfoot), that Lucian borrowed from the Ignatian literature, we must decisively reject. If the reader examines the '*testimonia veterum*' concerning

---

[1] *Sat.* I. 3. 133; cf. I. 120; 2. 3. 35. *Pers.* I. 133.

[2] Cf. Aubertin, *Senèque et St. Paul;* Martha, *Les Moralistes dans l'Empire Romain;* Boissier, *La Relig. Romaine;* Havet, *Le Christianisme,* 4. 413.

[3] Cf. further Seneca, *De Vit. Beat.* 18. *Ep.* 29. 1; Gellius 9. 2; Dion. *Disc.* 72, p. 628; Suet. *Vesp.* 13; Lucian, *Cynic and Demonax,* 3, *Dial. Mort.* 10. 9., 11. 3. Epictet. *Ench.* 66. 13, Diog. L. 6. 69, 71.

Polycarp and Ignatius, he will find little reason for believing that the drivelling letters connected with their names, as they lie before us, were known either to Irenæus, Tertullian, or Origen; rather, some slight data for the concoction of them are found in these fathers. And if, further, he examines the new vocabulary of these letters, the maudlin sentiment and mysticism, the ludicrously emphatic ecclesiastical spirit, he will be led to the conclusion that the fabrication of these letters belongs to a much later age. There is some ground for believing that Lucian's tract was used in their composition. The admirable painter of manners says that the report was that Proteus sent epistles to nearly all the cities of repute (ἐνδόξοις)—certain covenants, and exhortations, and laws; and certain elders after this he appointed by vote (ἐχειροτόνησε)[1] of the members of the society (τ. ἑταίρων), and called them *necrangels* and *nerterodromoi*[2] (messengers and couriers of the dead). Compare with these statements the following in 'Ignatius:' 'I write to all the Churches;'[3] 'I could not write to all the Churches.'[4] 'Appoint some one who shall be able to be called a God's courier (θεοδρόμος);[5] dignify him that he may go into Syria and glorify your unslothful love unto the glory of God' (!)

Lucian speaks of Proteus 'bound in Syria;' Ignatian letters, confused, talk of their hero as 'bound from Syria.'[6]

Zahn says that the description of the lavish liberality of the Christians in Lucian *depends* not on this or that passage of the Ignatian epistles, but on the whole of

---

[1] Cf. Acts 14. 23. [2] *Peregr.* 41.
[3] *Rom.* 4. 1. [4] *Ad. Pol.* 8. 1.
[5] Ib. 7. 2. Cf. *Sm.* 11. 2; *Phild.* 10; Zahn, *Ign.* 527.
[6] *Eph.* 1. 2, 21. 2. Cf. *Rom.* 2. 2, 5. 1; *Sm.* 11. 1.

them: an importunate begging of the question. Bishop Lightfoot finds 'much to say' for the 'view' that Lucian copied from those letters: we, where there is no evidence, find nothing to say for it.[1] To us it appears a monstrous waste of time and labour to pile up masses of learning in order to persuade us of the 'genuineness' of documents, so-called 'outbuildings of the house of the Lord,' from which any lover of simple piety and of vigorous thought and sentiment turns away in loathing and contempt.

On the whole, it would appear that Lucian has combined various traits from ideals of apostles, prophets, and martyrs current at the time in the churches, in the composition of his story. It was an age of romance, in which, as the example of Simon Magus reminds us, ideas of a supernatural character readily became embodied in the lives and adventures of fantastic persons; and through the thin veil of fiction we discern the figure of an apostle, who was held to possess means of communication with the world of the departed,[2] who appointed 'messengers to the dead,' who was sending letters to all the principal cities. Have we any contemporary Christian sources from which to correct this representation of Lucian's? Justin Martyr's *Dialogue* is supposed to have been written nearly at the same time, but we find no Polycarp, no Ignatius, no Paul, no great letter-writer here.

It is not until some fifty years or more that we find the Marcionite Apostle 'Paul' recognised by Tertullian, and his claims so jealously challenged, his supposed epistles so controversially examined. The

---

[1] Cf. Keim, *Celsus*, 145; Hilgenfeld, *Zeitschr. f. w. Theol.* 1874, p. 120, cited by Zahn, *Patr. Ap.* 327.

[2] The descent to Hades is in 'Hermas.'

probable inference is, that in Lucian's time the rumour of a great apostle's imprisonment and release and his wandering activity had reached the traveller's ears. The Gnostic and Antinomian party, under the leadership of Marcion, were carrying on their polemic with the reactionary or Catholic party, represented by Justin, Irenæus, and Tertullian. To the former party belongs the representation of the apostle in 'Galatians,' to the latter the counter-representation in the 'Acts;' while in other 'Pauline' epistles different currents of doctrine so meet and clash, that the discovery of a coherent and self-consistent 'Paulinism' has hitherto defied the efforts of modern interpreters.

If the mere name of 'Paul' in superscriptions and salutations be, as Tertullian argues, no evidence of the existence of such an apostle, then it will be difficult to find satisfactory evidence of the fact elsewhere. The only fact we can ascertain is that the Marcionites produced ten epistles as apostolic in their sense; and if these were ascribed boldly to an apostle of the highest possible pretensions, it was only in accordance with the inventive necessities and habits of theologians. They did but meet the demand and craving confessed by Tertullian in reference to the Marcionite 'Gospel,' for 'fulness of title and due declaration of the author.'[1]

One of the strongest pieces of evidence to our mind, negatively, that the Paul who has so long captivated our admiration and love is not historical, positively, that he is the product, like all similar figures, of religious passion and imagination, is that Lucian, whose glance embraced the great seats of supposed Pauline activity, betrays no knowledge of any such

[1] *Adv. M.* 4. 2.

vigorous personality as having left his mark upon the Christian communities from a century before his time.

Lucian, on the other hand, is our best witness for the all-prevailing delight in the world of wonder which has anew in our time been laid bare in collections of folk-tales from Greece and the East. He himself with his cool head stands critically aloof, musing and moralising over the human appetite for lies, and the vainglorious love of notoriety.

'I would be glad to ask you what you say of those who free those possessed with dæmons from their fears, and who so clearly drive away ghosts by excantations. All know the Syrian from Palestine, the sophist in these matters, and how many lunatics rolling their eyes, their mouths filled with foam, he raises up and sends away whole, after ridding them of their affliction for a great reward.'[1] Whenever he stands by the prostrate sufferers, and inquires whence they came into the body, the sick man himself is silent, but the dæmon answers,—hellenising or barbarising,—whence he is, how and whence he came into the man; and the other adjures him, and if this does not prevail, he threatens, and so drives out the dæmon. 'Why, I have seen him going out, black and smoky of skin.' 'Such a sight,' replies the sceptic, 'is no great thing, Ion, for the very Ideas appear to you, which your father Plato shows,—a somewhat dim spectacle for us of duller vision!'

The best elucidation of the allusions of the passage is the emphatic statement of Justin of Neapolis, to the effect that the dæmons yield to the name of Jesus used in exorcism. He appears to cite a formula when he says, 'By the name of this very Son of God and first

[1] *Philops.* 16.

begotten of every creature, and through a virgin, born and become a man of suffering nature, and crucified under Pontius Pilate by your people, and who died and rose from the dead and ascended into heaven, every dæmon is exorcised and made subject.'[1] Origen connects in this rite 'the name of Jesus with the recitation of the histories' about Him. The second 'Apology' (wrongly ascribed to Justin) claims sole virtue for this exorcism over all other exorcisms and incantations (c. 6)

These hints are most important as to the explanation of the popular progress of the new cult. It was a time when all disease was thought of as the effect of dæmoniac possession, and when salvation meant cure both of body and of soul. The temples of Asklépios, pre-eminently the healing god in these times, were thronged by the sick, who resorted to incubation and awaited the nightly visits of the god. The Christiani must under these conditions have made their way by addressing themselves to the belief in *exorcism*;[2] and the rite itself was a means of propagating the 'histories' about Jesus, whencesoever those histories were first derived. The success of the rite meant the propagation of the historical creed. From this point of view the assertions of both the heathen and the Jews that the new religion was a kind of magic[3] were justified from the mouths of the apologists themselves; and if the Christian Church no longer recognises the powers of exorcists, modern ecclesiastical admirers of Justin

---

[1] *Tryph.* 85; cf. *Orig. c. Cels.* 1. 6.
[2] Cf. Lippert, *Christenthum*, &c., 112. 177 ff. Exorcism and Baptism are related as negative and positive sides of the same thing : the expulsion of the old, the putting on of the new nature.
[3] On Ben Satda (Jesus) declared to have brought Magic secretly from Egypt, *Bab. Schab.* fol. 104. 2; *Sanh.* 107. 2; Lightfoot on Mt. 12. 24; cf. Wuensche, *ad loc.*

can derive no advantage from his statements as to the peculiar efficacy of the rite. Modern thought is here in sympathy with Lucian. There are no limits to the realising power of excited and undisciplined imagination; and diseases which have their obscure root in the nervous system and the phantasy, may and do give way before powerful counter-impressions.

We are compelled to pause and remind ourselves how slight and vague at this late date (c. 165) are the contemporary records of the origin of the new faith. Lucian the Syrian knows that the strongholds of the *Christiani* are in Syria, Palestine, and Asia Minor. Justin the Samaritan more definitely names two villages of Samaria, Gitton and Kappateia, the homes of Simon and of Menander his disciple, both 'magicians.' The latter practised his art in Antioch. He knows, moreover, one Marcion of Pontus. The disciples of all these are called *Christiani*. These are distinct representations amidst the surrounding haze. And we know not how to resist the conclusion that the definite statement gives the only historical clue; that the Gnostics of the half-heathen Samaria were in fact the first Christiani; and that Simon Magus is the legendary representative of their mysteries and their theosophy. To follow up the subject in detail belongs rather to the criticism of the Gospels and the Acts of the Apostles. But we may remark that in the latter book (to which chronological criticism is inapplicable) Simon is still represented as the 'Great One,' or the 'Power of God,' a Mage, who commanded the universal astonishment and respect of the people of that land. He is further represented as a baptized believer in Jesus; yet that he will be a 'gall of bitterness,' is still supposed to be foreseen.

THE INTERNAL HISTORY. 257

The history of the Samaritans (or Cuthæans) is admittedly obscure. Josephus,[1] however, states their Persian origin, which may in part account for the introduction of Mithras and his mysteries. The violence of Pilate against the Samaritans led to representations on the part of the Samaritan Senate to the governor of Syria, in consequence of which Pilate was sent to Rome to answer to the emperor.[2] It seems just possible that the tradition of the crucifixion under Pilate (the place of which is never stated by Justin) came from a Samaritan source.

Talmudists have set before us the various and contradictory views of the rabbins on the religious *status* of the Samaritans (*Cuthim* or *Cuthæans*). But what particularly arrests attention is the statement that in rabbinic writings the term *Cuthim* has often been substituted for Sadducees or hæretics, *i.e.*, *Christians*.[3] The Cuthim are charged with denying that the resurrection can be proved from the Pentateuch:[4] it is supposed that Sadducees *or* Christians are meant. When the 'Cuthæans' are said to have frustrated the emperor's permission to rebuild the temple,[5] Christians, according to Jewish scholars, are meant. But the Cuthim are charged with hatred to the temple at an earlier period.[6] The Samaritans, again, are said to have idolised Joshua as an Ephraimite and as connected with Shechem (Neapolis); and to have expected the Messiah as

[1] *Ant.* 9. 14, 10. 9. 7.
[2] Ibid. 18. 4. 2.
[3] Edersheim, *Life of Jesus*, 1. 399.
[4] *Sanh.* 90 b.
[5] *Ber. R.* 64. Edersh. *u. s.;* Joel, *Blicke*, 1. 17; Frankel, *Palast. Ex.* 244; Jost, *Gesch.* 1. 48, n. 2.
[6] Joma, fol. 59 (Wuensche, *Beiträge*, p. 534), refers to the time of Alexander the Great, from whom the 'Day of Mount Gerizim' among the Jews was dated.

Prophet, who would convert all nations to their religion. Some hold that the idea of the Messiah as son of Joseph was of Samaritan origin.[1]

It is admitted (by Dr. Edersheim) that Samaria was in many respects a soil better prepared for the divine seed than Judæa.[2] For ourselves, whether the obscurity of the subject can be further cleared up or not, we must hold to the fact that Justin of the 'foolish Sichem'[3] or Nablous testifies to the existence before and during his time of Christiani who held the doctrines of Menander, the disciple of 'the Great One.' If, as on the evidence before us, we believe, our present Gospels and the Acts date from the period between Justin and Irenæus and Tertullian, then their pictures of Samaritans and Syrophenicians acquire a new and peculiar interest.[4] The historiographers of the new faith recognise the ancient antipathy of Jews and Samaritans, and skilfully seek to overcome it; while the 'Great One' is reduced to a pitiful inferiority to the great catholic apostle.

According to Irenæus and Tertullian, Simon the Samaritan gave himself out for the Power of the Highest, and declared that he had revealed himself among the Samaritans as Father, among the Jews as Son, and among the heathen as Holy Spirit; and that he had ransomed Helena from the brothel in Tyre. But in the *Philosophoumena*, ascribed to Hippolytus and belonging to the same period,[5] it seems that it was *Jesus* in Simon's doctrine who appeared as Son in

---

[1] Jos. *Ant.* 11. 8. 6; Grimm. *Die Samarit.* 99; Nutt. *Sketch*, &c., 40, 69 (in Edersh. *u. s.*).

[2] Cf. Ewald, *Hist.* 5. 279, 7. 180, E. T.

[3] *Siracid.* c. 50.

[4] The Samaritans claim to be Sidonians in Jos. *Ant.* 12. 5. 5.

[5] E. Miller, 1851. See. Hipp. 6. 14.

Judæa, and suffered the apparent death which the Gnostics only admitted.[1]

The notion of the Messias Ben Joseph or Ben Ephraim frequently mentioned by the Jewish writers, 'makes so much for the Samaritans,' observed Lightfoot, 'that one might believe it was first hatched among themselves; only that the story tells us that Messiah was at length slain; which the Samaritans would hardly ever have invented concerning Him. And the Jews perhaps might be the authors of it; that so they might the better evade those passages that speak of the death of the true Messiah.'[2] If this notion is of post-Christian date, when the belief in a crucified Messias was in currency, it seems to imply the recognition that He who had suffered was the Samaritan Messias, or of the Ten Tribes.[3] To suppose that the notion was invented to explain a text, Zech. 12. 10, seems to be insufficient reasoning. The remarkable thing is, that a son of Joseph, whose bones were admitted by the Talmudic writers to be buried in Sychem,—a descendant of Ephraim, the Samaritan tribe,—should be admitted a Messias at all. We cannot but suppose that old Samaritan beliefs about the Messias were in some way blended with that current of Gnostic teaching of which the fountainhead was Simon, the Great One (perhaps originally only the *Rabbi*) of that land. Cerinthus, Cerdo, and Carpocrates taught that Jesus was son of Joseph and Mary.

Combining as far as we can the representations of Lucian with what is known of the mixed religious life of Syrian Palestine, it appears to us that he has

---

[1] Bunsen, *Hippolyt.* 1852, 1. 39, cited by B. Bauer, *Christus*, &c., 311.
[2] *Heb. and Talm. Exerc. on Acts*, 8. 9. Cf. Schœttg. *Hor. Heb.* 1. 359. Wuensche, *Leiden d. Mess.* 109; Edersh. 1. 78, u.

his eye upon that form of Christianity which was earlier than the orthodox Christianity of Justin and the Fathers, a Hellenic, Gnostic, Gentile Christianity, in which there was little but the mere name Christus to remind of the current beliefs of Judaism. Originating amidst heathen and Jews, the new doctrine contemned the faith of both, and aimed at the establishment of a new Mystery. It spread through Samaria and Galilee, the Decapolis, to the coasts of Tyre and Sidon; and at the time of Lucian, Antioch was the great centre of its propagandist activity, whence it had spread through Asia Minor. So bold an innovation must have been accompanied with many extravagances and with a boundless enthusiasm, which sufficiently explains the strictures of Lucian. It is, we must believe, Gnostic apostleship that he had in view in his description,—that apostleship which was to be dignified with the name of Paul, and from which that of Simon Magus was finally dissociated.

The criticism of Lucian is directed against the excesses of a passionate and self-denying enthusiasm, founded upon a new discovered sense of Brotherhood and a common expectation of an absolute triumph over death and an immortal life. Considering from whom it comes, it is the best testimony to the prevalence of that exaltation of mind, that divine madness from which all the best and all the worst in the religious life springs. His account, to the end of the imprisonment of 'Proteus,' as well as his reference to the epistolary activity, certainly reminds of the pictures of Paul's activity; and at present we must conclude that Lucian had heard some rumour of the ascendency of a new doctrine among the Christiani, and of an opposition to it. The division among the Christiani to which Justin bears witness, seems to be the only contemporary explanation forthcoming.

From the *Pseudomantis* of Lucian, composed about 180, we gather only that the Christiani were classed along with the atheoi and the Epicureans by the impostor and excluded from his mock mysteries, no doubt on the ground of atheism, in the Pagan sense.

The *Philopatris*, formerly assigned to Lucian, but now held to be of much later date, teaches the theology of Father, Son, and Spirit, and identifies this trinity with Zeus and the true God. Triephon says he will teach the nature of the All and of 'Him who was before all and the system of the All.' He had fallen in with 'a Galilæan bald of forehead, long of nose, who had gone up to the third heaven and learned the fairest things. He renewed us through water, guided us into the footsteps of the blessed, and redeemed us from wicked places.'[1] The sketch of 'the Galilæan' may be compared with that of Paul in the 'Acts of Paul and Thecla.'[2] In Tertullian's time the ascent is ascribed to Paul.

Had not Lucian openly named the Christiani, and that in a contemptuous manner, we might have been tempted to suppose that he was attacking their beliefs and traditions covertly under the name of Peregrinos Proteus. That a sect may be attacked, it must be first dreaded; that there may be a caricature, there must first be a portrait. But there is not a particle of evidence, so far as we know, that either Lucian or the Epicurean fellowship, with whom he so warmly shared admiration for the Master, the great lover of truth, regarded the Christiani as formidable claimants for the

---

[1] *Philopat.* 12.   [2] Tischendf. *Acta Apost. Apocryph.* 41.

spiritual rule of the world. And the like remarks apply to Apuleius and to Philostratos, whose picture of Apollonius of Tyana has been described as that of a 'pagan Christ.'[1] As the matter at present stands, there is as good reason for assuming that our Evangelists borrowed traits for their ideal from Apollonius, as for the contrary supposition.

Apollonius of Tyana in Cappadocia was a Pythagorean. He studied at Tarsus, and later at Aegae. He was a strict ascetic; and having visited Nineveh, Babylon, and India, returned to Asia Minor with pretensions to the possession of miraculous powers. He passed into Greece, thence to Rome, which he quitted in consequence of the edict of Nero against Magi, and travelled to Spain and Africa. He was with Vespasian at Alexandria.[2] Returning to Ionia, he was, in the reign of Domitian, accused of exciting an insurrection against the emperor, before whom he appeared at Rome. He escaped by the exertion of his supernatural powers; and he is said to have proclaimed the death of Domitian at Ephesus at the moment of its actual occurrence. He lived into Nero's reign. Here, then, was one believed at the end of the second century to have been a historical person. His biography was undertaken by Philostratos about the year 200, at the request of Julia Domna, the empress, wife of S. Severus, herself a Syrian of Emesa. Yet the Tyanæan comes down to us enveloped in a haze of supernatural

---

[1] See Dr. A. Réville's book on Apollonius.

[2] Cf. the miracles of Vespasian himself at Alexandria, Tacit. *Hist.* 9. 81, and the parallels in Mark 7. 33, 8. 23. According to Cudworth (4. 15), the god Serapis, at whose inspiration the cure was sought, was 'the devil' counterworking the Almighty in the plot of Christianity. But, according to the letter of Hadrian in Vopiscus, Serapis was the god of the Christians!

intuition. Proteus proclaims his birth to his mother; and a chorus of swans sing for joy. This new Reformer of the world heals the sick, casts out devils, raises the dead.[1] He is subject, like all spiritual beings, to sudden appearances and disappearances. He has adventures in the cave of Trophonios. A sacred voice calls him at his death. There is no difficulty in understanding this conception of a hero or god (the line cannot be sharply drawn between the two) in Hellenic belief, by which an actual life long passed away is suffused with supernatural and poetical colouring.[2] There is no reason to doubt that to the readers of Philostratus such an incarnation of the Divine in Asia Minor some two centuries agone, was as credible as the analogous incarnation in Palestine at a like distance of time to the Christiani. The belief in magical beings was universal; and phantasy always finds greater wonders in the dim distance than in contemporary nearness.

But now to revert to Lucian.[3] Another man of Tyana, a friend of Apollonius, and who knew 'the whole solemn tale' ($\tau\rho\alpha\gamma\wp\delta\prime\alpha\nu$) of him, became the trainer of the beautiful youth Alexandros, who turned out in due course a most imposing scoundrel, a Bandit, as Lucian calls him, who did not confine his depredations to Paphlagonia and other parts of Asia Minor, but extended them (in a manner of speaking) to the whole Roman empire. The illusive tricks

---

[1] Cf. Trench, *Miracles*, 64, 246, who believes that Philostratos had his eye on the Gospel miracles, but not that he wrote with hostility to Christianity.

[2] Eunapius, the neo-Platonist (c. 347), says the life of Apollonius should have been called the Epidemia of God to men, and that Apollonius was a being intermediate between the gods and men.

[3] Lucian, *Alexandros*.

which this Goete contrived with the aid of a tame serpent, were so captivating to the senses, that Lucian is almost willing to pardon the ignorant people of Paphlagonia and Pontus for yielding to the deception. When his contrivances were detected by intelligent persons, especially the Epicureans, the impostor turned against the latter with the utmost fury, and as it would appear, sought to bring them into odium by confounding them with Christiani. 'He said that Pontus was full of atheists and Christiani, who dared the worst blasphemies about him. They must be stoned and driven out, if they would have the god propitious.' At a kind of Mystery ($\tau\epsilon\lambda\epsilon\tau\acute{\eta}$) which he held, and which lasted three days, there was a Prorrhesis, or proclamation, similar to that made at the great Eleusinian mysteries, solemnly warning off atheists, Christiani, and Epicureans. The rite was in honour of Apollo and Asklépios. In some of his performances he uttered obscure sayings, as it seemed, in Hebrew or Phœnician. There are allusions in an oracle said to have been cited by him from the Sibyll, concerning a prophet and his doctrine of the 'first Monad' which point strongly to something like a Gnostic system. That the impostor (according to Lucian) sought to arouse odium against the Christiani as blasphemous, along with the Epicureans, of the rite of Apollo and Asklépios, is of course no proof that the Christiani themselves had not prophecies and theosophies of an analogous character connected with their Christos. Indeed it is evident that Lucian considered the Christiani the very class of people liable to have their passions of 'hope and fear' played upon by Goetes of the class of the Tyanæans and of 'Proteus,' whose very name hints an inner connection between them.

The position of Lucian as critic of all these votaries of new rites or renascent pagan rites, is clear enough. He looked upon them all as slaves of the tyrannic passions of Hope and Fear, and of those beliefs and phantasies which are generated from that source. And well might the miracle-loving impostor wage war 'without libation or herald' against Epicurus,— a fellow that utterly hated the truth found his proper foe in 'a man who had looked into the nature of things, and alone was acquainted with the truth in them.' The followers of Plato and Chrysippos and Pythagoras were his friends, and there was profound peace with them. But the undipped Epicurus—so he used to call him—was rightly his greatest enemy, because he made laughter and sport of these things.[1]

What will strike every reader in this admission is the combination of that imaginative philosophy of which the great father was Plato, with the practice of the lowest arts of magic in the agoræ of the cities of Asia Minor by this Goete. And this is precisely what characterises the Mages or Gnostics whose origin is referred to Simon of Samaria.[2] They held *teletæ* or mysterious initiations, without which in fact we can hardly conceive of a new religion making way in the second century; they maintained an esoteric doctrine of their Christ or Jesus; and they invented an allegorical theology, the whole impress of which is that of an effort to make good the assumption of a new Revelation to mankind by means of new mediatorial beings. The very mixture of Hebrew or Phœnician in

[1] C. 25. Cf. 61.
[2] Origen expressly maintains the magical efficacy of mysterious names, used by Persian Magi, Egyptian, Brahmans, and Hebrews, *c. Cels.* 1. 24.

the utterances of Alexandros has its parallel with the Gnostics and their Achamoth, &c.

At the time under study there were no gods more sought after in Greece and Asia Minor than Apollo, whom we may call the national god of the Hellenes, and his son Asklépios.[1] They were emphatically the Sótéres, the Saving Healers, the Purifiers and Atoners for peoples of Hellenic origin in these later times. We may not enter upon details here; but it seems clear that Christus, the new god, as every Hellene must have regarded him, found no more formidable rival on Hellenic ground than Asklépios. Or, to generalise, the divine human being of the new rite was opposed to the same conception under other names long deeply fixed in the Hellenic heart. And the practical proof that the idea of the Virgin-born came from Hellenic religion we derive from the Apologist Justin himself.[2] One of the most striking things in his embarrassed defence is the manner in which he is sensible of the force of the *argumentum ex analogia* in respect to divine births from maidens, and his entire inability to meet it, except by assuming a devilish imitation. We have seen that the Ebionite and Gnostic tradition of the Son of Joseph was in all probability the elder; and if so, the transition to the tradition of the Son of the Virgin Mary sprung up on ground where Hellenic beliefs had taken root.

To us the narratives in Philostratos and in Lucian are among the most remarkable 'evidences of Christianity' in the true sense of that phrase. They throw light upon that intense yearning after a Saviour God

---

[1] See Thræmer's art. s. v. *Asklépios*, in the new *Lexicon d. Griech. u. Röm. Myth.* 1884. Nothing is more beautiful than the expression of the healing god in plastic art.   [2] *Apol.* I. 21; *Tryph.* 69.

and after salvation in the comprehensive acceptation of the word, and upon that strong 'disposition to believe' that the dreams of the heart have been realised, without which the luxuriant growth of religious legend cannot be understood. We must hold that the 'tragedy' of the Tyanæan was known by heart in Asia Minor at the same time that the tragedy of the 'impaled sophist in Palestine,' as Lucian speaks, was known; and that the coincidences between them are due to the common life in the supernatural from which they sprung.

It is the same kind of evidence which we find in the contemporary Apuleius (c. 170), another great traveller, and one who made it his business to obtain initiation in the most renowned Mysteries of the world. The advantage of comparing Apuleius with Lucian is similar to that gained by comparing Epictetus. As the latter draws for us the portrait of the true or ideal Cynic, so Apuleius, in defending himself against the charge of Magia, reveals to us the true Mage.[1] He is, according to the designation of those times, simply a philosopher, a Platonist, and a Pythagorean, or more generally an eclectic. The pursuit of philosophy is to him a religion; and secret worship is the means whereby he realises the presence of the divine, as philosophy has taught him. His account of his initiation into the Mysteries of the great goddess, the one great Spirit revealed under many forms and names to mankind, is full of poetical and religious impressiveness. He means by this great 'Nature parent' no abstraction, but a personal being, the Queen of heaven and of the spirits of the departed. He alludes to Mithras as her chief priest, and to the 'sacrament of

---

[1] Apuleius is often classed with Apollonius as a Mage. Cf. Cudworth, 4. 15.

the holy warfare' in which the initiate is to rejoice. The preliminary baptism to which he is subjected seems exactly to correspond to the representations of the rite in the Catacombs.[1] When the profane have all been removed, and he is clothed in a rude linen garment, he is led by the priest to the penetralia of the sacrarium itself. 'You may perhaps ask with some anxiety, my attentive reader, what was then said, what done? I would speak if I might, you should know if you might hear. But ears and tongues would contract the like mischief of rash curiosity. But I will not torture you with a craving perhaps religious—with a protracted anxiety. Hear, then, but believe, what is true. I approached the confines of death; I trod the threshold of Proserpine, I was carried through all elements, I returned. At midnight I saw the sun sparkling with candid light; I advanced to the presence of the gods below and the gods above, and adored from near at hand. Lo, I have told thee things that though heard, thou must ignore.' The ceremonies of the third day closed with a *jentaculum religiosum*, and the 'legitimate consummation of the Teleta.' There is no reference to Christiani or Christus: the deities honoured are Serapis, Isis (the many-named queen of heaven), Fortuna, and Mithras the chief priest. And yet—removing these names—there is nothing of which the description in general so powerfully reminds us as the actual ceremonies of the Greek Church at the present day, which again lineally descend from the antique Mysteries. And here is one of many branches of proof that Christianity, at first a Teleté or Mysterium of 'Gnostic' introduction, had so to say its tap-root in

---

[1] "Sueto lavacro traditum præfatus Deum veniam, purissime circumrorans abluit."—*Met.* 11.

Hellenic religion and the related mystic philosophy. It will be remembered that Lucian spoke of the *Teleté* of the Christiani and of their priests and *Grammateis*. Apuleius here offers another point of coincidence. 'When we came to the very temple, the high priest (*sacerdos max.*) and those who carried before the divine effigies, and those who had been previously initiated in the reverend penetralia, were received within the cubicle of the goddess, and dispose in due order the breathing simulacra. Then one of those whom all called Grammateus, standing before the doors, having called the body of the Pastophori (this is the name of the sacrosanct college), as to an assembly [from a lofty mound], prefaced favourable prayers: To the *great prince, and the senate, and the knights, and the whole Roman people*, to the nautic ships and all that are ruled under the empire of the world by ours (*nostratis*); then he announces in the Greek speech and rite thus: To *the peoples remission!* (λαοῖς ἄφεσις). The joyous shout of the people followed.

The reader may ask, Granted that here are striking analogies to the rites and teaching of the Greek Church in the time of Basil and Chrysostom, yet how can the Christiani be connected with this confusing syncretism of Serapis, Isis, Fortuna, and many-named deities of one essence? The answer is, through the Gnostic or Pythagorean teaching of the Monad, the beginning of all, and the cause of all good things. 'He (Pythagoras) mystically set forth,' says an apologete, 'by means of symbols the dogmata of his philosophy;'[1] 'by an allegory he teaches that there is one only God.' Under this indifference to names and forms, this habitual apprehension of the spiritual essence revealed in

[1] Pseud. Just. *Cohort.* 19.

all, the ground was open for the introduction of any
new divine name, which only seemed to add richness
to the Pleroma of Deity; under any name the whole
idea of Divine Providence might be realised. Thus
Pliny the elder shrewdly observes that the real universal deity is Fortuna.[1] It is clear, under such conditions, that the Christian *Teleté* might and did make
way rapidly amidst a crowd of deities, whose rites so
closely resembled its own. There is some actual evidence that in a state of thought so careless of names
and national distinctions in religion, the Christiani
were confounded in Egypt with the worshippers of
Serapis. The Emperor Hadrian says, 'Those who
worship Serapis are Christians, and those who call
themselves bishops of Christ are in fact worshippers of
Serapis. There is no Jewish president of a synagogue,
no Samaritan, no Christian presbyter that is not an
astrologer and augur or quack healer. Even the
patriarch, if he comes to Egypt, must to please one
party show reverence to Serapis, and to please the
other, to Christ.' The Alexandrians 'have only one
God, and to Him the Christians, the Jews, and all
peoples of Egypt pray.'[2] If the letter be not genuine,
it is evidence only of what was thought by the writer
of the biography of Saturninus, about the year 300,—
namely, that Christianity at Alexandria was in close
affinity both to the Judaism and the Paganism of that
city. It was in short a much wider creed than the
'apostolic' and 'catholic' ecclesiastical doctrine of
Irenæus and Tertullian. We are led surely back to
the same result as before. If for momentary con-
venience we may cover with the garb of Gnostic or
Philosopher both Philonian Judaism and Pythagorean

[1] *N. H.* 2. 5.   [2] Flav. Vopiscus, *Saturnin.*

mysticism and monadism in Egypt, then it was from the Gnostic creed, with its recognition of the common element in all religions, and its publication of a new evangel and a new revelation, that Christianity sprang.[1]

[1] Pythagoras on the Unity of God, and His immanence in the World. See the citations in Clem. Al. *Protr.* c. 6, § 72, ed. Klotz, Cyrill. Al. *adv. Julian.* i. p. 30, Min. Felix, *Oct.* 19, Lactant. *D. I.* 1. 5, Salvianus *de gub. Dei* 1. 3.

CHAPTER XI.

CELSUS AND ORIGEN.

WE come now to Celsus, against whom Origen writes, apparently without knowing clearly who his critic was.[1] The work referred to by Origen was called *True Discourse* (ὁ λόγος ἀλήθης); and the contents, as cited by the Father, certainly give no other impression than that of a truth-loving spirit in this neo-Platonist, as Celsus is believed to have been. The like cannot always be said of Origen's defence. Celsus attacks the secret and illicit associations of the Christiani. He appears to regard the Agapé as the sacrament of a *synomosia* or secret confederacy, analogous to that of Catiline, cemented by the cup of blood. Origen does not cite this historical example; but he approves those who form secret associations in order to put to death a tyrant. And therefore the Christiani are justified in forming a league against 'him who is called the devil,' their tyrant! Celsus says in effect that 'the legend' (ὁ λόγος) was of barbarous, *i.e.*, foreign origin, and that it came through a Greek mould. And Origen actually confirms this conclusion, the general result of our previous inquiries independently of him: that the study of Hellenic philosophy and religion leads to the accept-

[1] I. 8.

ance of Christianity. In the modern way of statement, the religion defended by Origen is genetically explained from Hellenic sources. He adds to this the argument from the prophecies and from signs and wonders. Now if this latter argument, as it is stated from Justin onwards, can convince no educated man of the present day, because it has no scientific or historic premisses to rest upon, there remains only the conclusion, quite satisfactory and intelligible to the modern mind, that the new Religion is in fact the Reformation of old Hellenic religions, with the introduction of some elements from Oriental sources.[1]

Again, Origen admits that the morality of the Christiani is a common human possession; and that their opposition to idolatry is common to them with the teaching of Heracleitus, of Zeno, and of the Persians.

If Celsus says that it is by the names of spiritual beings and the use of incantations that the Christiani exert their power, nothing is more strongly confirmed by the statements of Justin and of Origen himself, concerning exorcism by the use of the name of Jesus, and the recitation of the 'Histories' relating to Him. If the good Father, who himself was too truth-loving to escape the charge of 'Hæresy,' talks of Celsus' criticism as 'malign,' we must refer this to the same polite convention of controversy which the late amiable Archbishop of Dublin complied with, when he charged Hierocles, another 'truth-lover,' with 'blind hate,' and the moderns, Blount[2] and Wieland, with 'hate, malice, and dexterity.' The interests of truth and of a sect

---

[1] Celsus (6. 22, 24) cites the Mysteries of Mithras as the origin of some things in Christianity. Origen wonders why those of Mithras rather than of Eleusis or others are named.

[2] Author of *Philalethes*.

are independent; nor can either well be served save at the expense of the other. Origen, in professing to defend sectarian pretensions, really concedes all to truth; and his combat with his critic is obviously a sham fight. He admits that Christianity is a mystery like those of the Greeks and barbarians, and that it has an esoteric doctrine, only maintaining that the outline of the creed is publicly known.[1]

When Celsus says that Christians are flighty, believe without logic, like those who follow soothsayers and Mithræ and others, and who glory in the foolishness of faith for faith's sake (1. 9), no one will deny that this represents the dissension between the educated man and the illiterate religionist of the present day. His remark is fair; and who that knows the position of the Catholic pastor at the present day, must not admit that 'the teaching of the multitude to believe without reasons,' which the Father defends, is a practice without which the work of the Church could not go on? Origen assumes that man must believe in some sect or other, must beg the question in favour of this or that teacher; and there was no third between him and his critic, to maintain, like the modern, *Je n'en vois pas la necessité*. But Celsus so far 'holds the field,' that it is clear, if the question must be begged, it should be begged in favour of the old wisdom over the new. How indispensable it was to the Christiani to appropriate the Old Testament, on this very ground— the need of the sanction of Antiquity—we have seen from Justin. We have seen this again in Origen; but his attempt to maintain the assumption of the priority of Jewish wisdom over that of the Hellenes, and the indebtedness of the latter to Moses, and again the originality of circumcision with the Jews, rather than with the Egyptians, only suggests reflection and inquiry. In truth, this urgent need of the support of Jewish antiquity, so clearly revealed in the leaders of the Catholic movement from Justin onwards, as distinguished from the Gnostics, seems to prove the dominance of Hellenised Jews in that movement—in other words, the ascendency of Philo over Pythagoras at the end of the second century. Through the instinct of self-preservation—the strongest instinct we know—and by dint of hard assertion, a position was conquered for the Old Testament in Christianity, or for Christianity in the Old Testament, which has so long remained unassailed. The results of modern exegesis of the Old Testament have shown more and more clearly, what is patent from the apologists themselves, that the dependence of the new religion on the prophets was from the first forced and artificial. Not an unsound exegesis, but the passion for antiquity on the part of the anti-Gnostic, anti-Hellenic party among the Christiani, accounts for their extraordinary enterprise of depriving the Circumcision of their right to enjoy and interpret their sacred books in their own way. The dilemma was consequent enough—'either you must remain a Jew, and follow the Jewish interpretations of the Scriptures, or you must be a Gnostic Christian and find an independent basis for the new religion.'[1] But school logic is not the governing power, neither in political nor in ecclesiastical life, and Catholicism continued to occupy the centre between the 'right wing' of Ebionitism and the 'left wing' of Gnosticism.

To return to Celsus' criticism. Peculiarly instructive are the pictures which he gives of the progress of

[1] Cf. Harnack, *Dogmengesch.*, 1886, p. 218.

the new religion among the masses, so closely paralleled by what we have seen of the progress of Methodist and Salvationist sects in our own time. It is, he says, the ignorant and the unintelligent, it is slaves, women, and children who make the best converts. There is a strong prejudice even against education; and the popular teachers of the market-place would not venture near a meeting of wise men (3. 49). And the Father in effect admits that there must be milk for babes, as strong meat for men of understanding (5 I f.). Moreover, the philosophers also invite slaves to virtue. Celsus does not approve that ignorant artisans, the 'local preachers' of the time, who would not venture to open their mouths in the presence of their lords, assume a tone of conceit and dogmatism with women and children, and stir up in them contempt towards their natural superiors. In the shops of the leather-sellers and the fullers, and in the *gynaikeia*, these things were going on; and doubtless, at whatever expense to family peace, at great gain on the whole to morality. Women were drawn away from vice, from theatres and dancing and superstition; and youths were restrained, by solemn warnings on the destiny of the soul, from the temptations of their age (3. 56). It appears indeed at first sight, as if the new religion did not promote with equal strenuousness to those of the heathen, purity of thought and life in those who came to participate in the Sacraments. Hellenism, like Judaism, tended to produce an ethical aristocracy. Those only were invited to the participation of the Mysteries, who were pure from all pollution, whose souls were conscious of no evil, those who were of clean hands and sober tongues, who lived well and justly. But to the new kingdom of God were called sinners, simpletons, chil-

poisoners, sacrilegious criminals and robbers of the dead, were all invited (3. 59). Justly, Origen draws a distinction between the invitation of the sick in soul to be cured, and of those who are in health, to the knowledge and study of divine things (60 ff.). They only are properly initiated in the Mysteries of Jesus who are holy and pure; and it is admitted, these distinctions being observed, that in principle the Hellenic mysteries and the new Mysteries are at one.

But Celsus thinks that an actual preference is given to sinners; and here again it must be admitted that many refined Christians of the present day are with him, when they observe how partially the parable of the Two Sons in the Gospel is explained, and how common it is to glorify converted prodigals, to the disparagement of those whose walk has been blameless. And Celsus doubts, like many in our time, the reality of the Conversion of sinners inveterate by nature and custom; to which it is replied that heathendom itself recognised its reality in significant examples; that no rational soul is by nature evil; that the difficulty of change lies in the will; that choice and practice will avail in difficult moral endeavour, much as they avail in the all but impossible feats of the acrobat in the theatre. But we need not dwell upon this interesting discussion, in which there is little that has not a present-day bearing. The remarks of Celsus are not 'slanders' nor 'calumnies,' for any dispassionate reader. They are the fair criticisms of a man of culture, and apparently of piety; they express, like a noted modern essay, the reasons of the 'aversion of men of taste from evangelical religion.' They are aristocratic in temper; therein lies their one-sidedness. This world can never be composed of men like Celsus.

The vulgar whom Nature kindly supplies the defect of knowledge with proportionate self-conceit and self-confidence, will always be what their name implies. They do not understand a doctrine of virtue which teaches

> 'How to climb
> Higher than the sphery chime.'

They need that 'Heaven should stoop' to them; and, converting their immediate persuasions into forms of retrospective and prospective intuition, they will see this sublimity of condescension as a fact. And indeed a fact it is, the fact of Christianity, although in a better than the poor local and physical sense; for the Doketic touches the truth on the positive, as well as the negative side.

The criticisms on the policy and practices of the Christiani in this work are fair enough; and are fairly met by Origen. But where his Apology, like those of Tertullian and Justin, fails, is that he does not and cannot show that Christianity is any other than an Innovation and a Revolt against the old order of things, as Celsus declares it is.[1]

But we have already transcended our limits in referring to the arguments of Origen, whose activity belongs to the third century. Except that he is a nobler man than Justin, he has no advantage over his predecessor. He can only repeat the flimsy old statements that the new religion is contained in the prophets, and meet the unmistakable analogies to Hellenic and Persian religions adduced by his opponent, by pointless declamation.

We cannot repress the suspicion that these blustering Apologies, whether offered to educated Jews or

---

[1] Cf. Havet, *Le Christianisme*, 4. 400 ff.

Greeks, were not so seriously meant as at first sight appears. They were evidently intended for the greater Christian public, whose notion of Truth was of something to be fought for and won by their party at the expense of the opposite faction. Unfortunately, with the exception of this unknown Celsus, the pagan, and the unknown Tryphon, the Jew, in Justin, those who maintained 'the other side' in the debate are lost to us, for the most part, during this stirring period. As the matter stands, the worthy Fathers have allowed it to appear to posterity, that they had the worst of the historical and exegetical argument; and perhaps we credit them with too childish a simplicity of judgment, when we assume they were the dupes of their own sophistries and unfounded assertions. Unfortunately, so long as the impatient popular mind insists on begging the questions of history in its own favour, so long will ecclesiastics of ability be found to respond to the demand, and the corruption of intelligence must go on. Happily, we approach, if we have not already arrived at, a time when at least the same degree of freedom and candour that obtains in societies of men of science and letters will be encouraged, under the like conditions, in ecclesiastical communities.

And now briefly to sum up the results of our inquiry on the question as to the origin and early development of Christianity, as disclosed in the literature of the second century. The inquiry for us means, Who were the first Christiani? The evidence shows that this was not the first name of the new community, inasmuch as it seldom occurs, and where it does occur, has a stigma fixed upon it as if the mere *nomen*, as the apologetes say, were a ground of accusation and reproach in society. General appellations, like Brethren and

Sisters and Disciples, can hardly be pressed for historical meaning. On the other hand, the designations οἱ πιστοί and οἱ ἅγιοι, seem clearly to be of Hellenistic origin, and we may fairly conclude that the *Hagioi* were the Hellenistic Jews or Judaisers of the Diaspora, who formed the first nucleus of the Ecclesia. The combination of this name with that of Eklektoi reminds us that these were men who maintained the ancient prerogative of Israel as the chosen people, while they broke down the exclusiveness of Judaism by relaxing or doing away with the obligations of the ceremonial law, by their emphatic insistance on the leading articles of Morality, and in general by founding an universal monotheistic faith and church. These were not, strictly speaking, Christiani, neither in the sense of Messianists nor in the sense of Justin and the other apologetes. We might almost call them Philonians; and Philo never mentions the Messiah in express terms; while Josephus is reserved upon the same topic. We may infer that this class of Jewish religionists did much to leaven the Greek and Roman world with a pure and simple life-wisdom, similar to that found in the pages of Seneca, of Plutarch, and others. Since nominal Polytheism was widely giving way to a real though polyonymous Monotheism, proselytes to this Judaism mingled with Stoics and Cynics upon a common ground. But not among these Hellenists, who are soon lost to sight, can we discern that mighty enthusiasm which kindles the imagination of the masses, and which must be assumed to have caused the greatest religious revolution the world has seen. Nor could these self-emancipated Jews have ever formed more than a small element in the population of great cities. Again, they did not publish so much a new religion as the spiritualisation of the old.[1]

The speculations of Philo were closely cognate to those of Platonists, Stoics, neo-Platonists, and neo-Pythagoreans. They filled the mind of the educated world with a dream-life, with a new mythology, with the idea of a Mediator or mediators between the unknowable God and the material world. And had the new movement been confined to educated men, it seems probable that these creations of the poetic spirit would never have deserted their proper sphere, nor have become clothed with flesh and blood and assumed local habitation and name. But where the poet dreams, the people need to worship; where the former is satisfied with a transcendental truth, the latter need to realise that truth under forms of space and time. And thus the vision of the Logos was destined to give rise to an epic, the scene of which was *terra firma*. It is still a delicate point of criticism whether the ideals of the new religion were drawn more from a Hellenic and Roman or a Jewish source. We cannot but think that Philo, though in a hesitating way, practically surrenders the Judaism of the Circumcision,[2] as does the writer of 'Barnabas' (cc. 4-9) more definitely; and that the admission or claim to existence of a 'New People' breaks down the barrier between Jew and Gentile, and leaves the New People itself to be formed and trained by the influences of Graeco-Roman religion and philosophy. Whether we look to the philosophical leaders, and the sources of their inspiration, or to the masses of

---

[1] Cf. Siegfried, *Philo*, 159; Harnack, *Dogmengesch.*, 1886, p. 74 ff. He strongly protests against the use of the terms 'Jewish Christian' and 'Gentile Christian' as representing the historic truth.

[2] Cf. Havet, 3. 445.

the people and their practical spiritual needs, the conclusion seems to hold good, that the New Religion and the New People were of Gentile rather than of Jewish origin. No one will ignore the anti-ceremonial piety and morality taught by great voices among the prophets and in some of the Jewish 'apocryphal' writings; but all experience shows that the mass of the people need something more to satisfy their needs. They must have the Mystery, the sacramental initiation by which the nature is renewed, the exorcism, the baptism, the sacrifice by which the ever-dreaded influence of evil spirits is annulled, or their wrath and bloodthirstiness is appeased. We find scarce a trace of these needs in writings like 'Barnabas' and 'Hermas.' What we do find is that from the first the charge of Magic is brought against the Christiani, and association with the mysteries of Mithras. Theirs was a sacramental religion; nor can we find any evidence that Hellenic Judaism, with its simple moral teaching, its emphasis on fasting, almsgiving, and hospitality and the like, ever could or did captivate the imagination of the masses. Still less can this be said of the doctrines and phantasies of Palestinian Judaism. The discussion of these matters which still goes on among critics, without leading to unanimity of judgment, seems too much to ignore the popular and massive side of the new religion, as distinguished from the intellectual life of the times, by which it was nourished, and through which it won its way among the educated classes.

We still recur to the question, Who were the first Christiani? As far as we can gather from the evidence before us, it was the Gnostics, who from about the beginning to the middle of the second century bore and propagated the Christian name. It was they who were the real depositaries of the evangelical tradition; to them that we owe the statement concerning the fifteenth year of Tiberius and the descent of Jesus at Capernaum. Concerning their arch-father, Simon of Samaria, we have the statement in Justin and in Irenæus [1] that he practised magical arts in the reign of Claudius, a date which is valuable amidst the scantiness of such particulars. The distance of the Fathers from that reign, and the mysterious nature of the religion of the Simonians, their contemporaries, appears sufficiently to account for the legendary manner in which the person of Simon and his mysterious teaching are set before us. The Simonian priests were, according to Irenæus, exorcists and incantators, used philtres and charms, and held intercourse with Paredroi and Oneiropompoi. There were images among them, one after the type of Zeus, the other of Athena, which were explained as images of Simon and Helena; and doubtless it was these monuments which seemed visibly to confirm the current legend of the redeemed woman of Tyre. According to Irenæus, Simon and Helena were the real objects of the worship of the Simonians, and of their religious trust. It was Simon who brought salvation to men, appearing as a man among men, although not really such; he was thought to have suffered in Judæa, but had not really suffered. Salvation was by his grace, and not by righteous deeds; and the blessing included redemption from bondage to 'the angels who made the world,' nay, from the corruptible world itself. Menander is mainly a double of the ideal Simon in this representation. He, too, is said to have been an adept in 'Magic;' to have proclaimed

[1] *Apol.* I. 26; Iren. I. 23.

himself as a Saviour, sent forth from the invisible, for the deliverance of men. By means of 'Magic,' *i.e.*, by initiation into his Mysteries, the Gnosis was gained, by which the angels who made the world were overcome. Baptized into him, his disciples became victorious over death, and entered into the possession of immortal youth.[1]

To sift these statements is not too difficult. Of these Samaritans as persons we know no more than their names and the places of their activity. The rest of the tale is an account of their doctrine of Redemption and of their religious rites. Examples in the old religious myths of Hellas remind us how common it was to transfer ideas connected with god or goddess to the representative priest or priestess, upon whom the supernatural character is reflected.[2] There is no proof nor probability that these men represented themselves as Saviours: they spoke of a Saviour in the revelation of their mystery—namely, of Jesus, on whom Christ had at baptism descended. These men had seized upon the spirit and inner meaning of the Hellenic mysteries and others akin to them. They knew that they aimed at the purification and blessedness of the soul, by deliverance from evil spirits, and they carried on the old rites, building on the old beliefs, but in the name of a good and gracious and liberating God. One might say that the religion of Dionysos Eleutherios, with the solemn feast, analogous to the Pascha, commemorative of the annulment of human sacrifice by the self-sacrifice of a divine-human being once for

---

[1] Iren. I. 23; cf. Tert. *De An.* 50.
[2] Melampous, *e.g.*, the great Mantis and Healer. Cf. Héra-Médeia. Milchhöfer has remarked that most of the 'Heroes' resolve themselves into healing gods.

all, prepared the way for the new Mysteries of the Christiani.[1]

It is common enough to maintain in theory the unbroken continuity of religious life; but this continuity has never been clearly shown in the case of Christianity and the elder religions. We see in the line of Gnostics the true historic link between the old and the new world. In the labyrinthine track of ideas of the schools we soon lose our clue; the rites and customs to which the people cling with age-long tenacity amidst the shift and change of opinion, are the only certain indication of origins and history. Both Jews and Gentile philosophers, especially the Epicureans, unite in describing the founders of Christianity as Mages or Goetes; and the religion itself is said to be a new Mystery. From the Christian apologetes themselves we gather a practical admission that this was so. The rites of the seal—the mystic mark in the forehead—of baptism, of exorcism, of the Eucharist, are stamped with the characters of a secret religion. We know not against whom the obscure warnings in the hagiographic literature, 'Hermas,' 'Didaché,' 'Barnabas,' can well be pointed unless at teachers of the Gnostic type; while the later and laborious polemic of apostolic and Catholic Christians against them, only proves how deep and widespread their influence continued to be. The modern polemic of the Roman Church against the Freemasons offers an analogy to the attitude of the Fathers; and perhaps there is a historical connection here worth exploration. If, after all that has been written on the Origins of Christianity, the adequate cause of so mighty a movement in an immense popular enthusiasm has not yet been

[1] Cf. Lippert, *Die Religg. d. Europ. Culturvolken*, s. v. *Dionysos*.

laid bare, we may well invite closer attention to the activity of these spirits and their schools and churches in Samaria, Syria, Asia Minor, Egypt and Rome. We hold, on the evidence, that whatever influence Judaism in any of its forms had in preparing the world for an universal religion, Christiani would never have been heard of but for that Synkretistic system of doctrine and practice, combining Hellenic and Oriental mysteries, founded by Simon and his followers, and propagated in the congenial soil of heathendom. Further study of Samaritan, Syrophœnician, Persian, and Babylonian worship may lead to a clearer apprehension of the truth on this subject.

Hellas herself, whose rites had flourished again under Hadrian's fostering patronage, seems silent during these movements. Yet if, dismissing the silly physical explanations of her religious myths, we seek to penetrate anew, by Pausanias' aid, into her deeper life, we shall convince ourselves that the great truths concerning the soul and its salvation, the incarnation, death, and revival of spiritual beings, the reality of covenantal relations between them and their people, the belief in the necessity of vicarious Sacrifice, the vivid apprehension of a future life—were all firmly held. Here wide and patient investigation is demanded; and nothing but this will satisfy the conditions of so great a historical problem as the rise and growth of Christianity. It is, however, with the Asiatic Greek, in his converse with Oriental peoples and religions, that the question is more immediately concerned.

Two opposite influences have probably always conspired in furthering new religious movements: the influence of ascetic and the influence of woman. The Gnostics, with their pessimistic contempt for the material world, were in theory absolute ascetics. They taught abstinence even from marriage. Human nature being what it is, such principles were dangerous and even suicidal. That the practice of the noblest teachers corresponded to their preaching, there is no reason to doubt. Notably we have a high testimony to Marcion's sanctity from the lips of Tertullian himself. On the other hand, woman seems to have played a great part in the Gnostic fellowships. And the charges against the Gnostic friars that their austerity was subdued by the charms of their fair associates, have probably the amount of truth in them that might be expected from the nature of the case. Some traces of the influence exerted by the Sisters of the community may probably be found in the Thecla and the Phœbe associated with Paul. It remains for inquiry whether this latest apostle, this Ectroma, as he calls himself, in whose passionate declamation the outline of the Gnostic creed again comes clearly into view, in whom we have long been accustomed to recognise the mightiest personal force in the propagation of the Gospel, is not—either Marcion himself, or Marcus, or some other disciple of the great 'shipmaster of Pontus.' In any case, Paul is the apostle of the Gnostics and of Protestants. In popular phrase, one might be tempted to say that Paul rose again in Martin Luther; but more correctly, he never lived, and can never die.

But now, if the Gnostics were the first Christiani and the real authors of the innovation, whence this enigmatic name? The ordinary assumption, with which we started, is that Christiani = disciples of Christos, and that Christos = Messiah of the Jews. But there seems to be no way of connecting the Gnostic Christos with the Messiah of the Jews, even if we had a more distinct and self-consistent picture of the expected Messiah of the Jews than is actually the case.[1] Was he a moral or a political or a theological conception? Various and conflicting answers are given by students of the Old Testament and of rabbinical literature. One thing seems clear, that he was thought of as Ben David. Now, where in our early Christian literature is it taught as a leading truth of history or theology that Ben David has come, has suffered, has offered an atoning sacrifice for sins, and founded a spiritual kingdom? Where is the evidence that the Jews thought of Ben David as 'the Anointed' *par excellence;* or that the first Christians thought of their Christ Jesus as essentially Ben David?

Until these questions shall be satisfactorily answered, we may suggest the possibility of an illusion still subsisting in reference to the names Christos and Christiani. These were once interchangeable among the Romans with *Chréstus* and *Chréstiani;* and the latter form survives in the French *Chrétiens*.[2] If we are correct in our statement that Gnostics were the first propagators of the new religion, then the truth probably is that he whom they owned as the 'Good God,' in opposition to the Old Testament God, was the *Chréstos* who descended on Jesus in the form of a dove at His baptism. Some confirmation of this view is afforded by the remarkable emphasis laid on the words *chréstos*,

---

[1] Cf. Dr. Edersheim's (*Life of Jesus the Messiah*, i. chap. 5) chapter on '*What Messiah did the Jews expect?*' 'There was *a fundamental antagonism* between the Rabbis and Christ.' 'Jesus was *not* the Messiah of Jewish conception,' p. 164. After this—apart from dogmatic assumptions—what becomes of the Thesis of Dr. Edersheim's book?

[2] Other old forms, *chrestienté, kerstienté, crestienté, crestianité, crestinité.* F. Godefroi, *Dict. de l'ancienne langue Française*, 1883.

chrēstotēs, and the occurrence of a new and singular verb, *chrēsteuomai*, in our documents. Justin Martyr[1] quotes from an unknown source : ' Be ye good (χρηστοί) and pitiful, even as your Father is good (χρηστός) and pitiful.' And again in the *Trypho*[2] the exhortation occurs, with the motive, ' for the Almighty God we see to be good (χρηστόν) and pitiful.'[3]

In the ' First Epistle of Clement ' we read the saying, not found in any of our Gospels,

$$\text{ὡς χρηστεύεσθε, οὕτως χρηστευθήσεται ὑμῖν.}^{4}$$

And again in the next chapter,[5] the same verb occurs (χρηστευώμεθα), where it is difficult to determine whether goodness is to be shown to the seditious persons just mentioned, or whether brotherly love is meant 'according to the compassionateness and meetness of Him who made us.' A confused reminiscence of passages in the Psalms and Proverbs follows : 'The good (χρηστοί) shall be inhabitants of the land,' &c. How came these words to be thrust in without contextual connection ? Lipsius sees an allusion to the nomen *Christianum*, and with good reason.[6] But how could this be brought in with any effect, except for those whose ear was accustomed to the pronunciation *Chrēstianoi* ? The like remark applies to Justin's connection of τὸ χρηστόν with the Name in his Apology,[7] which led the older editors with reason to

---

[1] *Apol.* I. 15.   [2] c. 96.
[3] V. Ps. 24. 9, 33. 8, 106. 1 ; Lc. 6. 35. Cf. the remarkable iteration of χρηστότης in Rom. 11. 22, cf. 2. 4, Eph. 2. 7.   [4] 13. 2.
[5] 14. 3. Cf. *Supern. Relig.* I. 224 ff. The same verb in New Testament, 1 Cor. 13. 4.
[6] Gebh. and Harn., *ad. l.*
[7] C. 4 ; cf. c. 12, where Christos is said to be the author of the name.

adopt the reading Chréstianoi in that place. Can we suppose that the new people were at first called by the one name or the other indifferently? Hardly so. The Romans were familiar with names like Chréstos, Chréstilla;[1] and Suetonius' reference to Chrestos may be here recalled. If, then, the new people were called after one 'Chrestos,' this name had no connection with the Jewish Messiah. If after 'Christos,' then the problem recurs, Whence this name, which those who adopted it do not appear to have particularly associated with the idea of Anointing (except by verbal suggestion) nor with the idea of the Jewish Messiah, except in polemics?[2]

Tertullian is, so far as we know, the first to explain that the odious name is derived from 'unction;'[3] but he says that the Romans pronounce it *Chrestianus*. In that case it is 'composed of sweetness or benignity!' So late as Lactantius the pronunciation was *Chrestus*, not *Christus*, and he says the change of the letter is an ignorant error. But why did not Roman ecclesiastics ever speak of *Unctus* or *Delibutus?* The statement of Tertullian is but evidence of how he desired that the name should be spelt; but the question is, Who gave this nickname to those who had before been called Nazoræi (according to Epiphanius)[4] and how did they pronounce it? The Fathers seem to have been at a loss to explain what the adopted name meant; several said it meant '*we* are anointed.'[5]

---

[1] Bœckh, *Inscrr.* 1723, 194, 516; Cic. *Ad. Fam.* 2. 8; Martial, 2. 31.
[2] See the vague statement in Ps. Justin, *Apol.* 2. 6.
[3] *Apol.* 3. Cf. Lact., *De Ver. Sap.* 4. 7.
[4] Hær. 29. p. 56. Suidas, s. v., says this was in Claudius' reign.
[5] Suicer, s. v. In a mystic calculation of Gnostics, Hippol. *Philos.*

If the name was originally *Chréstianoi*, then the connection with *anointing* or the *Anointed* are but after-thoughts.

To the above evidence should be added that from the use of the word χρηστός in classical letters in conjunction with such synonyms as δίκαιος, ἐπιεικής, εὐμένης, φιλάδελφος, φιλάνθρωπος, φιλόπατρις, &c.[1] This throws a collateral light on many passages in early Christian literature.[2]

Again, the evidence of Greek inscriptions shows that the epithet χρηστός, so constantly employed to denote the honoured Hero or Departed friend, was analogous to μακάριος or μακαρίτης, the 'sainted one.'

In Christian inscriptions, the earlier appear always to have the form Chrest or Chreist, that is, the Gnostic form.[3] The Gnostic belief in Chrestos, the 'good God,' the connection of all Gnostics with Simon Magus in the reign of Claudius, the reference of Suetonius to 'Chrestus' in that reign, are coincidences not to be neglected.

The conclusion seems probable that from that time the worshippers of Chrestos were themselves designated 'the Chréstoi,' and that the Romans corrupted

324–5 (Migne), the name of the Son is spelt χρειστος, and is said to consist of four letters.

[1] Stephanus, *Thes.*, ed. Hase and Dindorf, Paris 1865, s. v.
[2] See especially the 'Epistle to Diognetus,' 9. 1, 2, 6, 10. 4.
[3] Dr. J. B. Mitchell, *Chrestos*, 1880, p. 12, says: 'Careful search through the Christian inscriptions, numbering 1287, in the fourth vol. of Bœckh.'s *C. I.*, 1877, fails to discover a single instance of earlier date than the third century wherein the word is not written Chrest or Chreist.' In this useful tract the author further points out that the monogram ☧ = χρηστός, p. 34. Among the Egyptians, οἱ χρηστοί were 'the justified.' Sir G. Wilkinson, *Manners and Customs of the Egyptians*, 1878, 3. 69.

the name, from misunderstanding, into Chréstianoi. The introduction of Jewish and Catholic names like Hagioi for a time replaced the earlier name in the Church. Finally, the Roman nickname was adopted by the Fathers, partly from necessity, partly, it would seem, from a desire to ingratiate themselves with the Romans; at the same time altering it, from polemical motives.

If the reader thinks that we ascribe, without sufficient foundation, priority as well as greater energy of thought to the Gnostics in the propagation of the new faith, we will remind him that it is from the admission of Justin himself, our first extant apologete, so amply confirmed by Irenæus and Tertullian, our inferences are drawn. What is the great point of dissension between him of Neapolis and his contemporary Marcion? It is that Justin will not believe in the Theomachy of the Hæresiarch, nor admit that the Old Testament prophets must be set aside. On the contrary, the infallibility of 'the prophetic spirit' is the corner-stone of his system, if he can be said to have one. But he makes an absurd use of the old Scriptures; and we cannot believe that fantastic discoveries of Trees and Crosses and Caves and the like in those books ever did much to produce or confirm faith among the people. It is more to the point to inquire what Justin and his fellows had in common with Marcion? The Sacraments, so far as we know, were common to both, and the central belief in the Crucifixion, and the observance of the Day of the Sun. If these things were essential to the new religion, and if they point certainly not to Jewish but to heathen origins, and to Samaria as the first place of their institution, then we see not how our conclusion is to be resisted. Dissenters from a majority are not necessarily of later origin; nor can it be proved that 'the Hæretics' of the second century broke away from elder churches, disregarded a 'Canon' they never heard of, condemned an authentic and unbroken tradition from the earliest times, or mutilated an extant evangelion to serve their own theological passions and purposes. It is time that we should attend to their impressive silence, rather than to the vociferation of Tertullian; and shake off the slavish illusions under which the scholarly, as well as the ecclesiastical world, has been as it were for so many centuries spellbound. The spiritual originality of the first two centuries was with the Gnostics: there lay their merit and—their crime!

As far as we can be said to know Marcion[1] from the reflections of him in Tertullian's page, he is revealed to us as a great spirit, as one born to stamp his personality upon the time, and to give form to the aspirations after religious liberty. He was evidently profoundly religious by temperament; he felt God to be revealed as the God of love and compassion in his own soul, and seems to have needed no other evidence of the reality.

> 'Der Gott, der mir im Busen wohnt
> Kann tief mein Innerstes erregen;
> Der über allen meinen Kräften thront,
> Er kann nach Aussen nichts bewegen.'[2]

Had he that contempt for the external work of the Creator[3] which he is represented by Tertullian as

---

[1] *Quis enim non tam suis notus est, quam extraneis?* is the Marcionite position. Tert. *Adv. M.* I. 11.

[2] From Harnack, *Lehrb. d. Dogmengesch.* 211.

[3] He thought the deliverance of man by the supreme goodness of 'his God' preferable to 'all the locusts,' Tert. *Adv. M.* I. 17.

cherishing? There may be some gross exaggeration here, due to the misrepresentation of his 'Antitheses.' If he was not a dialectic thinker, if he viewed life under extreme contrasts of light and shade, this might readily lead to unreality and to exaggeration on the part of his opponents. Clearly he believed that if ' 'twas great to speak a world from naught, 'twas greater to redeem.' His oppositions of spirit to flesh and matter, of Gospel to Law, of the God of compassion to the God of severity and wrath, perhaps all resolve themselves into the contrast of the light within his own clear breast to the darkness of a world enslaved to its lusts and its sensual imaginations—a world under the 'yoke of the Law' and of the Creator. But those watchwords which we have been so long wont to consider 'Pauline'—Grace, and Faith, and Freedom—are Marcion's watchwords. So, too, is the ascetic which guarded his doctrine against licentious abuse. That he absolutely forbade marriage is stated: here and in other matters we should compare Tertullian's[1] statements with the evidence of 'Luke'[2] and of the 'Pauline' Epistles. For doubtless an important historical truth has been conveyed in the legend of some of his followers that it was Paul who sat on the right hand and Marcion on the left of the Saviour; and, again, that the advocate or spirit of truth to be sent from the Father was in reality the 'Apostle Paul.'[3] The statement is exceedingly instructive, because it shows that these men thought of the 'apostle' as another spiritual being, even as the first Apostle, who had descended

---

[1] Tert. 1. 29, 4. 11, 17, 29, 34, 38.
[2] Luke 20. 33 ff. is here remarkable.
[3] Origen in Luc. *Hom.* 25. Against Celsus, 6. 53, Origen shows that Celsus ascribed the belief in the Two Gods to Christians in general,—a proof of its wide diffusion.

from heaven at Capernaum in the remote and dim foretime. But the necessity of this apostle to the imagination of the so-called Hæretics, corresponded to the necessity on the Catholic side of the Apostle Peter. The Catholics had the last word; and have contrived by an effort of poetic imagination to represent their chief apostle as the elder in election. As far as the evidence goes, we must hold that Peter is rather the later and the feebler creation, called forth by the intense jealousy of the Marcionite apostle. No one who has attentively studied the manner in which the figments of 'Apostolic' authority, 'Apostolic' inspiration flowing through a line of bishops, of an inspired 'Canon' or rule of faith, of a New Testament, consisting of writings originally anonymous, for which authors were found in 'apostles' or 'apostolic men'—sprung up, will think our conclusions other than strictly critical. Fixing our eyes upon the year 200 as our terminus, this work of selection and rejection, of the indorsement of undated and anonymous documents in the interests of ecclesiastical necessity, was still going on.[1] At last, in 'Apostolic' Church orders, constitutions, canons, the full chorus of the twelve steps upon the world-theatre, having divided the lands among them,—appointing bishops and presbyters and deacons and readers and widows, and each casting in his little 'parcel' of moral sayings for the edification of the audience. When we dismiss these spectres, the 'Apostles' remain for the historian as nebulous as they were in the days of Justin.

[1] About 150 there was *no* collection of Christian writings on an equal footing with the Old Testament, *no* new writings regarded as inspired and authoritative texts; *no* canonical New Testament so late as 200 known at Antioch. Harnack, *Lchrb.* 1886, 273 ff.

We are content to close by pointing out that Marcion is the real 'fruit-laden tree' of the latter half of the second century. His opponents are angry with him because he will not defend or reason out his creed; but their own unhappy apologetic attitude in contrast, hints where strength really lay.[1] The God of pure goodness and love Marcion taught was an unknown God, till Christ revealed Him.[2] He had compassion on men who were under the rule of the malignant Creator; and Christ, the 'spirit of salvation,' appeared among men to proclaim a *new* kingdom,[3] and to invite the weary and heavy-laden to Himself.[4] It was the believers in the Creator of the world who put Him to death on the Cross, thus unwittingly serving His gracious ends; for His death became the ransom by which the God of love redeemed man from the dominion of the world-Creator. The effect of the transaction was that they who hope on the Crucified are assured of release from the power of the Creator and of translation into the kingdom of the good God. How, it may be asked, is the docetic notion that the death of Christ was only in semblance, reconcilable with that of the redeeming sacrifice by the death on the Cross? The only way in which we can understand the contradiction is by referring to old beliefs and feelings in Hellenic and probably other religions. The dramatic forms of the cults were accepted as solemnly sacramental and efficacious (*simulata pro veris habita*); and the *mimésis* of sacri-

---

[1] 'State truths of sentiment and do not try to prove them. There is a danger in such proofs.'—Joubert in M. Arnold, *Essays*, 234.

[2] We understand the Christ of Marcion to be the good God Himself revealed (*i.e.*, ὁ χρηστός.) Cf. Harn. 206 n.

[3] Tert. 3. 24; *Orig. c. Cels.* 6. 53.

[4] Tert. on Luke, bk. 4, *Adv. Marc.*

fice, at least in late times, availed instead of the actual human sacrifice. Then again, there was the cannibalistic notion that the dæmon who thirsted for blood and took up the soul of the victim into himself might be deceived: an explanation of the Atonement stated in the crudest way by the Greek Father Basil. The Creator of Marcion's theology is *just* in the sense of one who exacts his due, and is hardly, if at all, distinguishable from one of the dæmons of the old local creeds, who held the land in his power, and exacted the life of the fairest youth or maiden as a condition of its weal. And the notion was here also that the Creator had been deceived and overcome by—in short, a trick. Christ, as a spiritual being, was untouched by death; and (according to the account of the Armenian Esnik) 'Jesus came down a second time in the form of His Godhead to the Lord of creatures, and held judgment with Him because of His death.' Jesus demands that the Creator shall surrender Himself, because He has broken His own law which denounces death against the shedder of blood. The Creator replies: ' Because I have put Thee to death, I give for Thy satisfaction all those who shall believe on Thee that Thou mayest do with them what Thou wilt.' Then Jesus left him and stirred up Paul, and showed him the Price, and sent him to preach that we are bought with a Price, and that all who believed on Jesus are redeemed from this ' Just One' to the ' Good One.' [1]

All theories of a ransoming death rest upon a dualism explicit or implicit; and it is for this reason that all attempts to combine the Atonement with the modern conception of a perfectly good God and Father have failed. It is from Marcion that we learn the meaning

[1] Harnack, *Lehrb. d. Dogmengesch.* 1886, 209, n. 1.

of the text, 'I came not to call the righteous, but *sinners* to repentance;' and again, 'Fear not them that kill the body.'[1] It was sinners, not the just of the Old Testament, but those who were disobedient to the Creator, whom Christ brought up from the Underworld;[2] and it is the soul only, not the body, being an earthly thing, that is capable of salvation.[3] In this emphasis on the redemption of the soul by detachment from the body, Marcion was but following the old teaching of Hellenic mysteries, as the myths of Thetis and of Démétér and their favoured boys remind us; and Baptism doubtless signified for him the entrance of a new soul.[4] There are old popular physiological and psychological notions at the bottom of such conceptions; no absolute innovation can take place in religion; and the more we think of it, the more we see in Marcion's antitheses or dualisms an attempt to expound a purely spiritual religion, and to detach the idea of the Sótér, or Saviour-god, from all complicity with his infernal counterpart. For in the case of Apollo even or of Dionysos, it is difficult to determine, from the study of myths and rites, whether it was more a good or a fiendish being that the people worshipped.

Marcion or his followers had an anonymous 'Gospel of the Lord' as well as 'Pauline' epistles. But to talk of the 'Canon' of Marcion (the word does not certainly appear till the fourth century) is an anachro-

---

[1] 'Sinners, the Homeless (ἀκλήρων), the very offscourings, as themselves say.'—*Orig. c. Cels.* 6. 53.

[2] Iren. I. 27. 3.

[3] Ibid.

[4] Both Irenæus and Tertullian charge Marcion with inconsistency in Baptism, because Water belongs to the Creator; an argument that might be extended to show that Marcion's positions are suicidal. Mystical intuitions will not bear these sharp dialectics.

nism.[1] Tertullian's statement about the mutilation of 'Luke' means that Marcion's Evangelion was the substratum of our 'Luke.' And if we follow the Fathers' comments on that Gospel, we may learn how much of its power and pathos is due to the great mystic or his followers; while the study of the Epistles in the light of Gnostic ideas may enable us ultimately to give a clearer account of that complex which has hitherto passed by the name of 'Paulinism.' But these matters lie beyond our present scope.

The followers of Marcion said that their master's separation of the Law and Gospel was not an innovation, but the restoration of the adulterated rule to its former simplicity.[2] In spite of Tertullian's passionate remonstrance, we must, especially with the writer of 'Galatians,' believe they were historically correct. The proof positive lies in the extraordinary vigour and influence of the Gnostic attack on the Old Testament, and the negative in the extraordinary weakness of those who tried to find Christianity in the Old Testament.[3] We who have long known where the *verba et voces*—the master-spells of our religion—lie, refuse to trace them to Haggadistic and Cabbalistic ineptitudes.

If Simon of Samaria, in the reign of Claudius, was the pioneer of the new faith, then a century later Marcion was its reformer, and the true critic of its traditions. The 'Pauline' letters, in spite of interpolations, still speak for him, and he must still be heard. The contemporary of Justin, perhaps he had heard of the remarkable discovery of the 'Twelve Apostles,'

---

[1] Harnack, 276, n. 3, 278, n. 2.
[2] Tert. *Adv. M.* 1. 20.
[3] See *Ib.*, bk. 3.

illiterate men who had set out from Jerusalem at some undefined epoch[1]—those superlative sinners, as 'Barnabas' calls them; that they had been discovered—in the second chapter of Isaiah! Perhaps he had heard of the further remarkable discovery in some source unknown of the 'twelve bells' on the high-priest's robe which symbolised them! These discoveries could hardly have had any effect upon Marcion. Did he admit the existence of the Twelve at all? We see no proof nor probability of it, seeing that their very names were unknown to Justin so late as about 160, when Marcion was possibly no longer living. Tertullian writes against him as if he were living, apparently from the year 207; and in this interval of forty or fifty years, the whole legend of Peter and the other apostles must have sprung up;[2] and the opposed representations of 'Galatians' and the 'Acts' have been produced by writers who had their eyes upon each other. The former is Marcionite, the latter anti-Marcionite or 'apostolic,' in the new and fictitious sense. And it is remarkable that while Tertullian would force the 'Acts' upon the Marcionites if he could, he himself is compelled to accept 'Paul' and the discomforting Epistle to the Galatians at their hands. Remarkable also, that though this epistle did not come into 'the Canon' with flying colours (as Loman says), that it came in at all; while by a truly tragic fate (as Harnack says) writings of a more Jewish cast were excluded.

'Marcion,'[3] says the last-named scholar, 'criticised

---

[1] *Apol.* I. 39; Isa. 2. 3. Cf. *Tryph.* 106. Cf. Tert. 4. 13, and his phantasies on the twelve springs of Elim, twelve gems of Aaron's robe, and twelve stones from the Jordan.

[2] In *Tryph.* 106 the curious digression about Peter speaks for itself.

[3] *Ldb.* 213.

Tradition from a *dogmatic* standpoint. But would his undertaking be well conceivable, had trustworthy accounts of the Twelve and their doctrine been extant at the time, and had they been influential in wide circles? The question may be answered in the negative. Thus Marcion supplies weighty evidence against the historical trustworthiness of the opinion that the Christianity of the multitude was actually based upon the tradition of the Twelve Apostles.' . . . Then what becomes of Him who was 'born out of due time?' To Marcion time and freedom of inquiry have at length brought a noble revenge. 'He was a religious character, yea, the only independent religious character that we know before Augustine in the ancient Church. His efforts confirm the experience, that a religious community can only be founded by a religious spirit that expects nothing from the world.'

The Christian world presents a wonderfully variegated picture at the close of the second century. Amidst two sects of Ebionites on the one hand, and several Gnostic sects on the other, two objects command our attention; the ghostly figure of the great Ascetic confronted by the 'great Church' itself, destined, under the proud Catholic and Apostolic name and pretensions, to so magnificent a career. It was then and still remains the Church of the multitude, and gradually absorbed into itself the spiritual treasures of all the schools and sects. The Gnostic ascetic and echoes of the Gnostic war of the Gods found their way into its forming the New Testament. Apologetes endeavoured to prove the harmony between the Old Testament preparation for the new Doctrine and the Wisdom of the Greek masters from Heracleitus to

Zeno ; and so made way for the ecclesiastical stroke of policy, by which the Heads of the community about the year 200 accorded to their fund of dogmatic teaching the character of the Catholic, Universal, and exclusively valid.[1]

[1] B. Bauer, *Christus u. die Cäsaren*, 317.

ADDENDA.

Page 13.

THE feast *Jom Trajanus.*—See the texts from the Talmuds on this subject in Selden *de Synedr.*, 3. 143, Graetz 4. *note* 14. Dr. Joel seems to stand alone in ascribing to Trajan rather than to Hadrian the permission to rebuild the Temple; *v.* Rosenthal in *Monatschr. fr. Gesch. u. Wiss. d. Judenth.*, 1880, p. 280. The period of especial embitterment of the adherents of the Temple against the *Minim* appears to have been from 118 to 132, when the insurrection under Bar-Cocheba broke out. To this period it can hardly be doubted the first *Apology* ascribed to Justin Martyr, the *Epistle of Barnabas* 16, and the martyrdom of Stephen refer, Acts 7.

It is certainly suggestive that the *Jewish* martyrs in *defence* of the Law and Temple, Schemaja and Achija (prob. = Lollianus and Pappus), Joel, *Bl.* 1. 17 *ff.*, should be connected with *Trajan* as the tyrant. Was not this the source of the invention about Pliny, and the *obstinatio non sacrificandi*, Tert. *Apolog.* 2 ?

Page 31.

Tacitus' *Annals.*—The passage in 2. 85 seems equally exposed to suspicion with that in 15. 44. It should be borne in mind that the question as to the authenticity of the *Annals* has never been settled. On the suggestion of forgery by Poggio Bracciolini in the fifteenth century, see J. W. Ross, *Tacitus and Bracciolini*, 1878, and Simcox, *Hist. of Lat. Lit.* 1883, 2. 207. Under these conditions, the passage must be cancelled from any list of early literary "evidences of Christianity." On the fabrication in Sulp. Severus, 2.

30. 6 (*Christians* in the time of Titus), see Illhardt *Hermes*, 1881, p. 195.

Page 40.

The *Procurator* Pilate.—For ἐπίτροπος as the *correct* Greek term, *v.* Strab. 3. 4. 20, 13. 2. 3, Plut. 2. 813 D, Jos. *B. J.* 2. 9, 2, Philo 2. 517. 14, Epictet. 3. 4. 1, Cels. in Orig. 1. 1569 B., Hdian. 7. 4. 5, 11. Who were the writers who employed the vaguer designations, *Hégemón, Præses, Vulg.* (Mt. 27. 2, Lc. 3. 1, where Tiberius is also a *Hégemón*), and *when* did they write?

What proof is there that a *Procurator* could exercise the *jus gladii*, and in particular, that Pilate ever exercised it? The answer is still, It is in the (*false*) passage *Ann.* 15. 44, together with some legendary Catholic *Acts* of martyrs! See Forcellini (1868), s. v. *Procurator* 7.

Page 251.

Lucian and the Cynics and Christians.—On this subject see J. Bernays, *Lucian u. die Cyniker.*

On reconsideration of this Tract, we hold it to be probable in the highest degree that it was written or interpolated in the fourth century, the great age of literary forgery, the extent of which has yet to be exposed. We date the Ignatian epistles from the same age; and the correspondences between them and the Tract in Lucian is probably due to the fact that they proceeded from the same writer, or from members of the same literary confederacy. It is in the fourth century that we hear of a *Cynic bishop*.

The testimony put into the mouth of M. Aurelius (Eus. *H. E.* 4. 13) to the constancy of the Christians may here be compared. And not until the mass of inventions labelled 'Eusebius' shall be exposed, can the pretended references to Christians in Pagan writers of the first three centuries be recognised for the forgeries they are. The reference in the Emperor's Meditations (11. 3) to *Christiani* is another of these interpolations.

INDEX.

Aboth, 57, 184.
Acts of Paul and Thecla, 178.
Acts of Thomas, 119.
Anab. Jesaiæ, 163.
Angels, 163.
Annals of Tacitus (15, 44), 3, 22, 28, 31.
Apollonius of Tyana, 262.
Apostles, the Twelve, 299.
—— of the Sanhedrin, 12.
—— and prophets, 52 ff.
'Apostle of the Hæretics,' 236.
Apostles, Jewish, 12, 55.
Apostolic Constitutions, 147.
Apuleius, 109, 267.
Aquila, 17.
Arnold, Matthew, 233, 296.
Asklépsios, 266.
Assumptio Moysis, 163.
Athenagoras, 2.
Aubé, 30.
Aurelius, Marcus, 243.

BAUDISSIN, 54.
Bauer, B., 1, 21 f., 25, 28, 78, 192, 214, 241, 244, 302.
Baur, F.C., 9, 219.
Baptism, 113.
'Barnabas,' Epistle of, 54, 66, 86, 91, 94, 96, 107 f., 166.
Basnage, 20.
Ben David, 71.
Ben Satda, 255.
Berachoth, 64, 191.
Birthplace of Jesus, 37.
Boeckh, 290.
Boissier, 250.
Browning, R., 36.

CARPOCRATES, 217.
Celsus and Origen, 272.
Cerinthus, 216.
Χρηστός, &c., 289 ff.
Chrestos, &c., 291.
Chrestus, 8, 19.
Christemporos, 65.
Christiani, in Nero's reign? 5, 31.
—— and Chréstiani, 12, 19.
—— no reference to, in literature of first century, 17.
—— Gnostic, 18, 46.
—— said to worship Serapis, 270.
Christus, the Gnostic, 18.
—— the Blood of, 206.
—— a proper Name in Tacit., 13.
Cicero, 290.
Circumcision, 107.
Claudius' Reign, 8, 234.
Clemens, Alex., 31, 223.
'Clement, Epp. of,' 153, 165, 171 ff., 206.
Clem. Recog., 49, 234.
Clinton Fynes, 16.
Cod. Theodos., 60.
'Confessors' (*qui fatebantur*), 7.
Critics and apologetes of Christianity, 243.
Cross, the, 204.
Crucifixion; the date unknown, 16.
Cudworth, 262.
Cynic, the True, 248 ff.

DARMESTETER, 210.
Derenbourg, 13.
Dernburg, 21.
De Rossi, 10.
Deutsch, 149, 164, 232.

U

INDEX.

Didaché, the, 11, 54, 71, 86, 146 f., 247.
Diogenes Lært., 210.
Dion Cassius, 4.
Domitian's Reign, 4, 25.

Ecclesia, the, 69 ff.
Edersheim, 20, 53, 257 ff.
Eleusis, Mysteries of, 232.
Ennoia, 214.
Epictetus on the Cynic, 248.
Eucharist, the, 116 ff.
Eucharistia, 73.
Eunapius, 263.
Eusebius, 12, 31, 165, 170.
Evangelion and Evangelists, 151.
Ewald, 258.
Exorcism, 255.

FAST DAYS, the, 85.
Frankel, 20.
Friedländer, 21.
Freudenthal, 232.

'GALATIANS, Epistle to the,' 239.
Galen, 220.
Gebhardt and Harnack, 91, 97, 110, 165, 209.
Gesta Pilati, 14.
Gloatz, 119, 123.
Gnostic *Gospel of Truth*, 222.
Gnostics: their Theology, 213.
Graetz, 16, 20, 55, 71, 78.
Grimm, 258.

HÆRETICS, the, 44.
Hagioi, 11, 52, ff.
—— Rites of the, 78.
—— Theology of, 157.
Havet, 30, 73, 82, 121, 203, 211, 234, 250.
Harnack, 15, 59, 65, 70 ff, 85, 88, 91, 118, 177, 192, 213 f., 220, 235, 295.
Hausrath, 9.
'Hermas,' 58, 66, 70, 87, 94, 95 ff., 97 f., 107, 109, 110, 147, 151, 159 ff.
Hilgenfeld, 201, 252.
Hippolytus, 223, 290.

Histor. Zeitschr., 85.
Horace, 75, 250.

IDEAL, the, among Jews and Gentiles, 189 ff.
Ideler, 16.
Ignatian Epistles, 66, 85, 125, 153 f., 172, 208.
Ignatius, 59.
Irenæus, 49, 71, 125, 178, 214, 217 ff.

JEROME, S., 19, 213.
Jesus; His descent to Capernaum, 226.
—— Mysticism on His name, 229.
Jews, references to, in Roman literature, 20 ff.
Joel, Dr., 7, 13, 16 f., 21, 216, 240.
Joma, 257.
Josephus, 22, 40, 79.
Joubert, 296.
Justin Martyr; on Birth of Christ, 33.
—— 'Memorabilia of the Apostles,' 34.
—— on the Prophetic Scriptures, 37.
—— on Mithras, 37.
—— on the Death of Jesus, 40.
—— on *Christiani*, 32, 46, &c.
—— *Apology*, 2, 32 f., 55, 94, 99, 112 ff., 118, 157, 167, 170, 200.
—— *Dialogue*, 12, 33, 76, 82 f., 88, 101 f., 121, 158, 200.
—— silence on Paul, 35.
—— are his supposed writings genuine? 39.
Juvenal, *Satt.*, 10.

KEIM, 109, 252.
Kessler, 232.
King, C.W., 121.
Kiss, the, 116.
Koffmane, 216.
Köstlin, 219.

LACTANTIUS, 2, 170, 290.
Laver, the, 95.
Lightfoot, Bishop, 15, 29 f., 156.

INDEX. 307

Lightfoot, Dr. John, 259.
Lippert, 45, 82, 111, 117, 122, 149, 219, 255.
Lipsius, Justus, 204.
—— R. A., 116, 172, 176, 204.
Logos, the, 158.
Loman, A. D., 16, 81, 215, 240.
Lucian, 33, 41, 45 f., 109, 232, 250.
—— *Peregrinos*, 41, 244. ff.
Lucius, 78.
Lucretius, 211.
Λύτρον in Legends, 191.

MARCION, 224, 293.
—— his Gospel, 226.
Martha, Mons., 250.
Martial, 290.
Massebieau, 146.
Merivale, 10, 16.
Messiah, the Suffering, 200.
Michael, the Angel, 162 f.
Minim, 12, 16.
Minucius, Felix, 195.
Mischna, 55, 63, 86.
Mitchell, 19, 291.
Mithras, 37, 82, 120, 204, 210 f.
Mommsen, 1, 60.

NABER, 79.
Names, magic efficacy of, 265.
Nazoræi, 290.
New Creation, the, 94 ff.
—— Law, 94 ff.
—— People, 94 ff.
Nipperdey, 24.

OORT, Dr. H., 13.
Orelli, 82.
Origen, 37, 214, 219, 265, 294.
Overbeck, F., 85, 213.
Ovid, 45, 211.

PAUL and Thecla, 215.
Paulus, jurist, 123.
Persian customs, 82, 164, 210.
Pesachim, 20.
Philo, 22, 72 f., 91, 187 f.
Pilate, Pontius: Epitropos or Hegemon, 40.

Pierson, Dr. A., 14, 79.
Pistis Sophia, 219.
Pliny and the Christians, 1 ff., 29.
Pliny the Elder, 21.
Preller, 45.
Plutarch, 210.
—— references to Jews, 9, 27.
Polycarp, 66.
'Prayer, the Lord's,' 146.
Proclamation, the universal, 97.
Pronoia, 214.
Prophets, in Jewish Christian literature, 61.
Psalter of Solomon, 20, 202.

RESURRECTION of the Dead, 210.
—— the, 177.
Rénan, 8, 230.
Réville, A., 262.
—— J., 121.
Ritschl, 172, 176.
Roman writers on the Jews, 20 ff.

SABATIER, 146.
Sabbath, the, 81.
Sallust, 123.
Samaritans, the, 257.
Sanclemente, 16.
Sanhedrim, 57, 61, 64, 180.
Schaff, 59, 74.
Schiller, H., 4, 7 ff., 10, 16, 18.
Schœttgen, 259.
Scholten, 22.
Seal, the, of the community, 107 ff.
Selden, 16.
Semisch, 103.
Seneca, his teaching, 22, 191 ff., 194 f., 230, 250.
Serapis, 262.
Simon Magus and Semo Sancus, 45.
—— romance of, 214.
Siracides, 91, 183 f.
Sophia, 183.
—— Achamoth, 220.
Sota, 184.
Spire, Joh. de, 31.
Stahr, 7.
Stein, Leop., 171.
Strabo, 79.

Strauss, 190.
Suetonius, 4, 21, 163.
Sueca, 174.
Sulpicius Severus, 31.
Sun-Day, 82.
Supernatural Religion, 32 f., 38, 171, 215, 224, 226.
Synkretism of Religions, 214, 232.

Taanith, 191.
Tacitus, *Annals*, 3, 22, 28, 31.
—— *History*, 9, 22, 26.
—— and the *Christiani*, 3, 9, 11, 31.
—— and Bracciolini's supposed forgery of the *Annals*, 304.
Temple, the, 88.
Tertullian, 2, 12, 29 ff., 71, 82, 88, 115, 121, 167, 170, 175, 178, 204, 210, 216, 224, 236 f.
Testaments of the patriarchs, 172.

Thræmer, 266.
Toland, 16.
Trumbull, 119, 122.

VALENTINUS, 219 f.
Vespasian at Alexandria, 262.
Vine, the, 73 ff.
Volkmar, G., 22.
Vopiscus, Fl., 270.

WEINGARTEN, 216.
Windischmann, 121.
Wisdom of Solomon, 91, 185.
World, end of the, 211.
Wuensche, 55, 65, 86, 174, 178, 211, 257, 259.

ZAHN, 126, 155, 251 f.
Zumpt, 16.